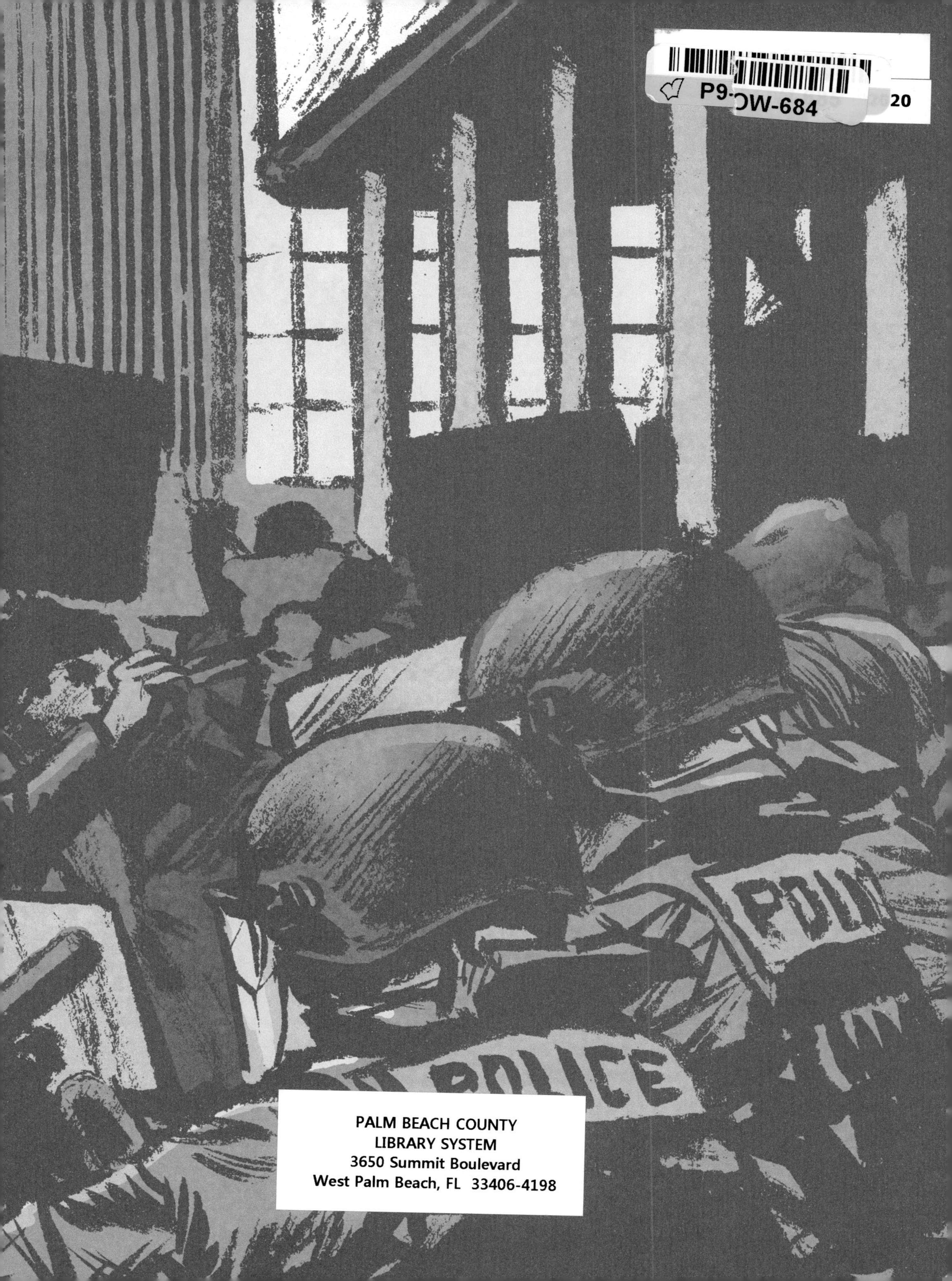
POLICE

SNOW PIERCER

THE PREQUEL
PART 1 : EXTINCTION

SNOWPIERCER

THE PREQUEL
PART ONE : EXTINCTION

WRITTEN BY

MATZ & JEAN-MARC ROCHETTE

ART BY

JEAN-MARC ROCHETTE

COLORS BY
JOSÉ VILLARRUBIA

TRANSLATED BY MARK MCKENZIE-RAY

LETTERING BY LAUREN BOWES

The world of Snowpiercer is based on an original idea by Jaques Lob.

Titan COMICS

Editor
Jake Devine
Designer
Dan Bura
Managing Editor
Martin Eden
Titan Comics Editorial
Jonathan Stevenson, Tolly Maggs
Senior Production Controller
Jackie Flook
Production Controller
Peter James
Production Assistant
Rhiannon Roy
Art Director
Oz Browne
Senior Designer
Andrew Leung
Sales & Circulation Manager
Steve Tothill
Senior Publicist
Will O'Mullane
Publicist
Imogen Harris
Senior Brand Manager
Chris Thompson
Commercial Manager
Michelle Fairlamb
Publishing Director
Darryl Tothill
Operations Director
Leigh Baulch
Executive Director
Vivian Cheung
Publisher
Nick Landau

SNOWPIERCER THE PREQUEL
PART ONE: EXTINCTION

ISBN: 9781785868832

Published by Titan Comics
A division of Titan Publishing Group Ltd.
144 Southwark St.
London
SE1 0UP

A CIP catalogue record for this title is available
from the British Library.

First edition: September 2019

Originally published in French as
Transperceneige: Exctintions (2019)

10 9 8 7 6 5 4 3 2 1

Printed in China.
Titan Comics. TC3246

SNOWPIERCER

THE PREQUEL
PART ONE: EXTINCTION

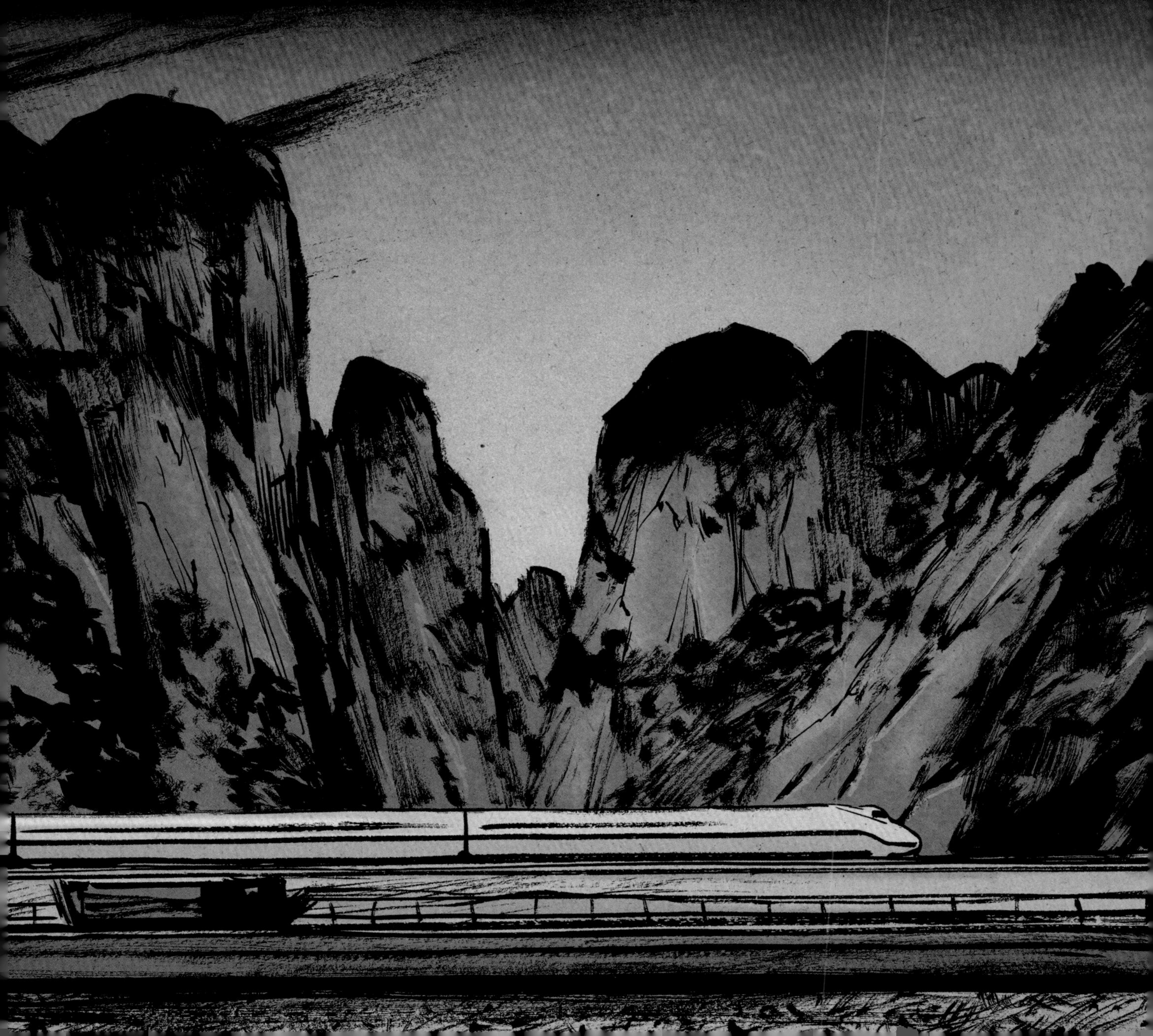

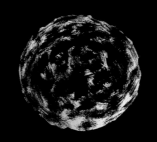

EARTH IS BEING RAVAGED BY A SEEMINGLY
INCURABLE DISEASE -- MANKIND.

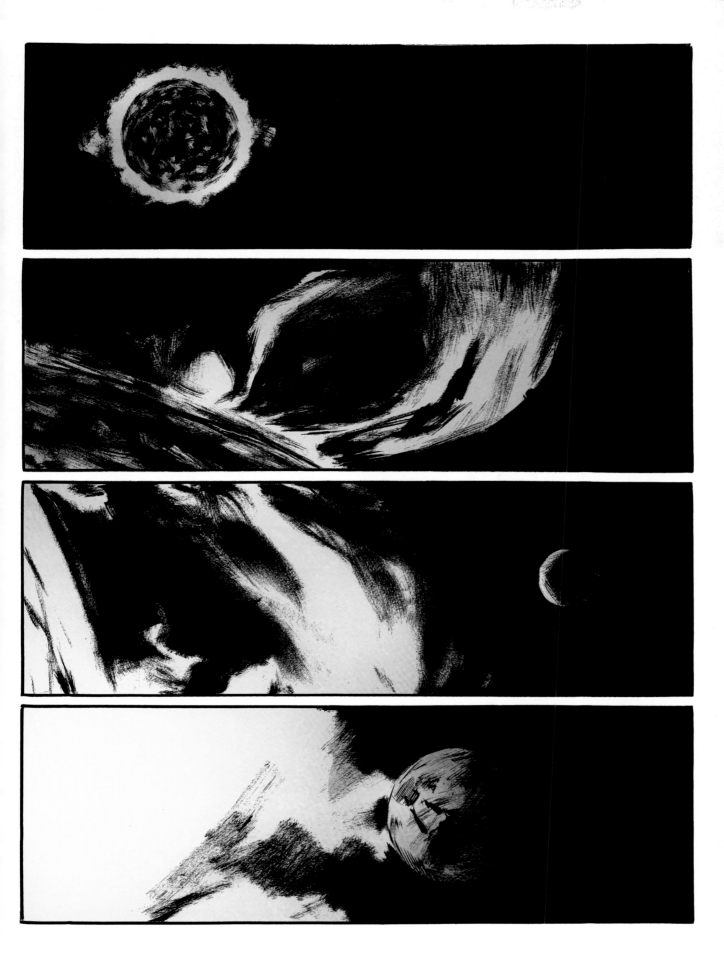

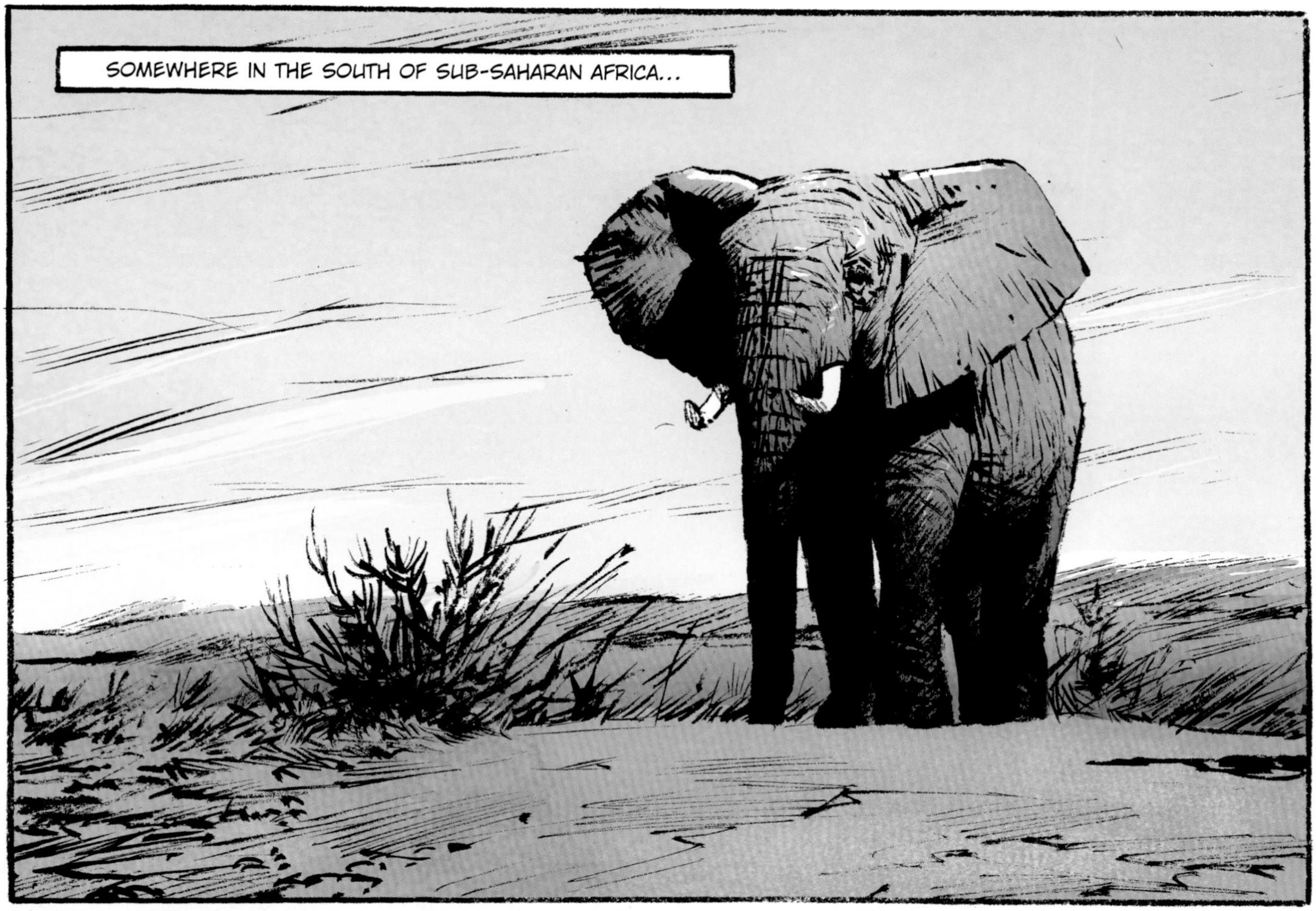
SOMEWHERE IN THE SOUTH OF SUB-SAHARAN AFRICA...

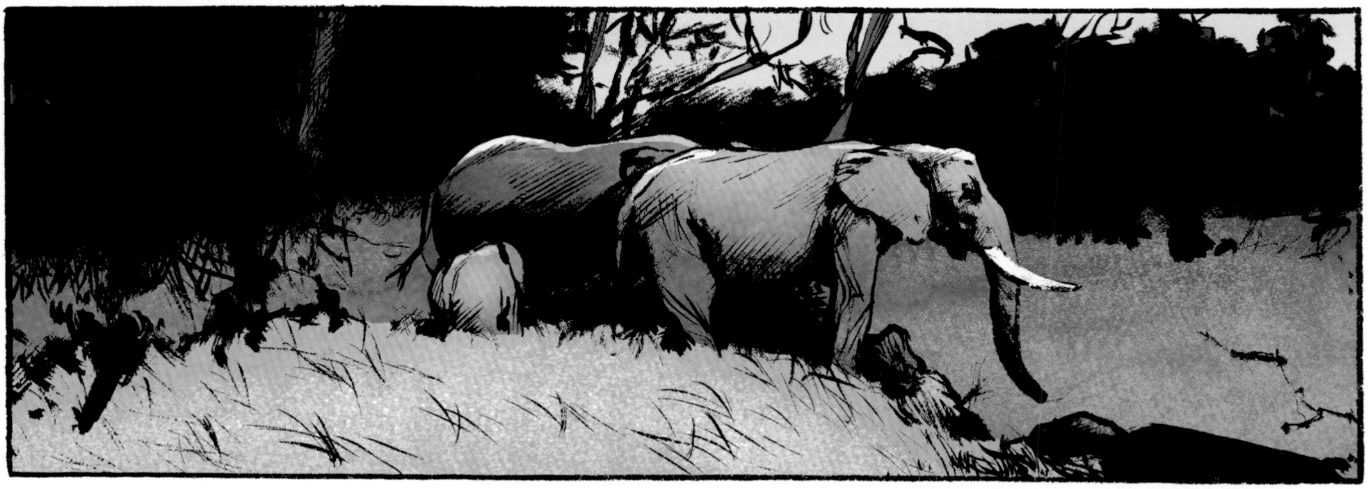

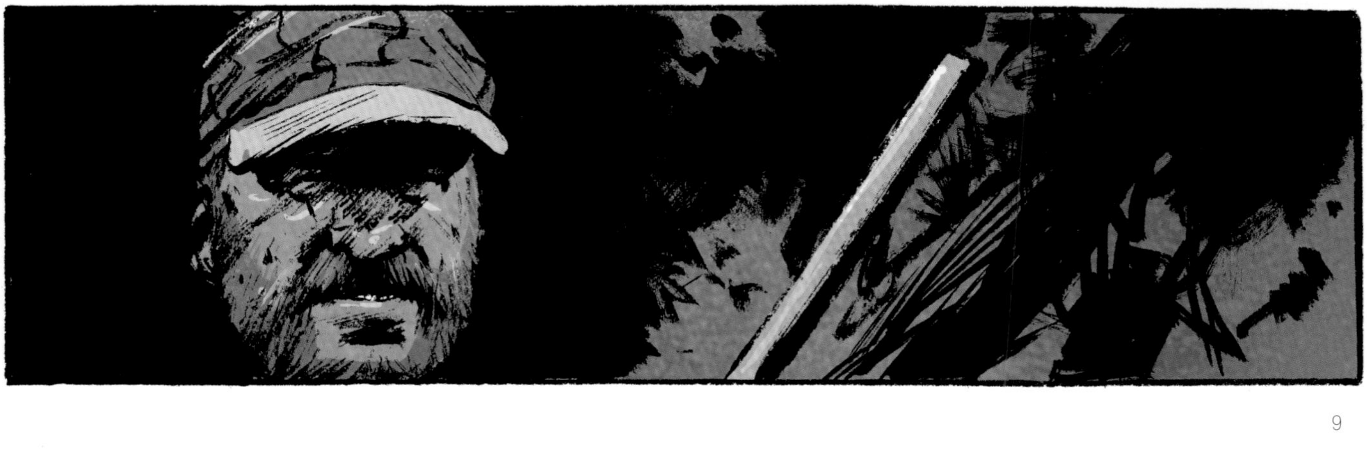

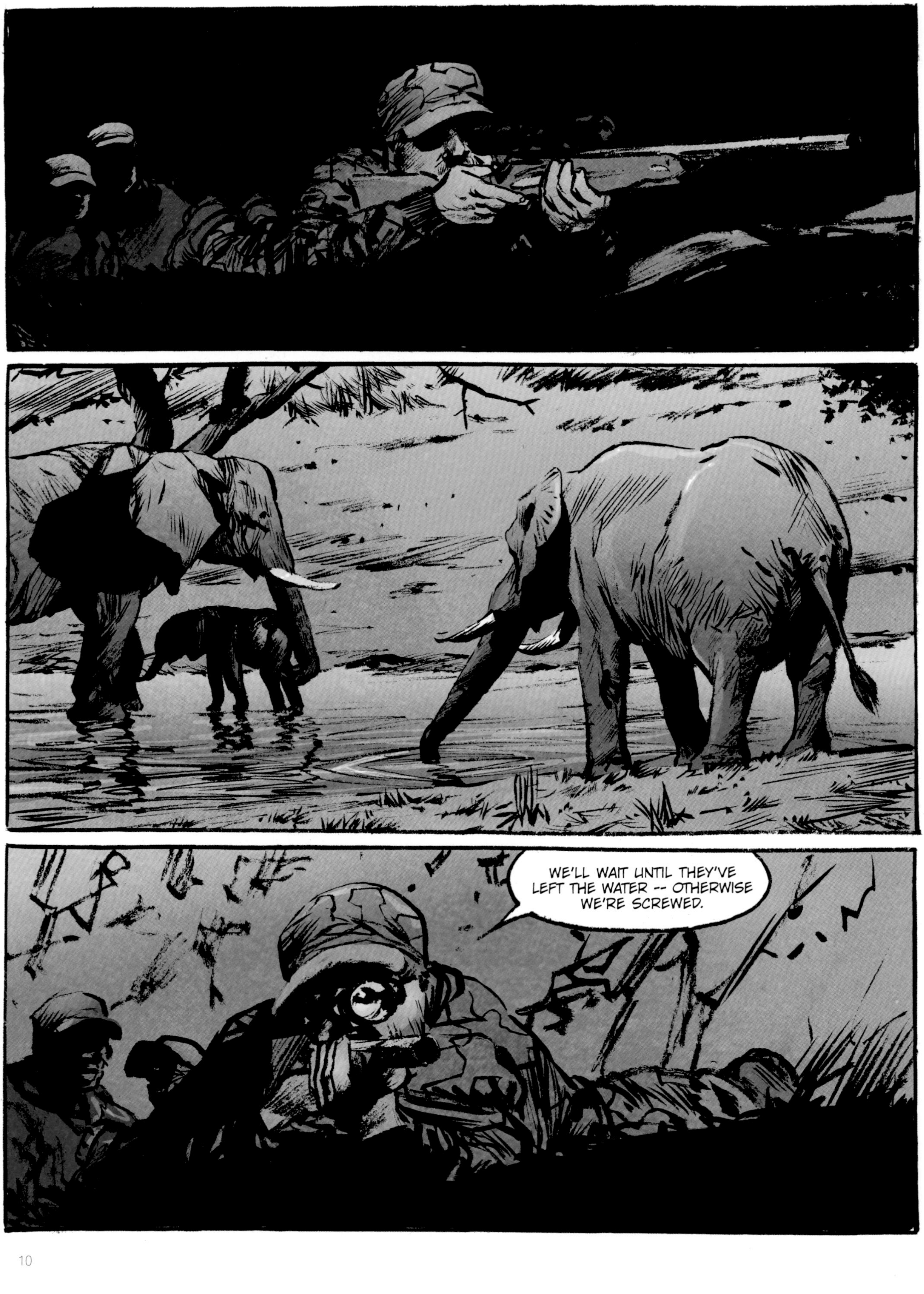
WE'LL WAIT UNTIL THEY'VE LEFT THE WATER -- OTHERWISE WE'RE SCREWED.

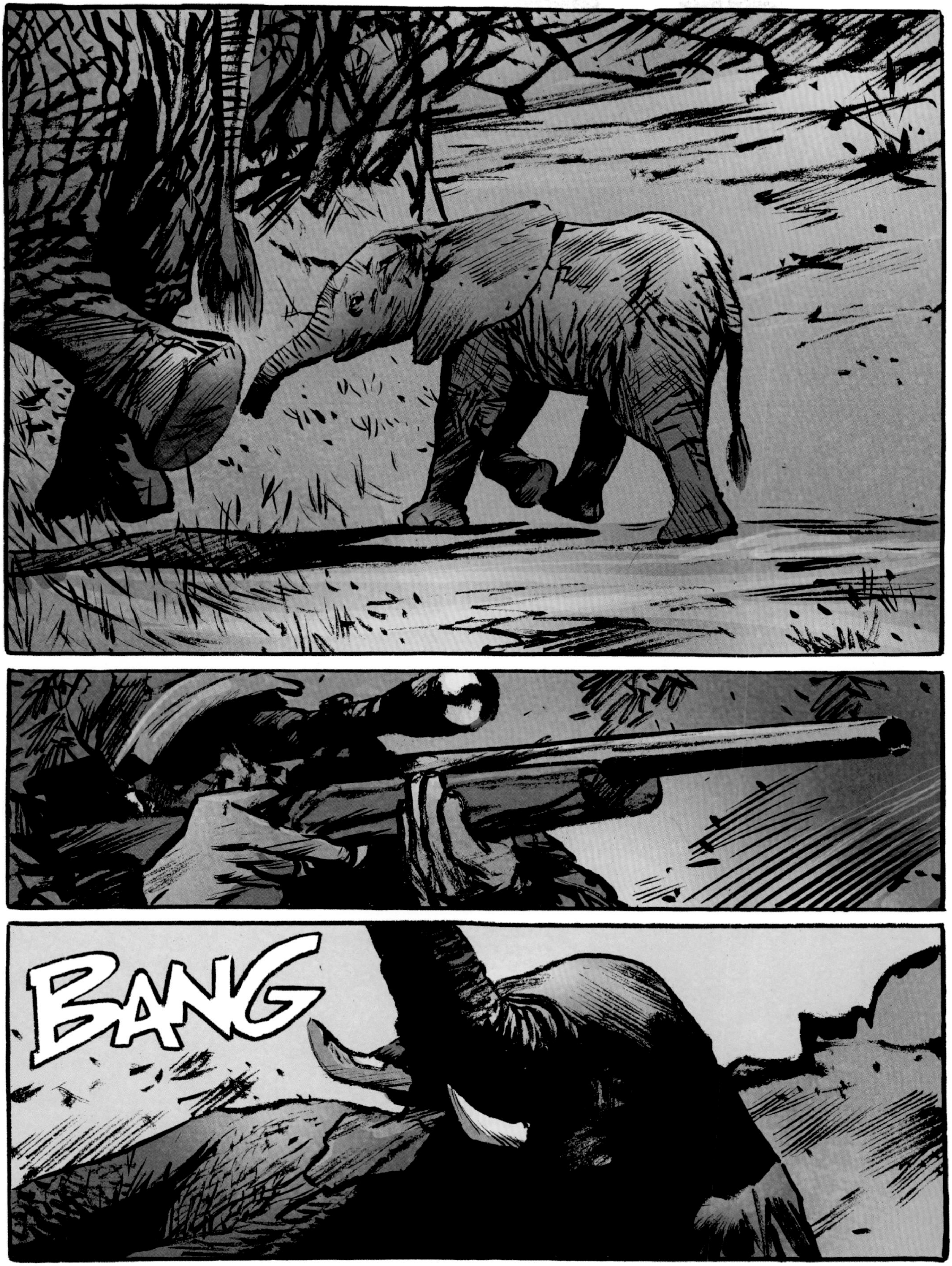
BANG

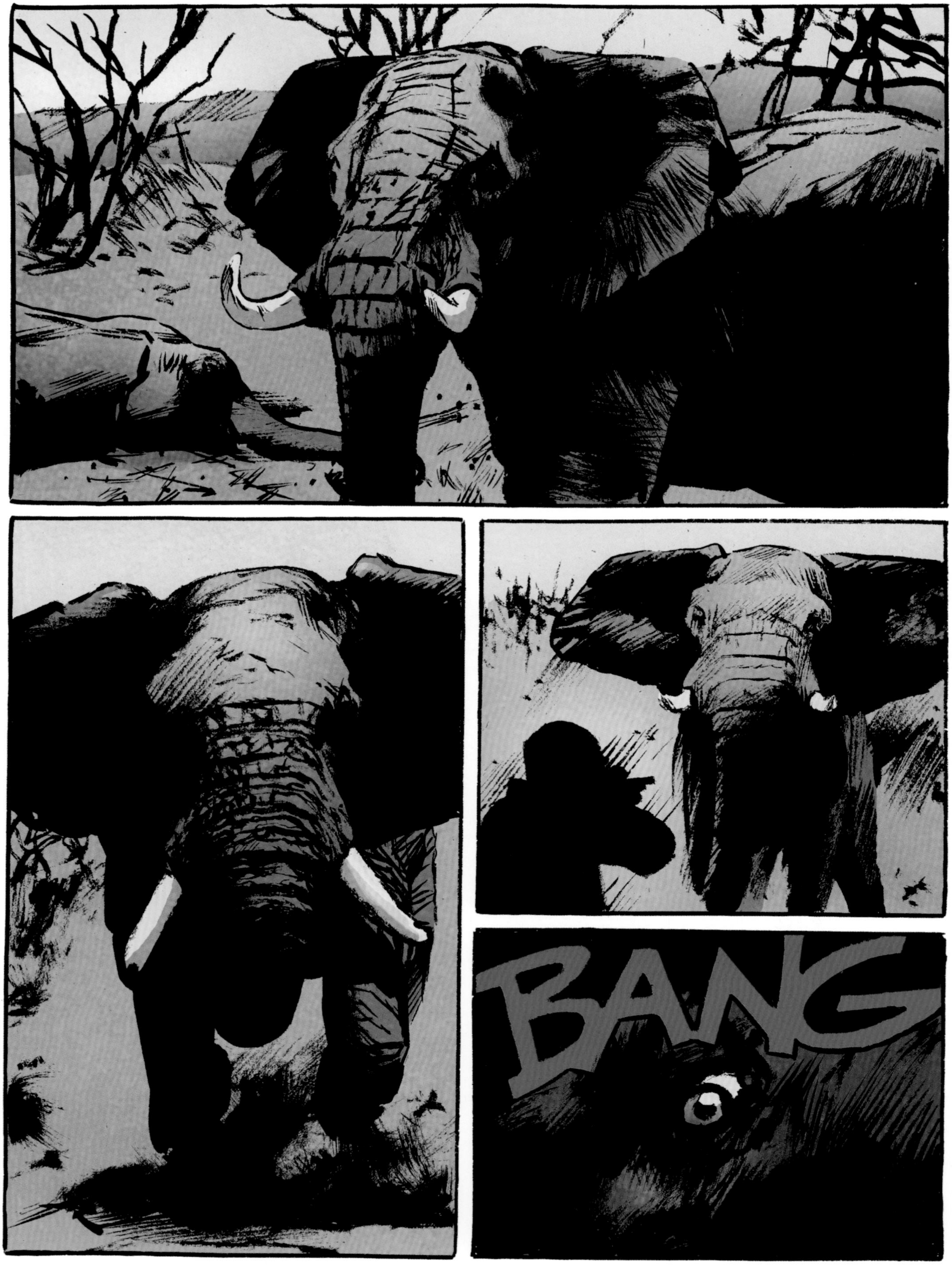
BANG

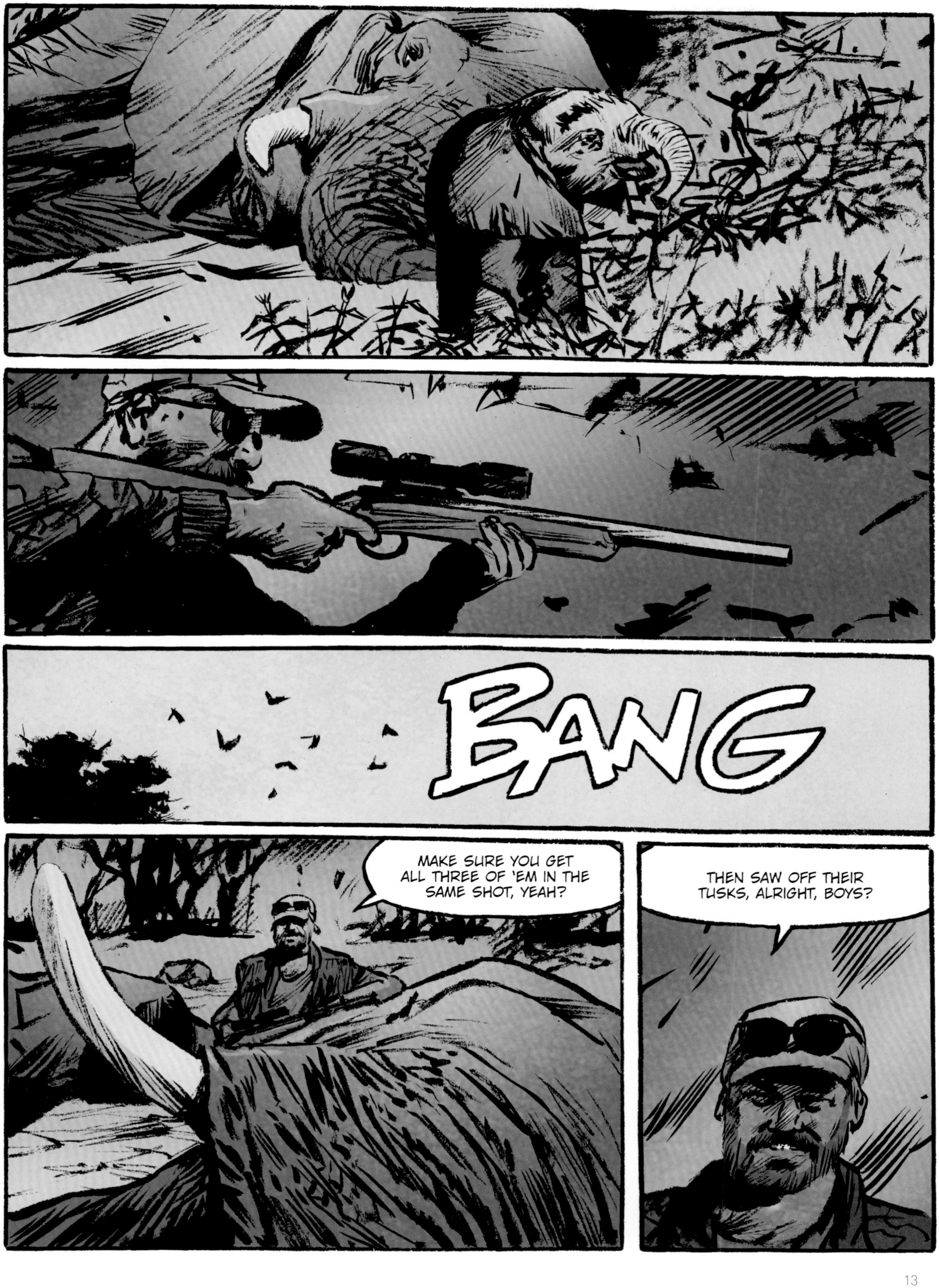
BANG
MAKE SURE YOU GET ALL THREE OF 'EM IN THE SAME SHOT, YEAH?
THEN SAW OFF THEIR TUSKS, ALRIGHT, BOYS?

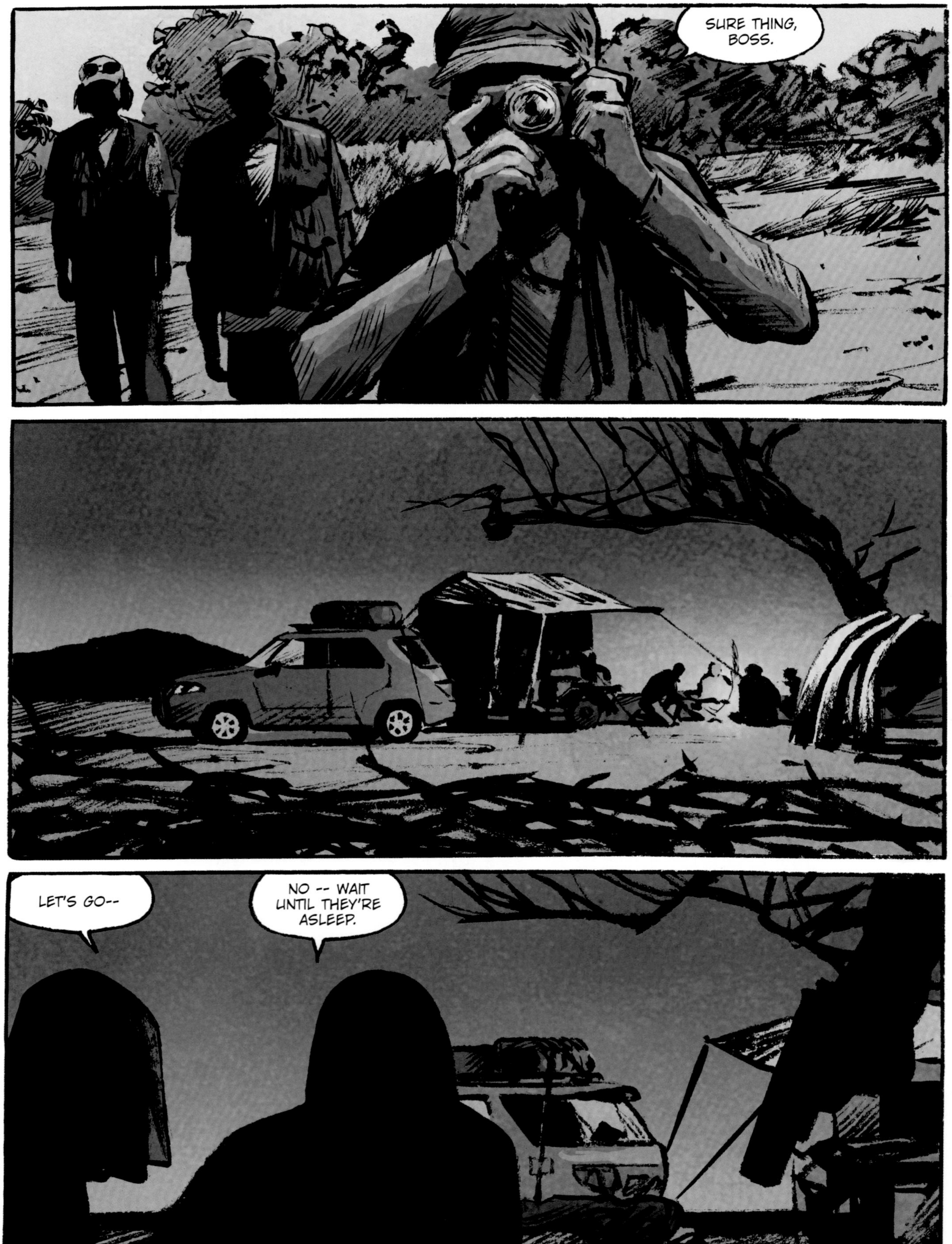
SURE THING, BOSS.
LET'S GO--
NO -- WAIT UNTIL THEY'RE ASLEEP.

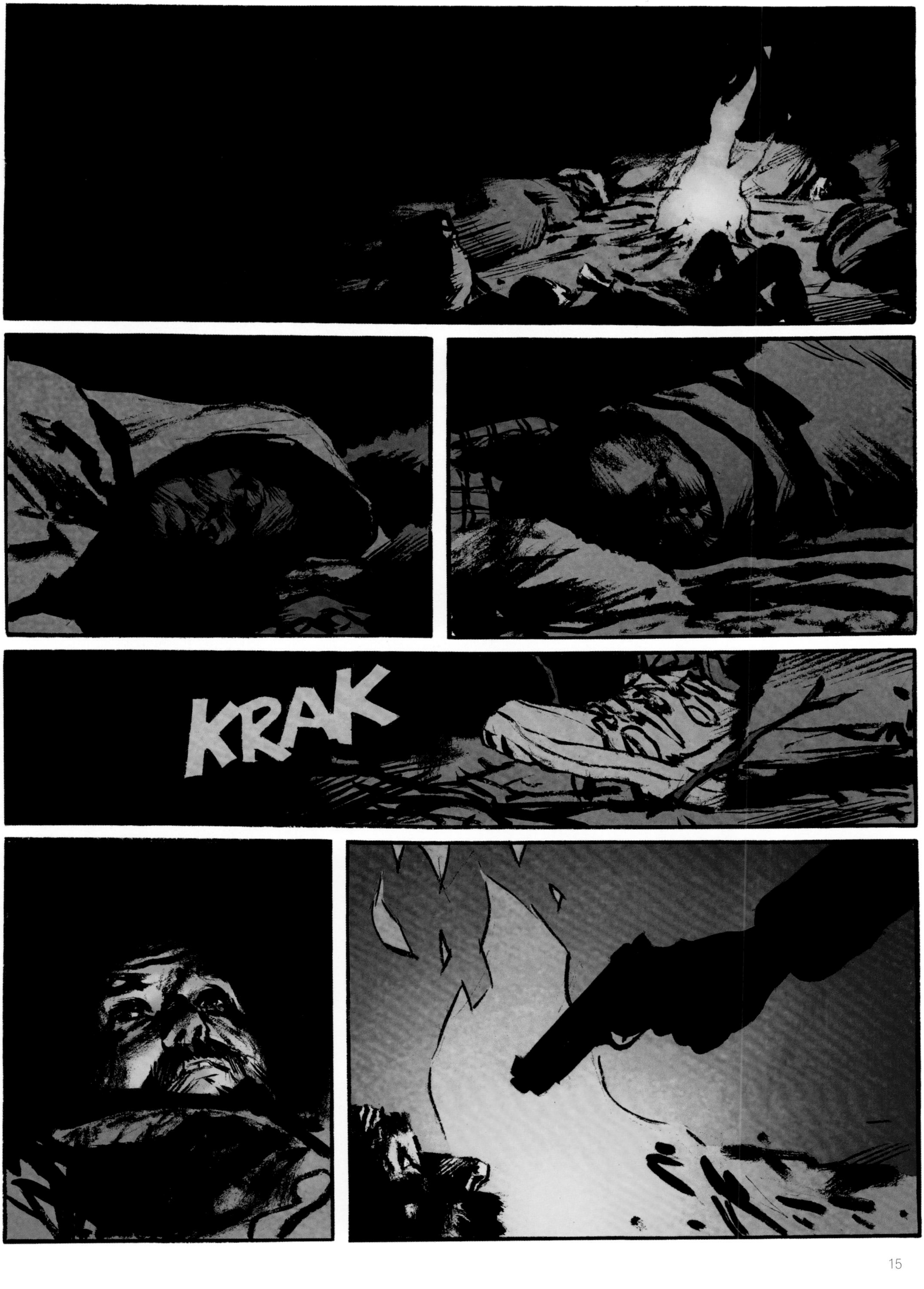
KRAK

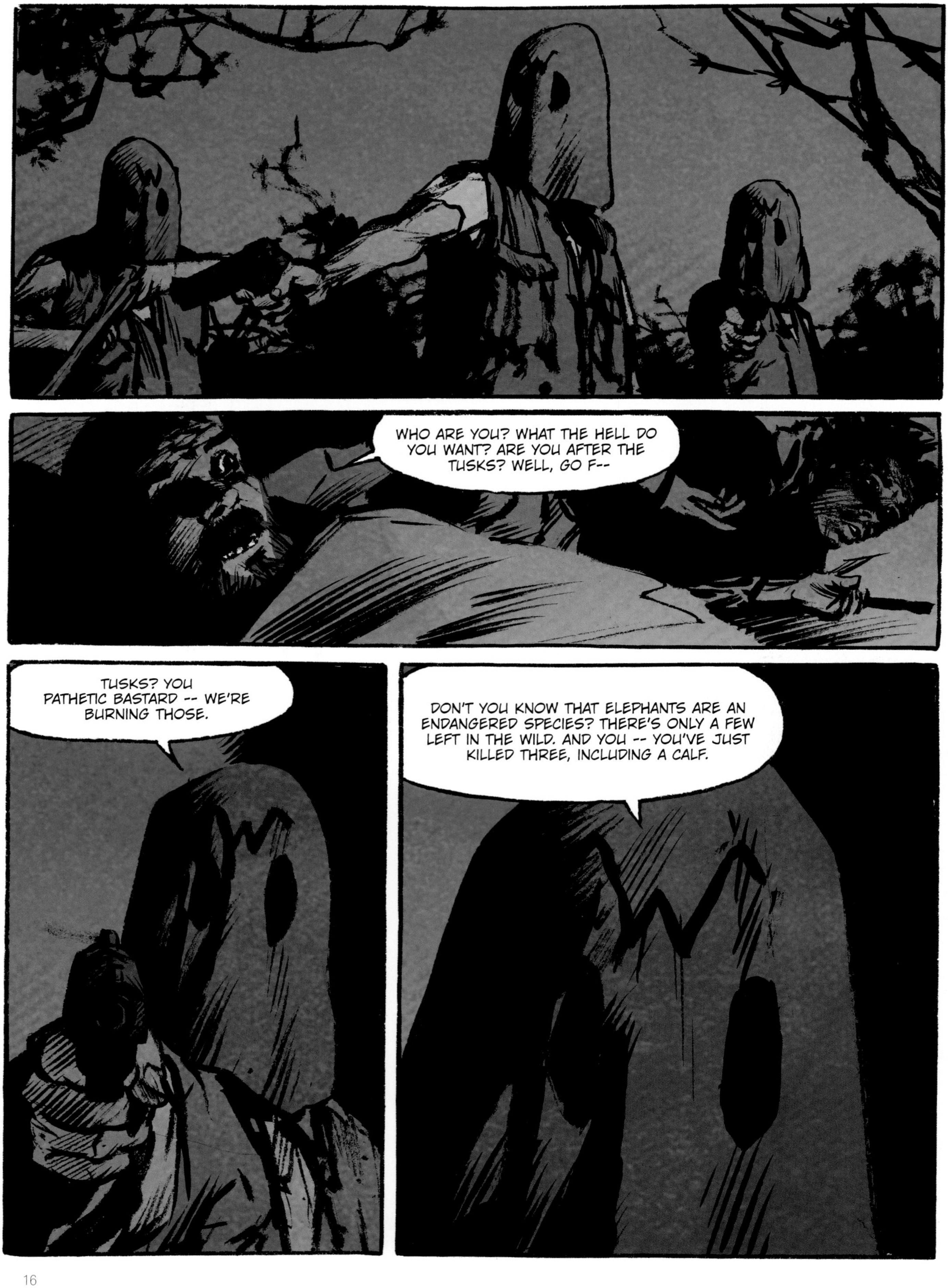
WHO ARE YOU? WHAT THE HELL DO YOU WANT? ARE YOU AFTER THE TUSKS? WELL, GO F--
TUSKS? YOU PATHETIC BASTARD -- WE'RE BURNING THOSE.
DON'T YOU KNOW THAT ELEPHANTS ARE AN ENDANGERED SPECIES? THERE'S ONLY A FEW LEFT IN THE WILD. AND YOU -- YOU'VE JUST KILLED THREE, INCLUDING A CALF.

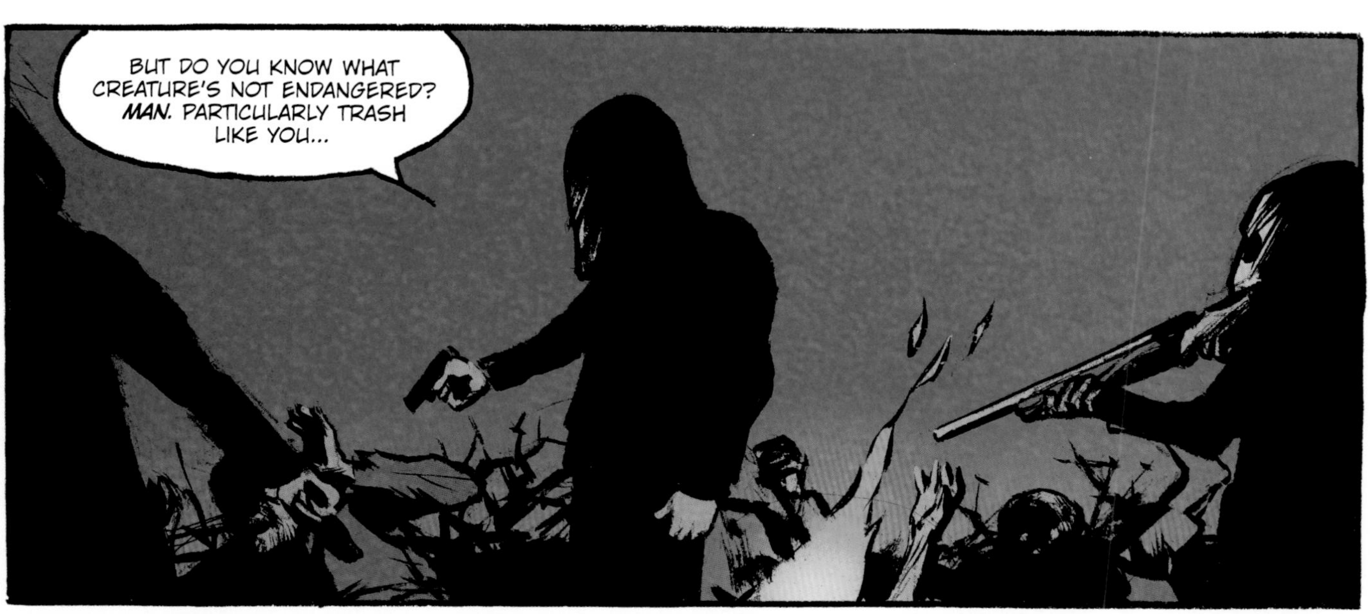
BUT DO YOU KNOW WHAT CREATURE'S NOT ENDANGERED? *MAN.* PARTICULARLY TRASH LIKE YOU...

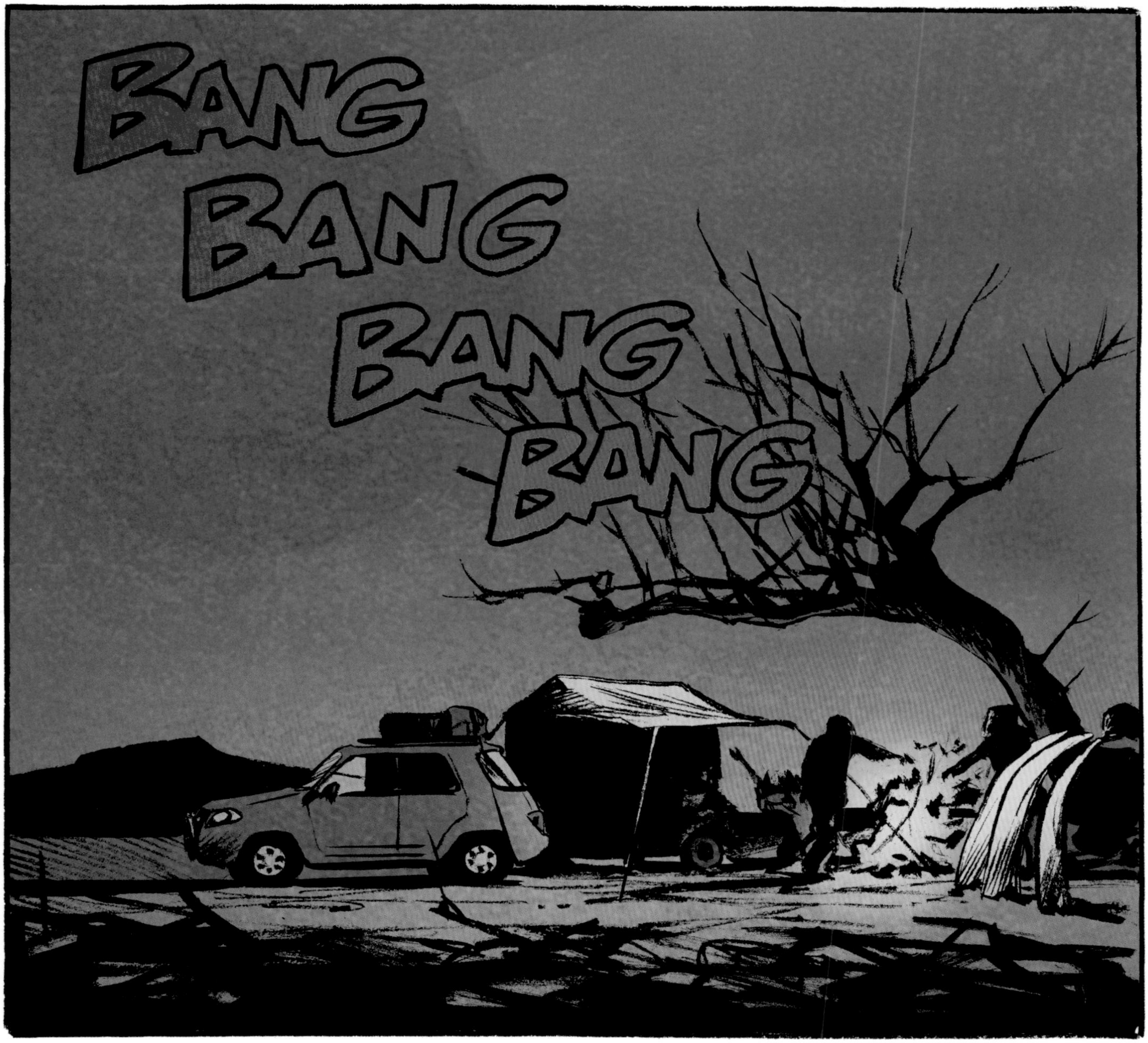
BANG
BANG
BANG
BANG

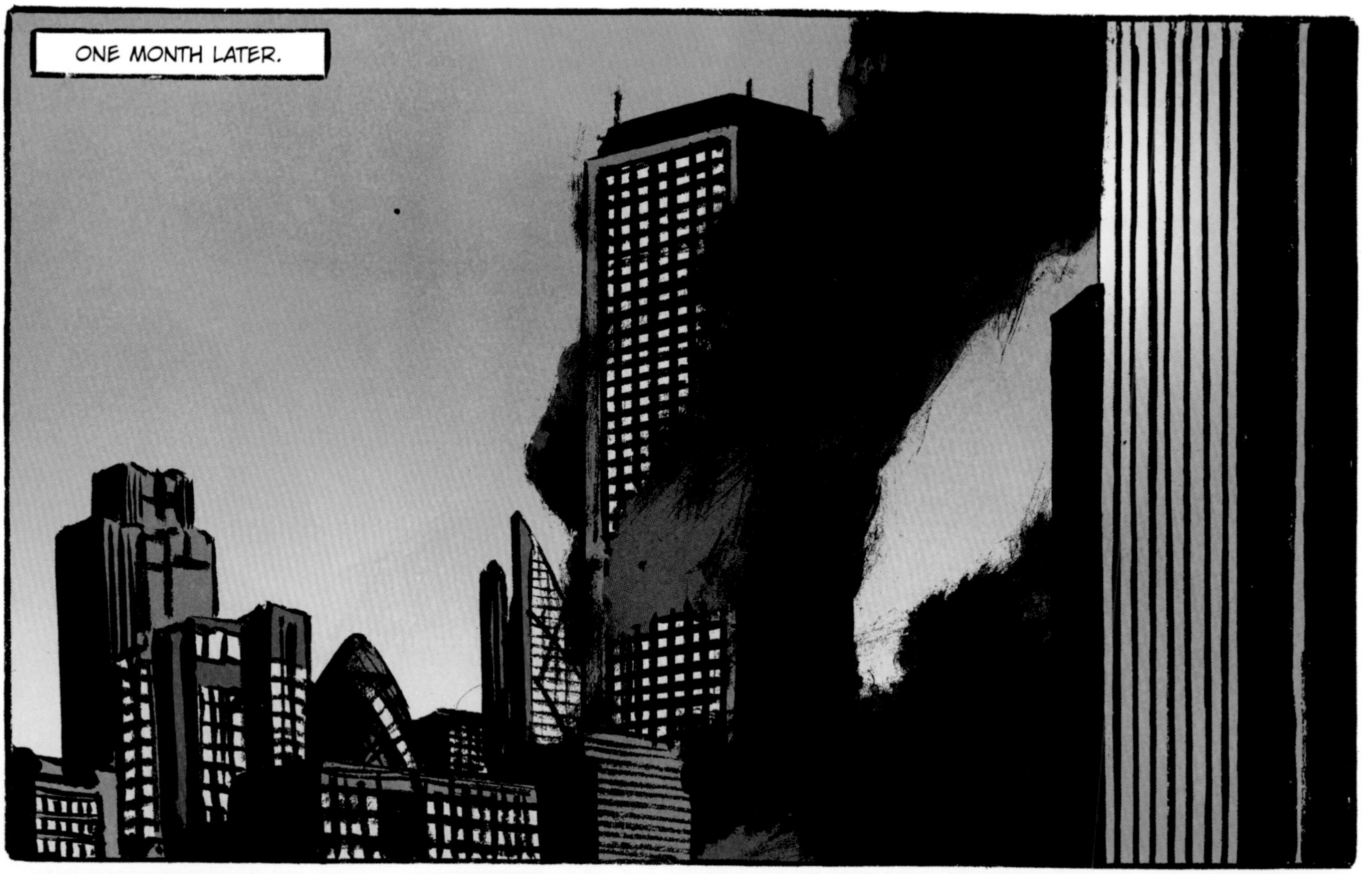
ONE MONTH LATER.

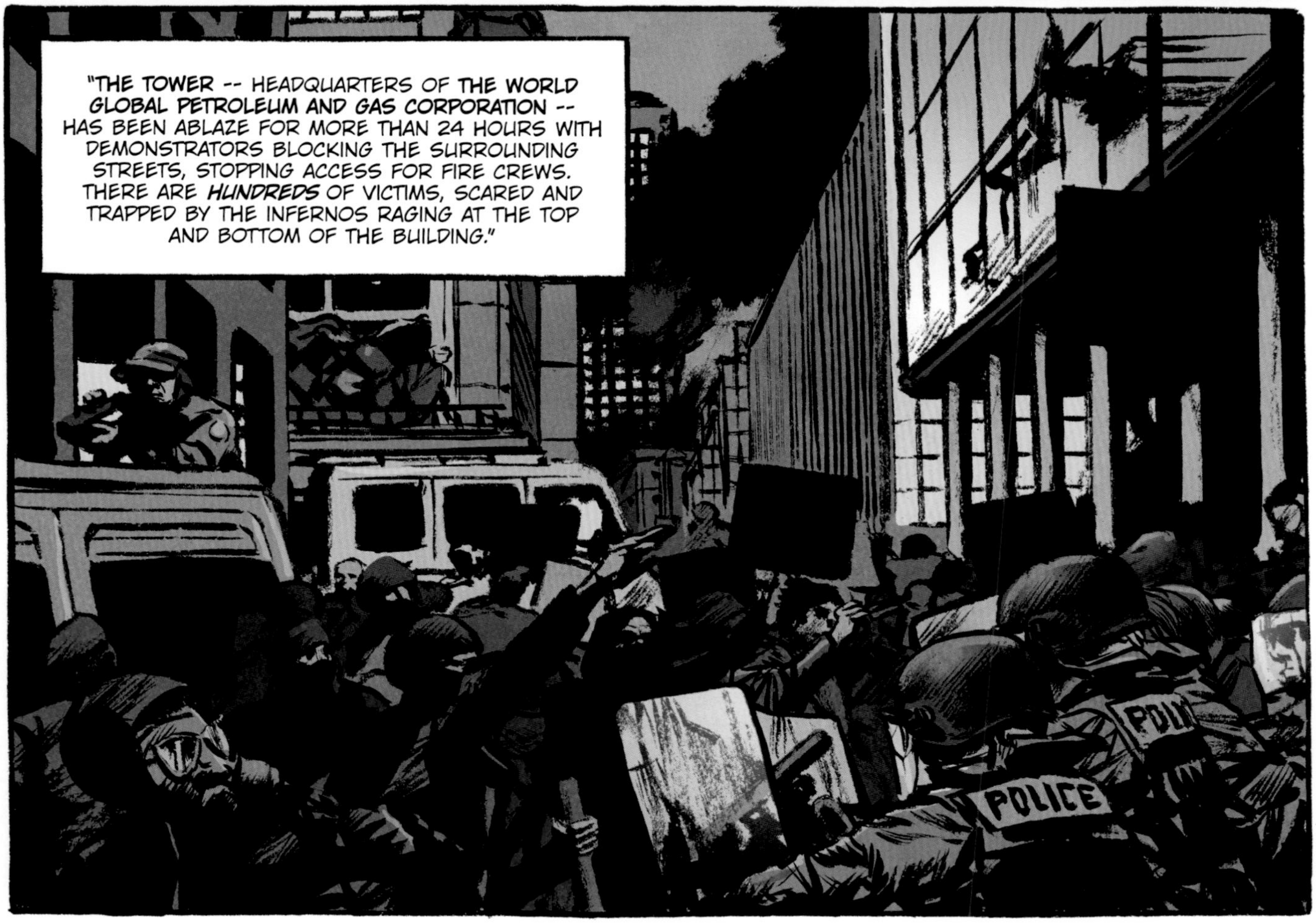
"THE TOWER -- HEADQUARTERS OF THE WORLD GLOBAL PETROLEUM AND GAS CORPORATION -- HAS BEEN ABLAZE FOR MORE THAN 24 HOURS WITH DEMONSTRATORS BLOCKING THE SURROUNDING STREETS, STOPPING ACCESS FOR FIRE CREWS. THERE ARE HUNDREDS OF VICTIMS, SCARED AND TRAPPED BY THE INFERNOS RAGING AT THE TOP AND BOTTOM OF THE BUILDING."
POLICE
POLI

THE SO-CALLED ECOLOGIST ACTIVIST ORGANIZATION -- *WRATH* -- HAS CLAIMED RESPONSIBILITY FOR THIS ARSON. I MET WITH ONE OF ITS MEMBERS EARLIER TODAY. WHAT FOLLOWS IS OUR CONVERSATION.

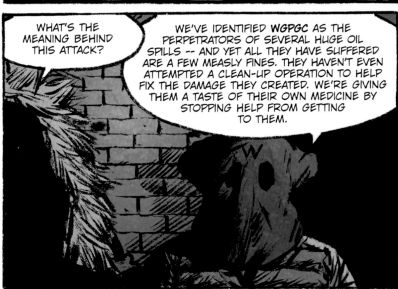

WHAT'S THE MEANING BEHIND THIS ATTACK?

WE'VE IDENTIFIED **WGPGC** AS THE PERPETRATORS OF SEVERAL HUGE OIL SPILLS -- AND YET ALL THEY HAVE SUFFERED ARE A FEW MEASLY FINES. THEY HAVEN'T EVEN ATTEMPTED A CLEAN-UP OPERATION TO HELP FIX THE DAMAGE THEY CREATED. WE'RE GIVING THEM A TASTE OF THEIR OWN MEDICINE BY STOPPING HELP FROM GETTING TO THEM.

SO YOU'RE SAYING THAT THIS IS A DELIBERATELY POLITICAL ATTACK ON WGPGC?

NO -- IT'S AN ECOLOGICAL ONE. AT THEIR RECENT AGM, WGPGC SHOULD HAVE AGREED TO SHARE THE RESPONSIBILITY FOR THE CLEAN-UP, NOT REWARDED THEIR SHAREHOLDERS FOR THEIR INACTION. OUR MESSAGE IS CLEAR -- WE *WRATHERS* WANT FEAR AND PUNISHMENT TO MAKE THEM THINK OTHERWISE.

BUT YOUR ACTIONS ARE BREAKING THE LAW. YOU'RE A CRIMINAL ORGANIZATION, RESPONSIBLE FOR DOZENS OF DEATHS!

IT'S NO WORSE THAN THE DESTRUCTION AND MURDER INFLICTED BY WGPGC. WE NEED THEM TO UNDERSTAND OUR MESSAGE IF THAT REQUIRES *SACRIFICES*...

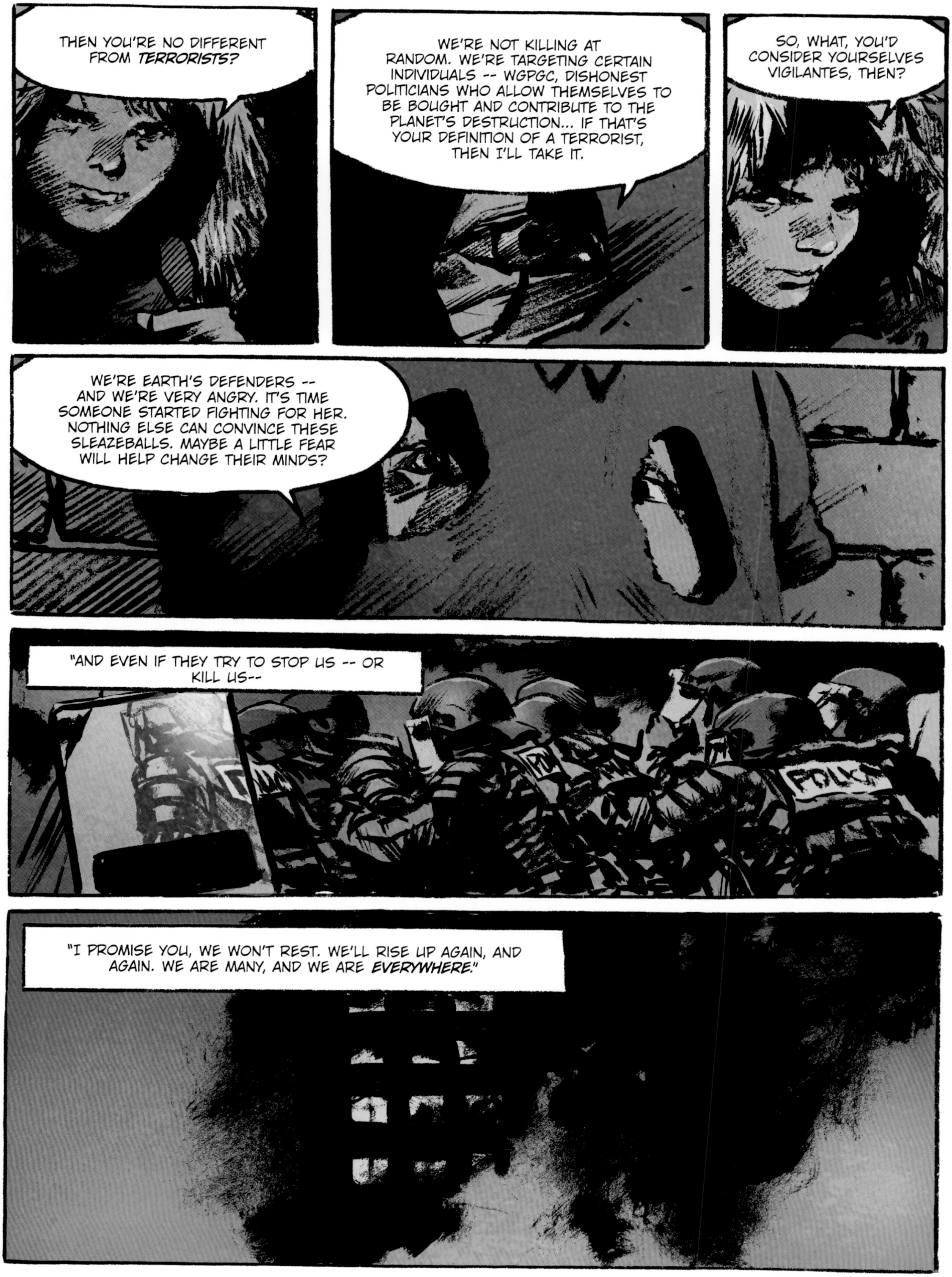
THEN YOU'RE NO DIFFERENT FROM *TERRORISTS?*
WE'RE NOT KILLING AT RANDOM. WE'RE TARGETING CERTAIN INDIVIDUALS -- WGPGC, DISHONEST POLITICIANS WHO ALLOW THEMSELVES TO BE BOUGHT AND CONTRIBUTE TO THE PLANET'S DESTRUCTION... IF THAT'S YOUR DEFINITION OF A TERRORIST, THEN I'LL TAKE IT.
SO, WHAT, YOU'D CONSIDER YOURSELVES VIGILANTES, THEN?
WE'RE EARTH'S DEFENDERS -- AND WE'RE VERY ANGRY. IT'S TIME SOMEONE STARTED FIGHTING FOR HER. NOTHING ELSE CAN CONVINCE THESE SLEAZEBALLS. MAYBE A LITTLE FEAR WILL HELP CHANGE THEIR MINDS?
"AND EVEN IF THEY TRY TO STOP US -- OR KILL US--
POLIC
"I PROMISE YOU, WE WON'T REST. WE'LL RISE UP AGAIN, AND AGAIN. WE ARE MANY, AND WE ARE *EVERYWHERE.*"

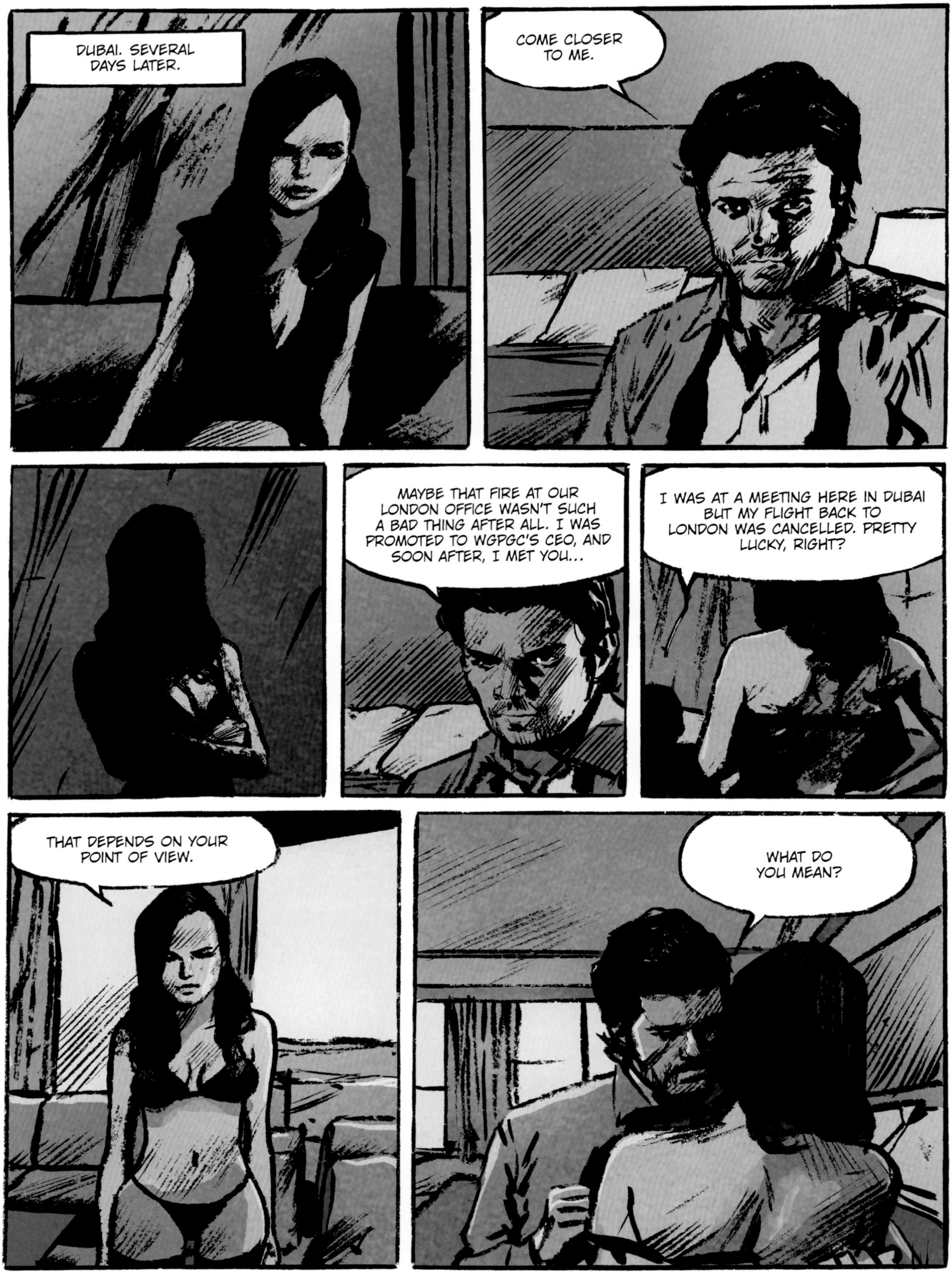
DUBAI. SEVERAL DAYS LATER.
COME CLOSER TO ME.
MAYBE THAT FIRE AT OUR LONDON OFFICE WASN'T SUCH A BAD THING AFTER ALL. I WAS PROMOTED TO WGPGC'S CEO, AND SOON AFTER, I MET YOU...
I WAS AT A MEETING HERE IN DUBAI BUT MY FLIGHT BACK TO LONDON WAS CANCELLED. PRETTY LUCKY, RIGHT?
THAT DEPENDS ON YOUR POINT OF VIEW.
WHAT DO YOU MEAN?

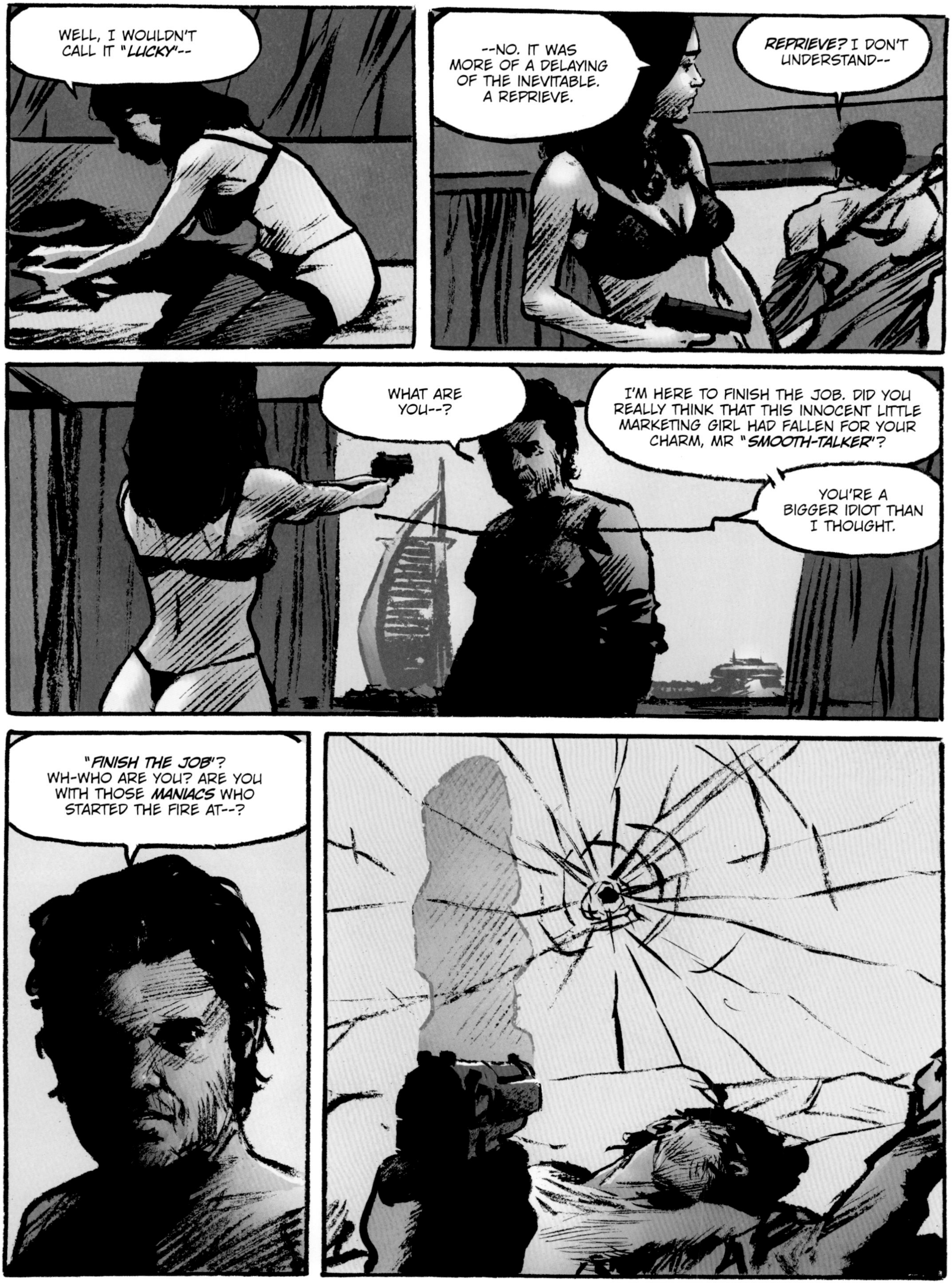
WELL, I WOULDN'T CALL IT "LUCKY"--
--NO. IT WAS MORE OF A DELAYING OF THE INEVITABLE. A REPRIEVE.
REPRIEVE? I DON'T UNDERSTAND--
WHAT ARE YOU--?
I'M HERE TO FINISH THE JOB. DID YOU REALLY THINK THAT THIS INNOCENT LITTLE MARKETING GIRL HAD FALLEN FOR YOUR CHARM, MR "SMOOTH-TALKER"?
YOU'RE A BIGGER IDIOT THAN I THOUGHT.
"FINISH THE JOB"? WH-WHO ARE YOU? ARE YOU WITH THOSE MANIACS WHO STARTED THE FIRE AT--?

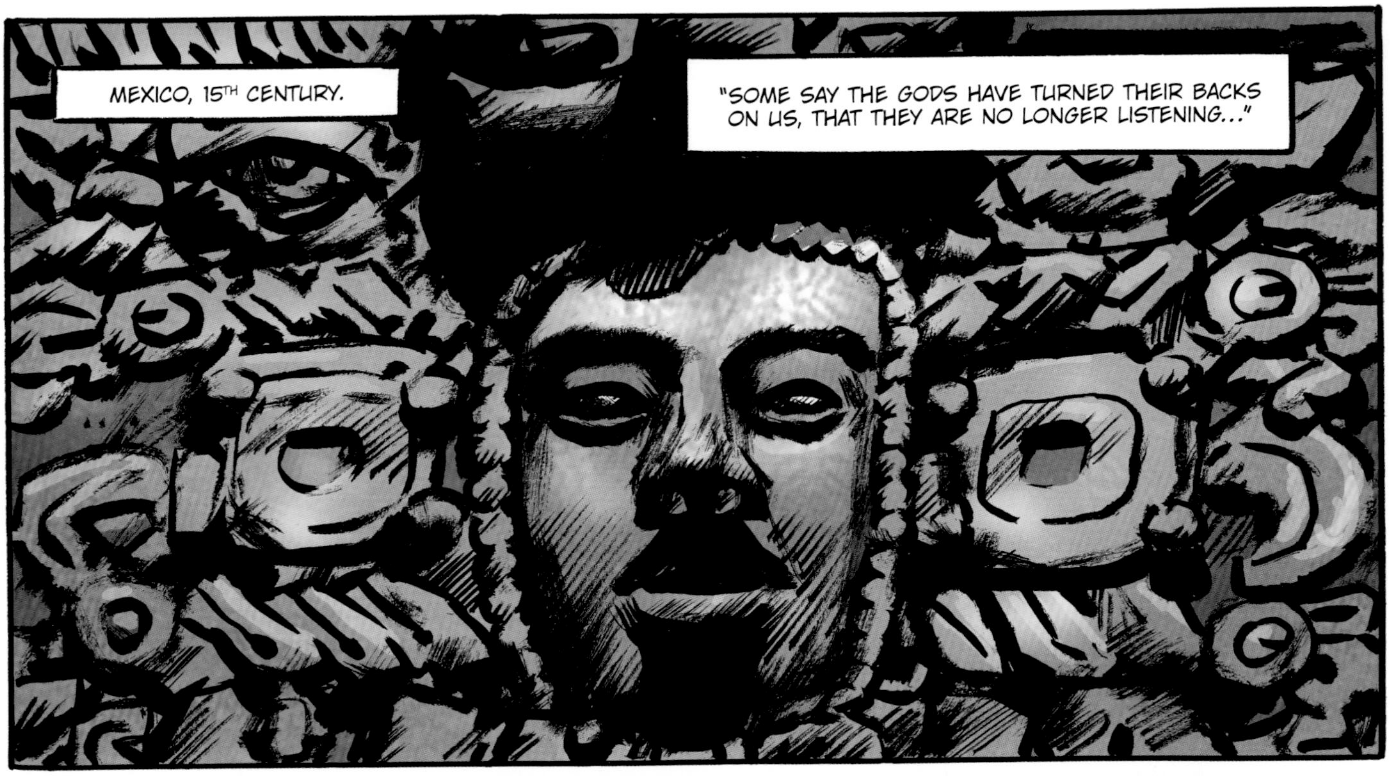
MEXICO, 15TH CENTURY.
"SOME SAY THE GODS HAVE TURNED THEIR BACKS ON US, THAT THEY ARE NO LONGER LISTENING..."
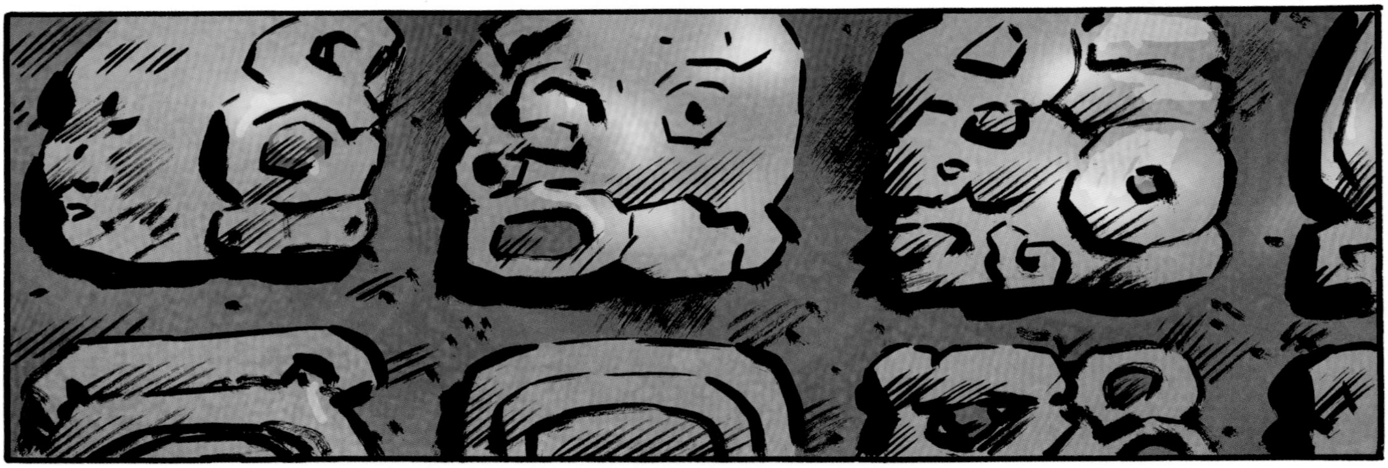
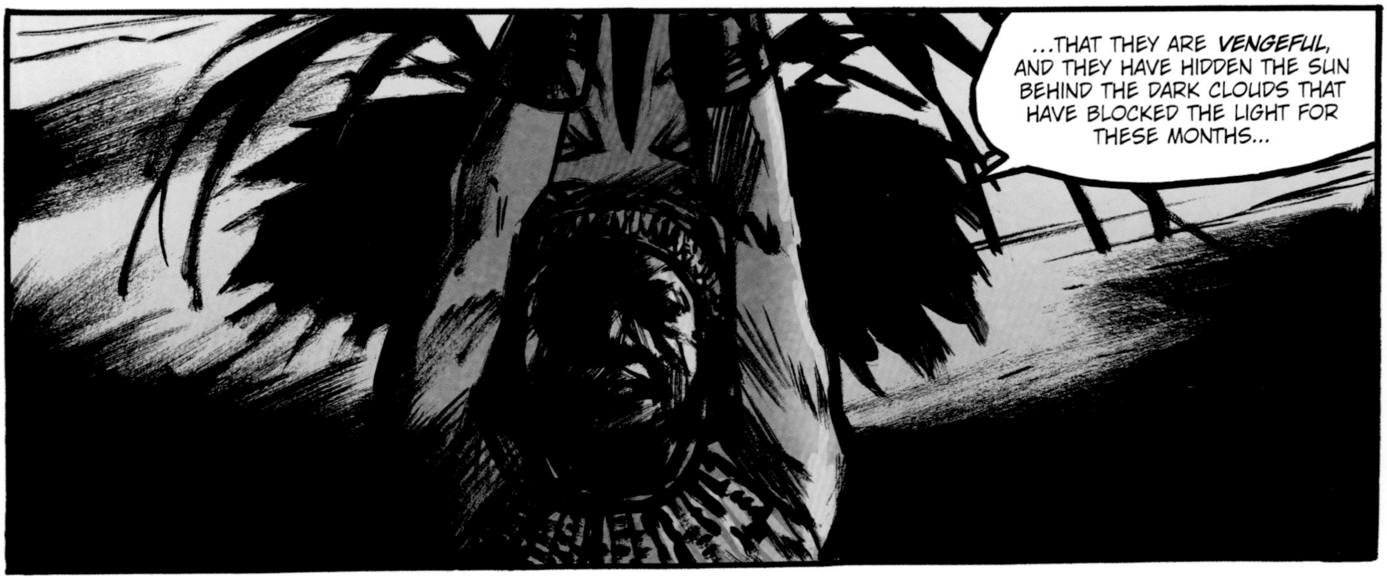
...THAT THEY ARE ***VENGEFUL***, AND THEY HAVE HIDDEN THE SUN BEHIND THE DARK CLOUDS THAT HAVE BLOCKED THE LIGHT FOR THESE MONTHS...

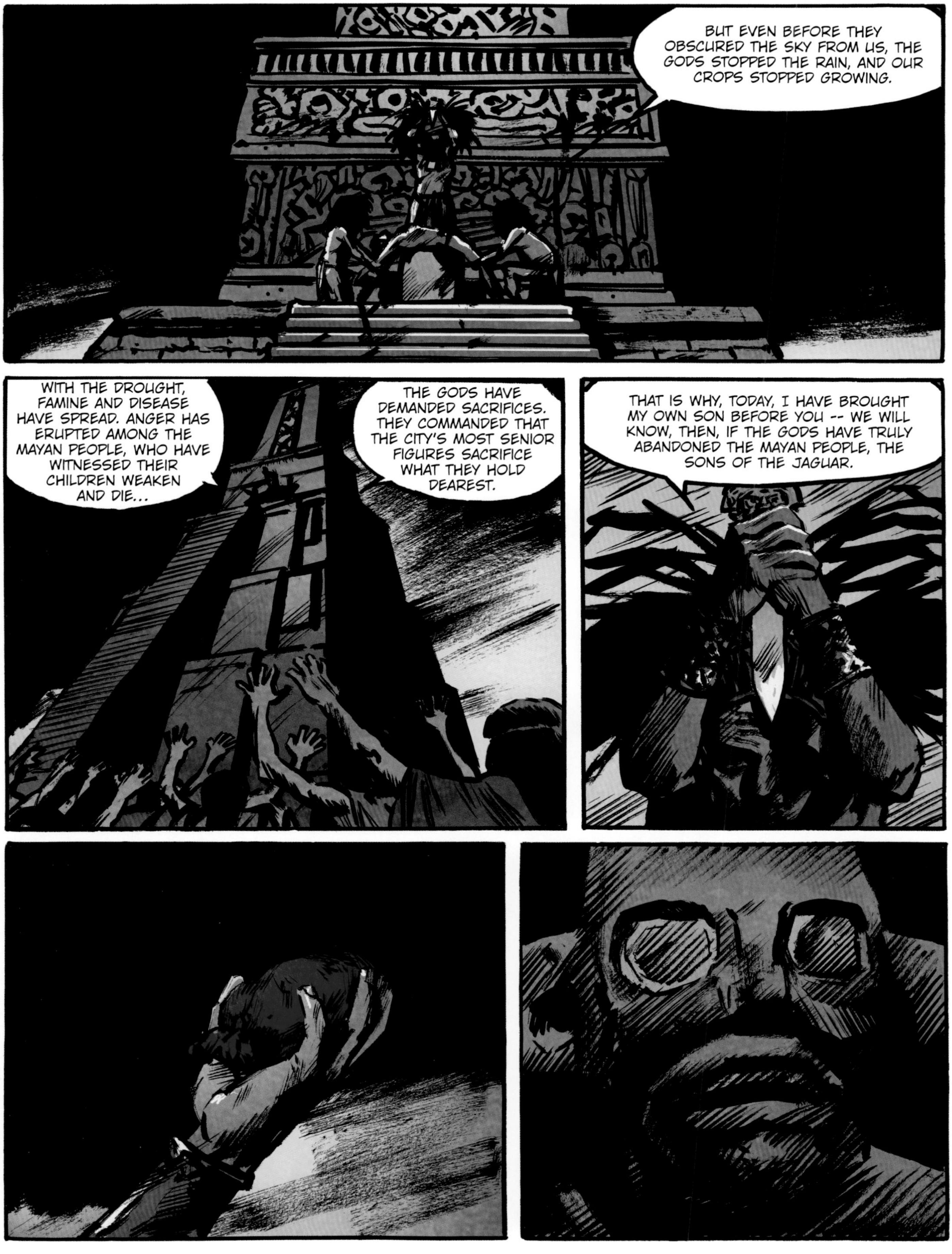
BUT EVEN BEFORE THEY OBSCURED THE SKY FROM US, THE GODS STOPPED THE RAIN, AND OUR CROPS STOPPED GROWING.
WITH THE DROUGHT, FAMINE AND DISEASE HAVE SPREAD. ANGER HAS ERUPTED AMONG THE MAYAN PEOPLE, WHO HAVE WITNESSED THEIR CHILDREN WEAKEN AND DIE...
THE GODS HAVE DEMANDED SACRIFICES. THEY COMMANDED THAT THE CITY'S MOST SENIOR FIGURES SACRIFICE WHAT THEY HOLD DEAREST.
THAT IS WHY, TODAY, I HAVE BROUGHT MY OWN SON BEFORE YOU -- WE WILL KNOW, THEN, IF THE GODS HAVE TRULY ABANDONED THE MAYAN PEOPLE, THE SONS OF THE JAGUAR.

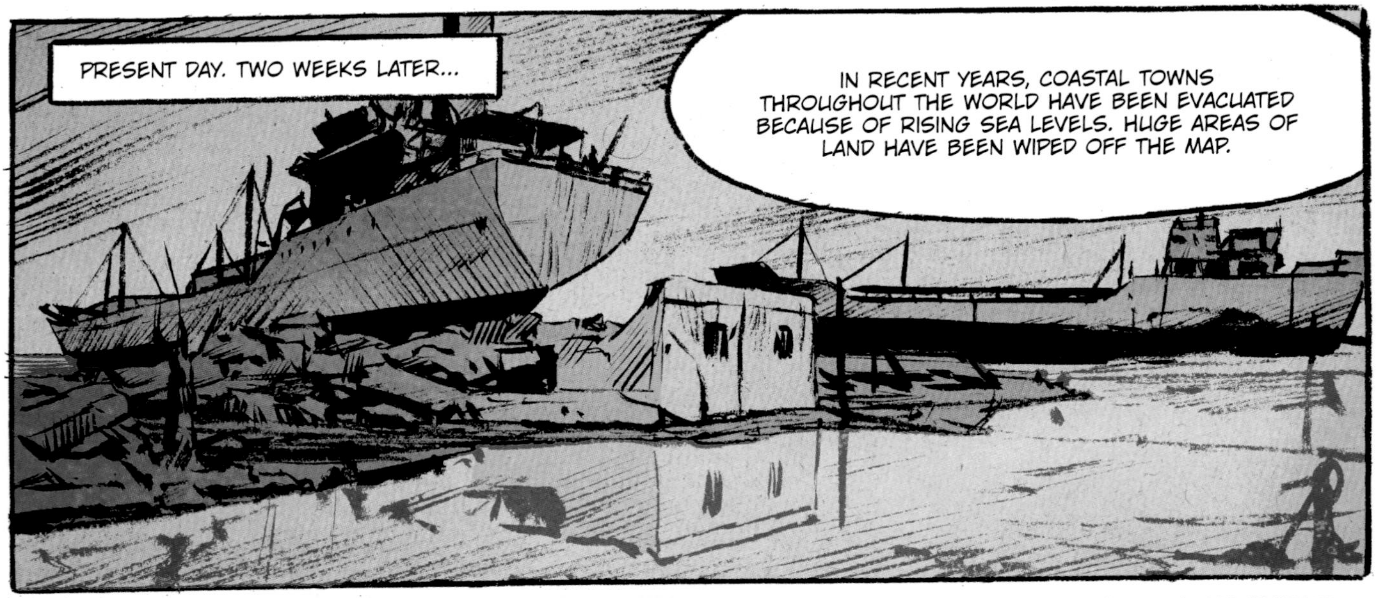
PRESENT DAY. TWO WEEKS LATER...
IN RECENT YEARS, COASTAL TOWNS THROUGHOUT THE WORLD HAVE BEEN EVACUATED BECAUSE OF RISING SEA LEVELS. HUGE AREAS OF LAND HAVE BEEN WIPED OFF THE MAP.

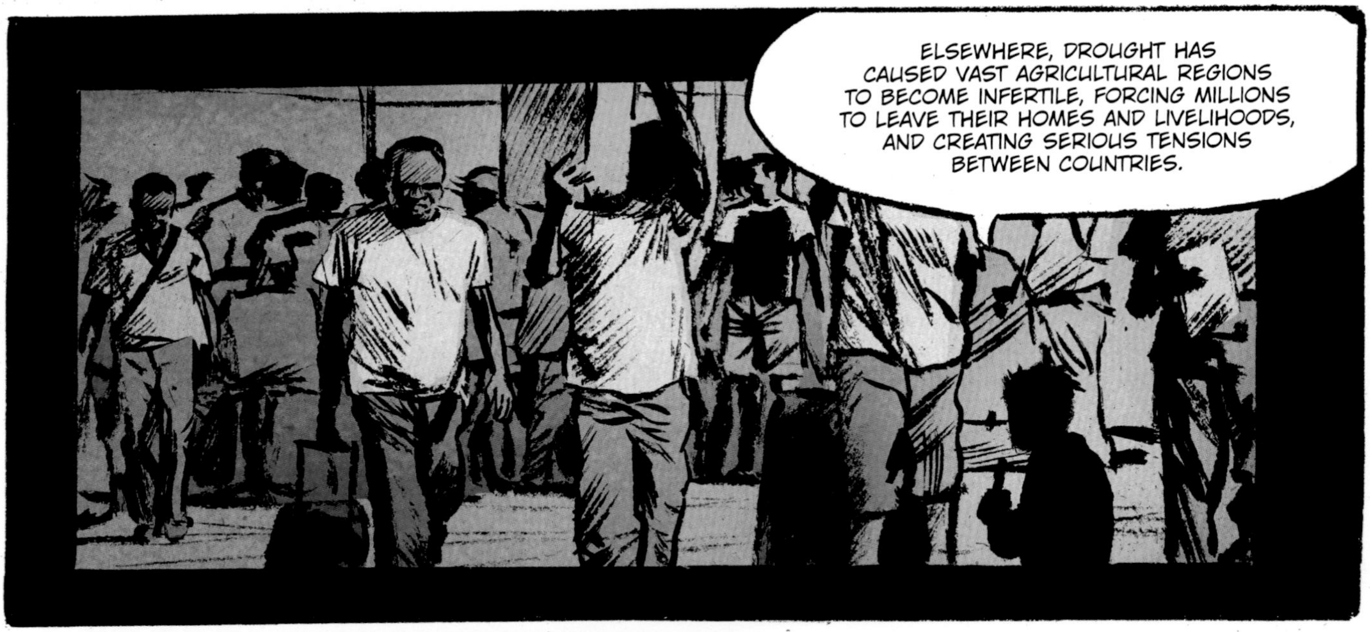
ELSEWHERE, DROUGHT HAS CAUSED VAST AGRICULTURAL REGIONS TO BECOME INFERTILE, FORCING MILLIONS TO LEAVE THEIR HOMES AND LIVELIHOODS, AND CREATING SERIOUS TENSIONS BETWEEN COUNTRIES.

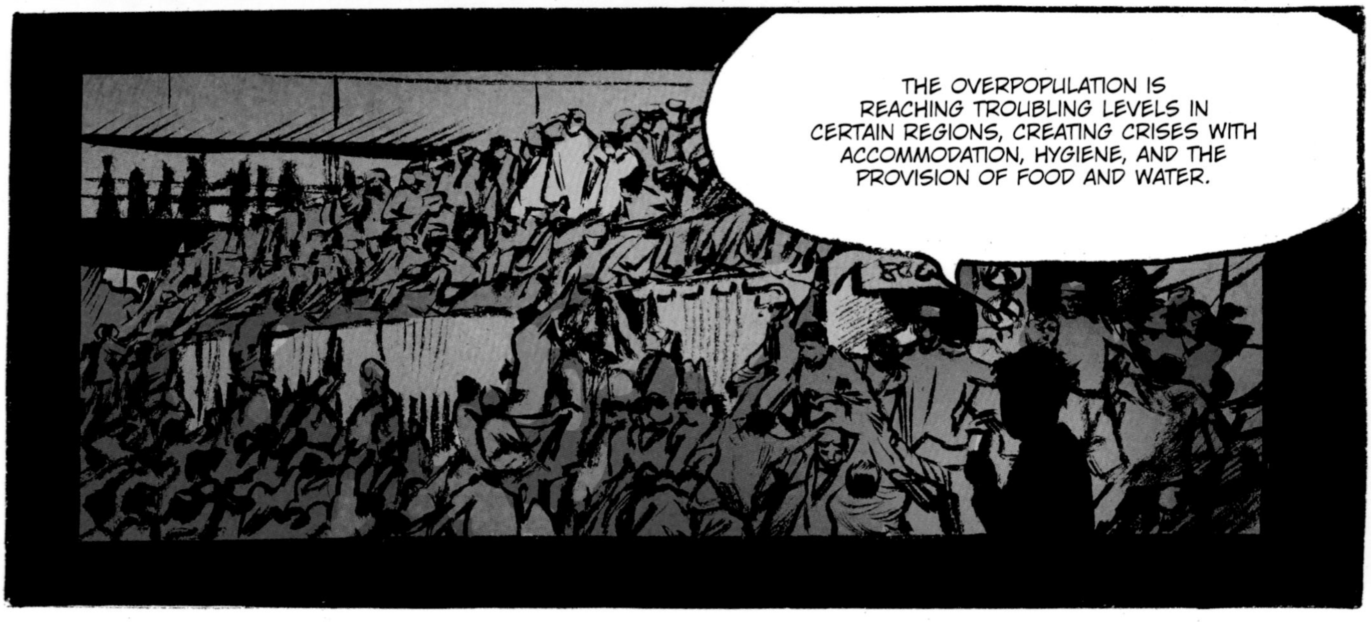
THE OVERPOPULATION IS REACHING TROUBLING LEVELS IN CERTAIN REGIONS, CREATING CRISES WITH ACCOMMODATION, HYGIENE, AND THE PROVISION OF FOOD AND WATER.

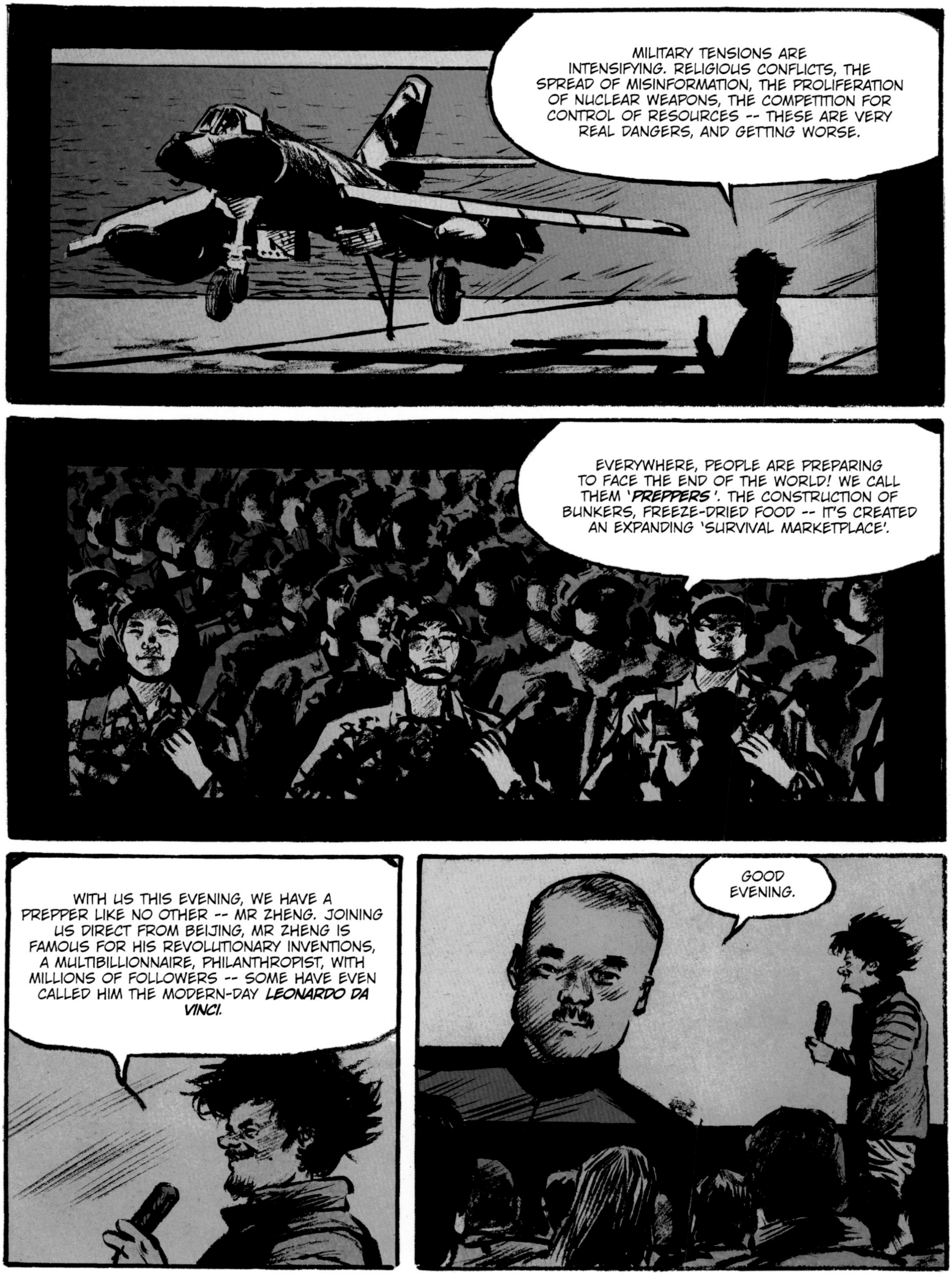

MILITARY TENSIONS ARE INTENSIFYING. RELIGIOUS CONFLICTS, THE SPREAD OF MISINFORMATION, THE PROLIFERATION OF NUCLEAR WEAPONS, THE COMPETITION FOR CONTROL OF RESOURCES -- THESE ARE VERY REAL DANGERS, AND GETTING WORSE.
EVERYWHERE, PEOPLE ARE PREPARING TO FACE THE END OF THE WORLD! WE CALL THEM '*PREPPERS*'. THE CONSTRUCTION OF BUNKERS, FREEZE-DRIED FOOD -- IT'S CREATED AN EXPANDING 'SURVIVAL MARKETPLACE'.
WITH US THIS EVENING, WE HAVE A PREPPER LIKE NO OTHER -- MR ZHENG. JOINING US DIRECT FROM BEIJING, MR ZHENG IS FAMOUS FOR HIS REVOLUTIONARY INVENTIONS, A MULTIBILLIONAIRE, PHILANTHROPIST, WITH MILLIONS OF FOLLOWERS -- SOME HAVE EVEN CALLED HIM THE MODERN-DAY ***LEONARDO DA VINCI***.
GOOD EVENING.

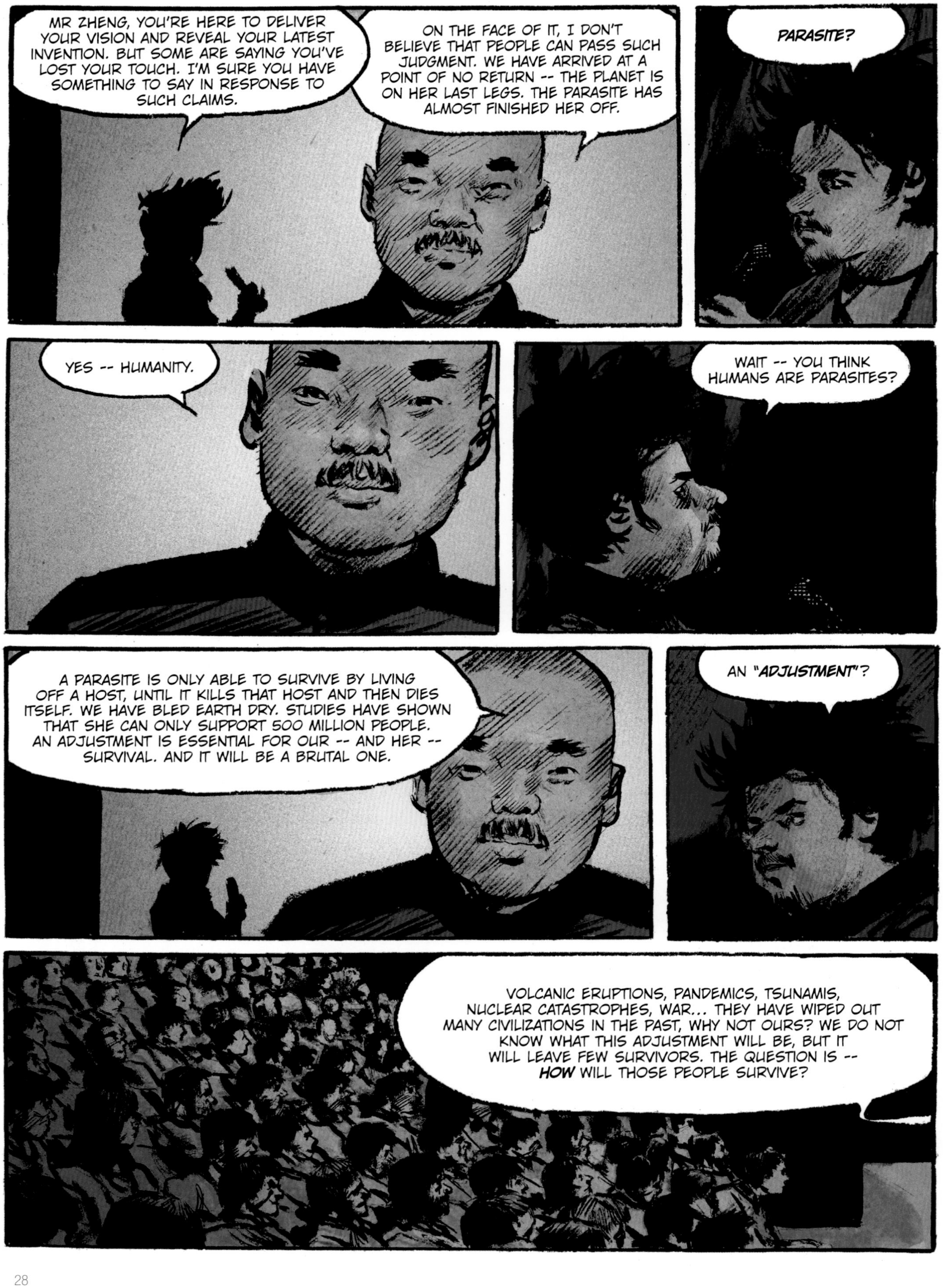
MR ZHENG, YOU'RE HERE TO DELIVER YOUR VISION AND REVEAL YOUR LATEST INVENTION. BUT SOME ARE SAYING YOU'VE LOST YOUR TOUCH. I'M SURE YOU HAVE SOMETHING TO SAY IN RESPONSE TO SUCH CLAIMS.
ON THE FACE OF IT, I DON'T BELIEVE THAT PEOPLE CAN PASS SUCH JUDGMENT. WE HAVE ARRIVED AT A POINT OF NO RETURN -- THE PLANET IS ON HER LAST LEGS. THE PARASITE HAS ALMOST FINISHED HER OFF.
PARASITE?
YES -- HUMANITY.
WAIT -- YOU THINK HUMANS ARE PARASITES?
A PARASITE IS ONLY ABLE TO SURVIVE BY LIVING OFF A HOST, UNTIL IT KILLS THAT HOST AND THEN DIES ITSELF. WE HAVE BLED EARTH DRY. STUDIES HAVE SHOWN THAT SHE CAN ONLY SUPPORT 500 MILLION PEOPLE. AN ADJUSTMENT IS ESSENTIAL FOR OUR -- AND HER -- SURVIVAL. AND IT WILL BE A BRUTAL ONE.
AN "*ADJUSTMENT*"?
VOLCANIC ERUPTIONS, PANDEMICS, TSUNAMIS, NUCLEAR CATASTROPHES, WAR... THEY HAVE WIPED OUT MANY CIVILIZATIONS IN THE PAST, WHY NOT OURS? WE DO NOT KNOW WHAT THIS ADJUSTMENT WILL BE, BUT IT WILL LEAVE FEW SURVIVORS. THE QUESTION IS -- *HOW* WILL THOSE PEOPLE SURVIVE?

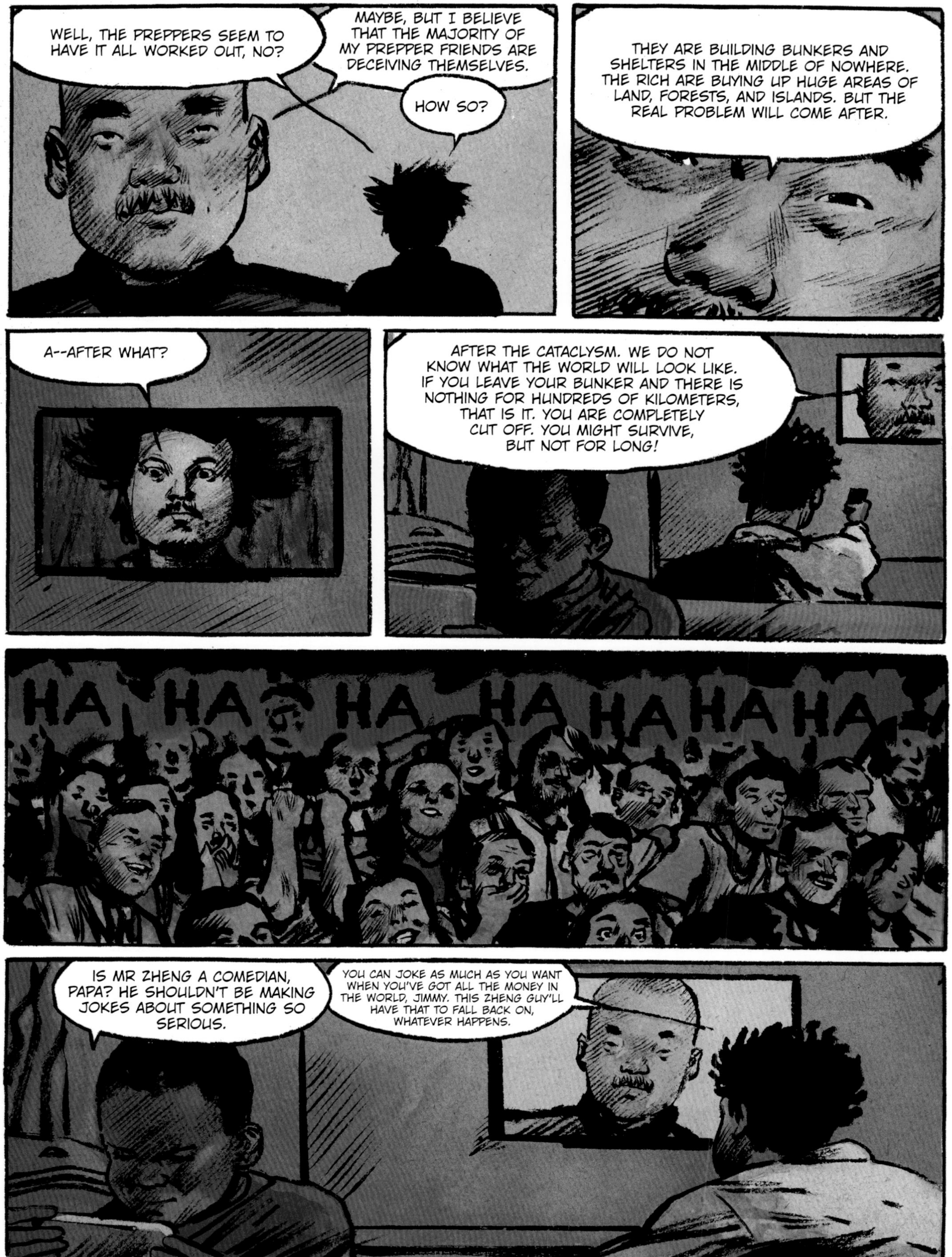
WELL, THE PREPPERS SEEM TO HAVE IT ALL WORKED OUT, NO?
MAYBE, BUT I BELIEVE THAT THE MAJORITY OF MY PREPPER FRIENDS ARE DECEIVING THEMSELVES.
HOW SO?
THEY ARE BUILDING BUNKERS AND SHELTERS IN THE MIDDLE OF NOWHERE. THE RICH ARE BUYING UP HUGE AREAS OF LAND, FORESTS, AND ISLANDS. BUT THE REAL PROBLEM WILL COME AFTER.
A--AFTER WHAT?
AFTER THE CATACLYSM. WE DO NOT KNOW WHAT THE WORLD WILL LOOK LIKE. IF YOU LEAVE YOUR BUNKER AND THERE IS NOTHING FOR HUNDREDS OF KILOMETERS, THAT IS IT. YOU ARE COMPLETELY CUT OFF. YOU MIGHT SURVIVE, BUT NOT FOR LONG!
HA HA HA HA HA HA HA HA HA
IS MR ZHENG A COMEDIAN, PAPA? HE SHOULDN'T BE MAKING JOKES ABOUT SOMETHING SO SERIOUS.
YOU CAN JOKE AS MUCH AS YOU WANT WHEN YOU'VE GOT ALL THE MONEY IN THE WORLD, JIMMY. THIS ZHENG GUY'LL HAVE THAT TO FALL BACK ON, WHATEVER HAPPENS.

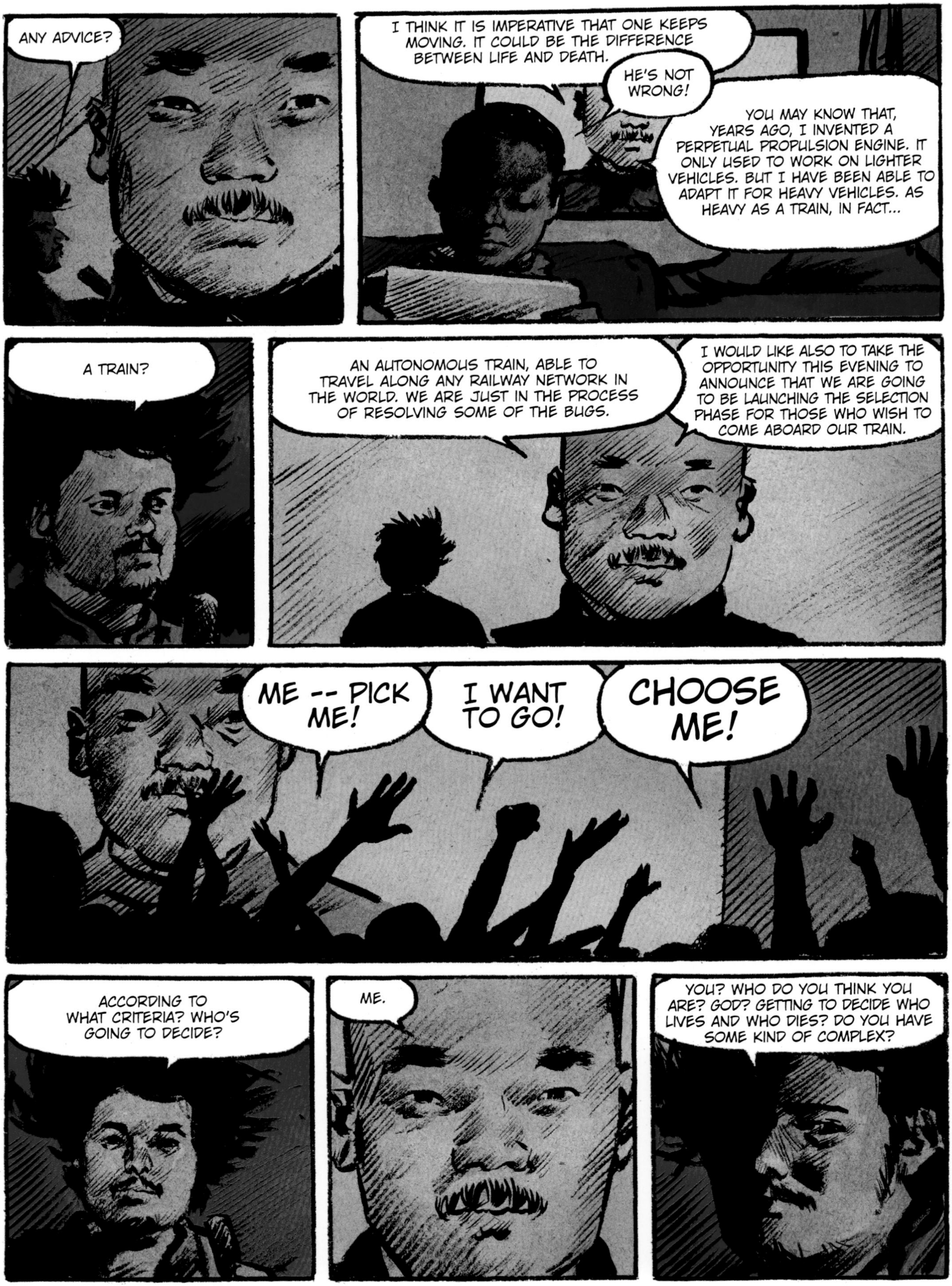
ANY ADVICE?
I THINK IT IS IMPERATIVE THAT ONE KEEPS MOVING. IT COULD BE THE DIFFERENCE BETWEEN LIFE AND DEATH.
HE'S NOT WRONG!
YOU MAY KNOW THAT, YEARS AGO, I INVENTED A PERPETUAL PROPULSION ENGINE. IT ONLY USED TO WORK ON LIGHTER VEHICLES. BUT I HAVE BEEN ABLE TO ADAPT IT FOR HEAVY VEHICLES. AS HEAVY AS A TRAIN, IN FACT...
A TRAIN?
AN AUTONOMOUS TRAIN, ABLE TO TRAVEL ALONG ANY RAILWAY NETWORK IN THE WORLD. WE ARE JUST IN THE PROCESS OF RESOLVING SOME OF THE BUGS.
I WOULD LIKE ALSO TO TAKE THE OPPORTUNITY THIS EVENING TO ANNOUNCE THAT WE ARE GOING TO BE LAUNCHING THE SELECTION PHASE FOR THOSE WHO WISH TO COME ABOARD OUR TRAIN.
ME -- PICK ME!
I WANT TO GO!
CHOOSE ME!
ACCORDING TO WHAT CRITERIA? WHO'S GOING TO DECIDE?
ME.
YOU? WHO DO YOU THINK YOU ARE? GOD? GETTING TO DECIDE WHO LIVES AND WHO DIES? DO YOU HAVE SOME KIND OF COMPLEX?

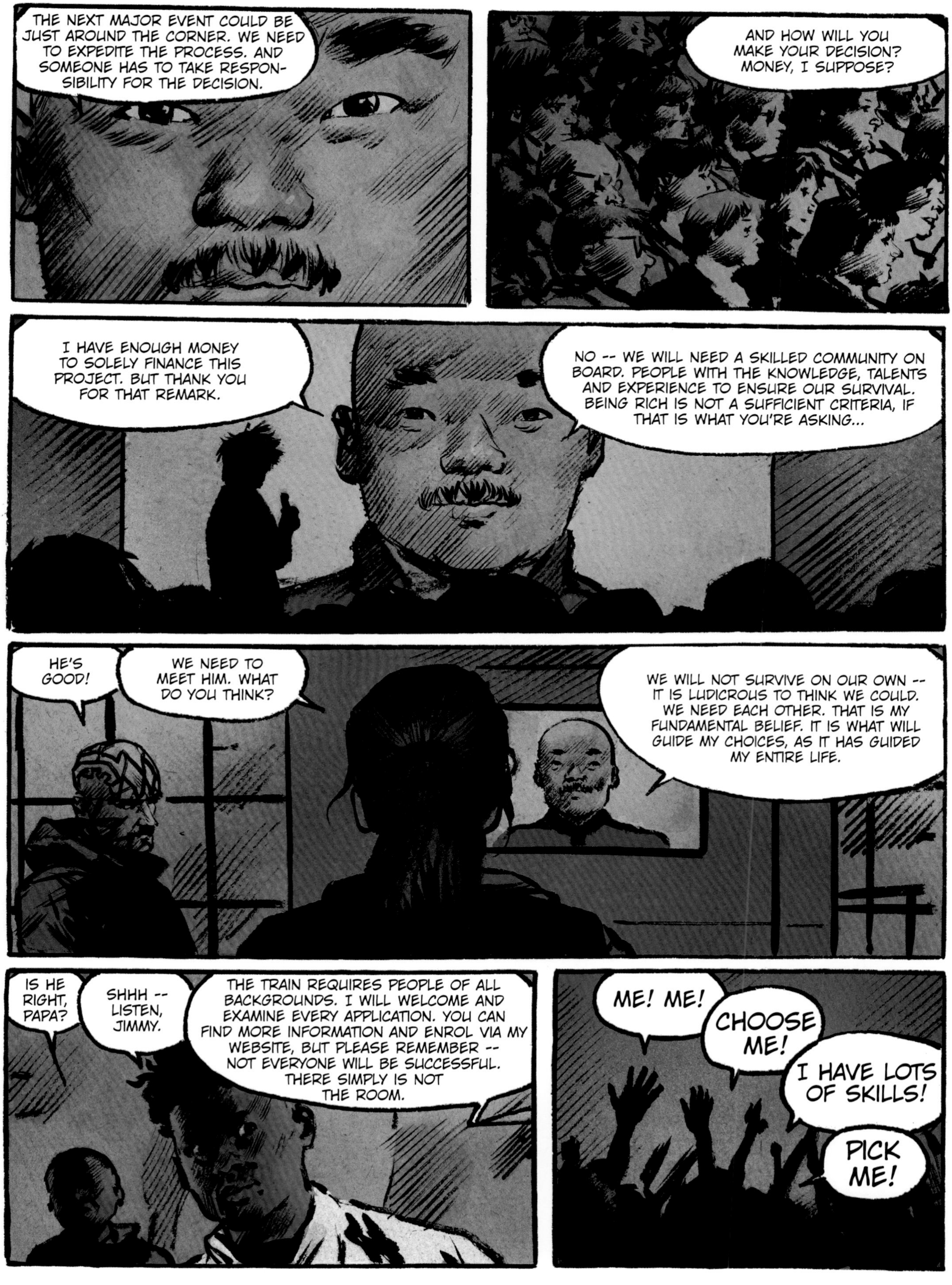
THE NEXT MAJOR EVENT COULD BE JUST AROUND THE CORNER. WE NEED TO EXPEDITE THE PROCESS. AND SOMEONE HAS TO TAKE RESPONSIBILITY FOR THE DECISION.
AND HOW WILL YOU MAKE YOUR DECISION? MONEY, I SUPPOSE?
I HAVE ENOUGH MONEY TO SOLELY FINANCE THIS PROJECT. BUT THANK YOU FOR THAT REMARK.
NO -- WE WILL NEED A SKILLED COMMUNITY ON BOARD. PEOPLE WITH THE KNOWLEDGE, TALENTS AND EXPERIENCE TO ENSURE OUR SURVIVAL. BEING RICH IS NOT A SUFFICIENT CRITERIA, IF THAT IS WHAT YOU'RE ASKING...
HE'S GOOD!
WE NEED TO MEET HIM. WHAT DO YOU THINK?
WE WILL NOT SURVIVE ON OUR OWN -- IT IS LUDICROUS TO THINK WE COULD. WE NEED EACH OTHER. THAT IS MY FUNDAMENTAL BELIEF. IT IS WHAT WILL GUIDE MY CHOICES, AS IT HAS GUIDED MY ENTIRE LIFE.
IS HE RIGHT, PAPA?
SHHH -- LISTEN, JIMMY.
THE TRAIN REQUIRES PEOPLE OF ALL BACKGROUNDS. I WILL WELCOME AND EXAMINE EVERY APPLICATION. YOU CAN FIND MORE INFORMATION AND ENROL VIA MY WEBSITE, BUT PLEASE REMEMBER -- NOT EVERYONE WILL BE SUCCESSFUL. THERE SIMPLY IS NOT THE ROOM.
ME! ME!
CHOOSE ME!
I HAVE LOTS OF SKILLS!
PICK ME!

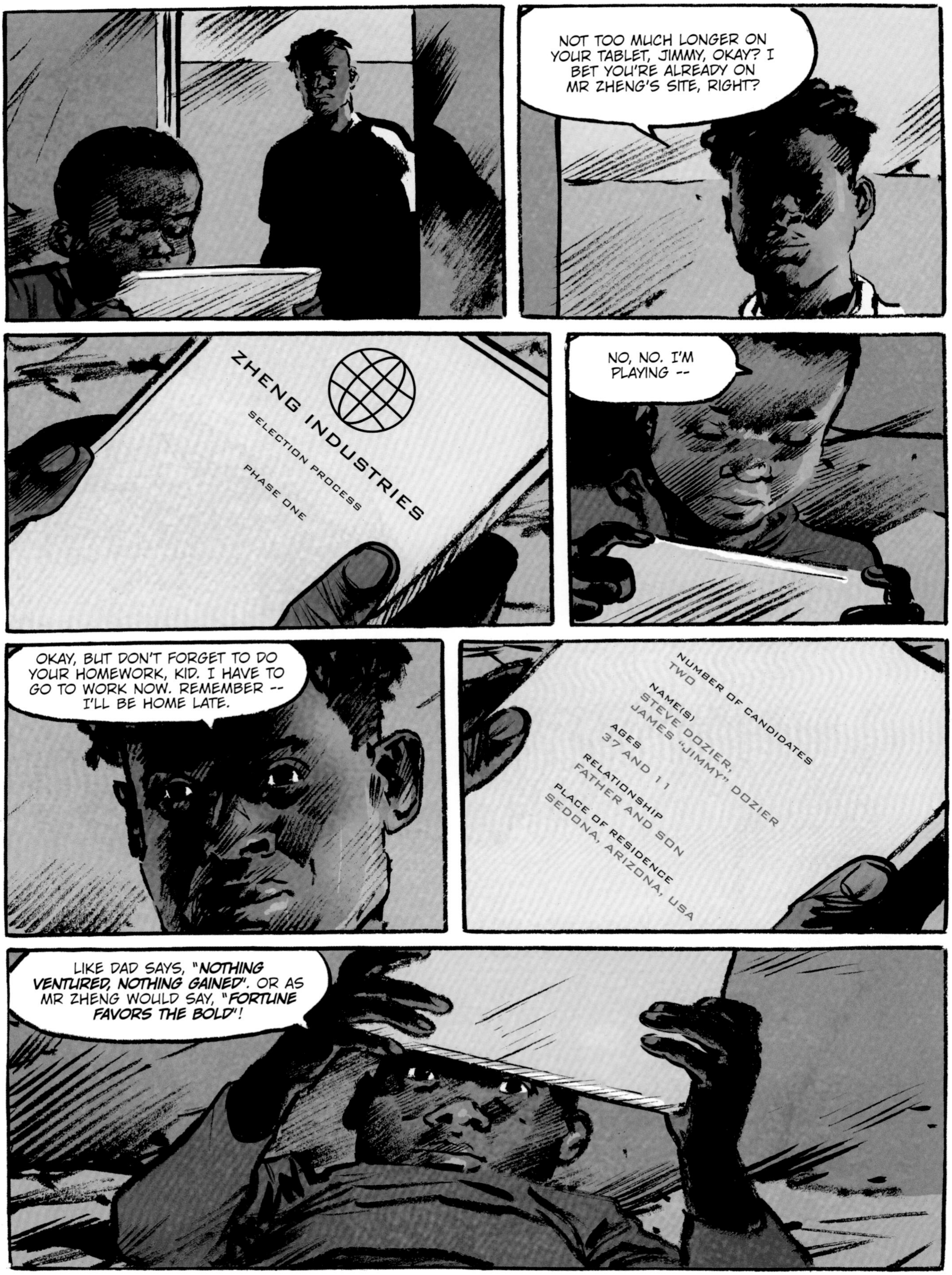
NOT TOO MUCH LONGER ON YOUR TABLET, JIMMY, OKAY? I BET YOU'RE ALREADY ON MR ZHENG'S SITE, RIGHT?
ZHENG INDUSTRIES
SELECTION PROCESS
PHASE ONE
NO, NO. I'M PLAYING --
OKAY, BUT DON'T FORGET TO DO YOUR HOMEWORK, KID. I HAVE TO GO TO WORK NOW. REMEMBER -- I'LL BE HOME LATE.
NUMBER OF CANDIDATES
TWO
NAME(S)
STEVE DOZIER,
JAMES "JIMMY" DOZIER
AGES
37 AND 11
RELATIONSHIP
FATHER AND SON
PLACE OF RESIDENCE
SEDONA, ARIZONA, USA
LIKE DAD SAYS, "**NOTHING VENTURED, NOTHING GAINED**". OR AS MR ZHENG WOULD SAY, "**FORTUNE FAVORS THE BOLD**"!

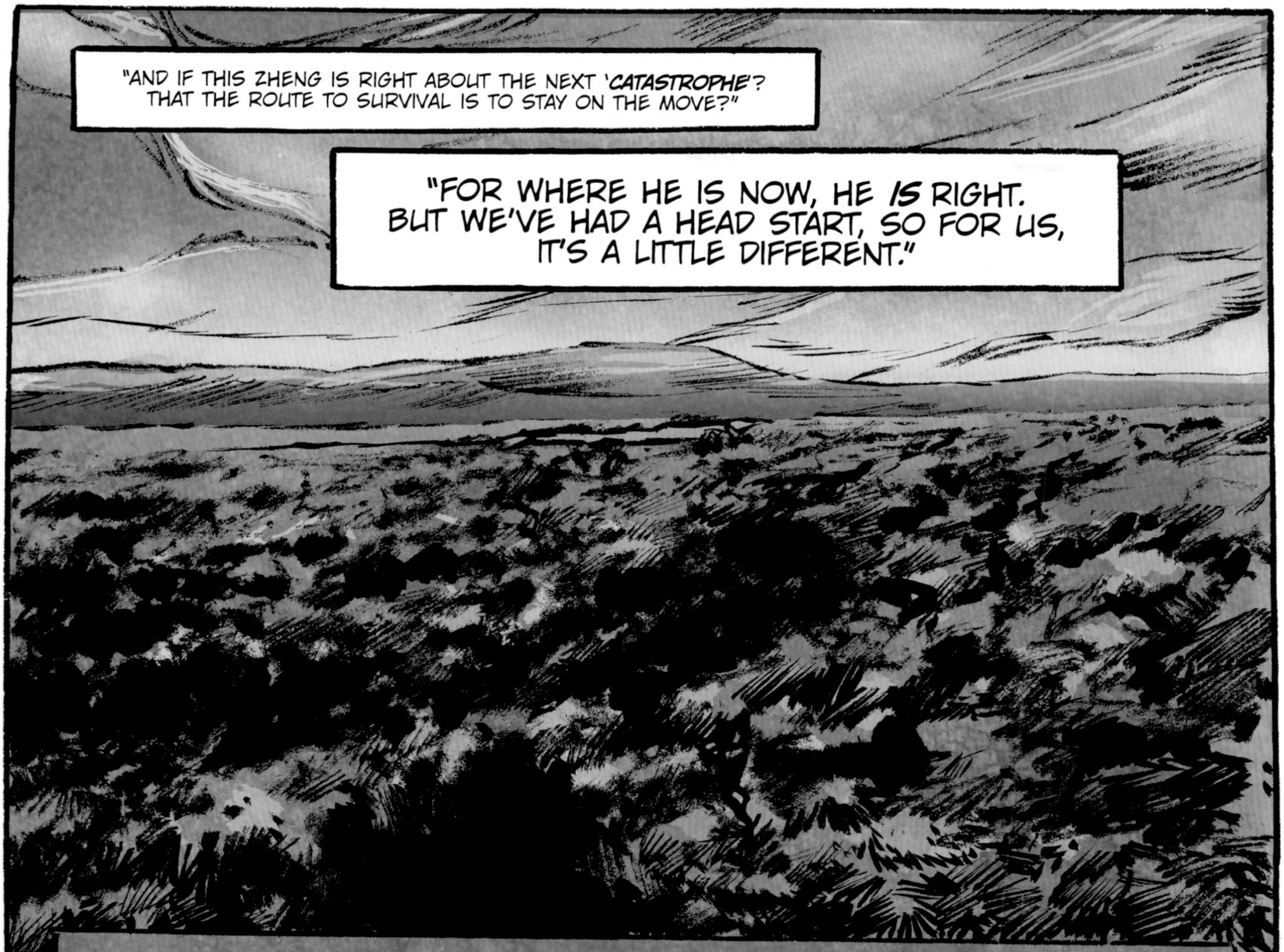
"AND IF THIS ZHENG IS RIGHT ABOUT THE NEXT '*CATASTROPHE*'? THAT THE ROUTE TO SURVIVAL IS TO STAY ON THE MOVE?"
"FOR WHERE HE IS NOW, HE *IS* RIGHT. BUT WE'VE HAD A HEAD START, SO FOR US, IT'S A LITTLE DIFFERENT."

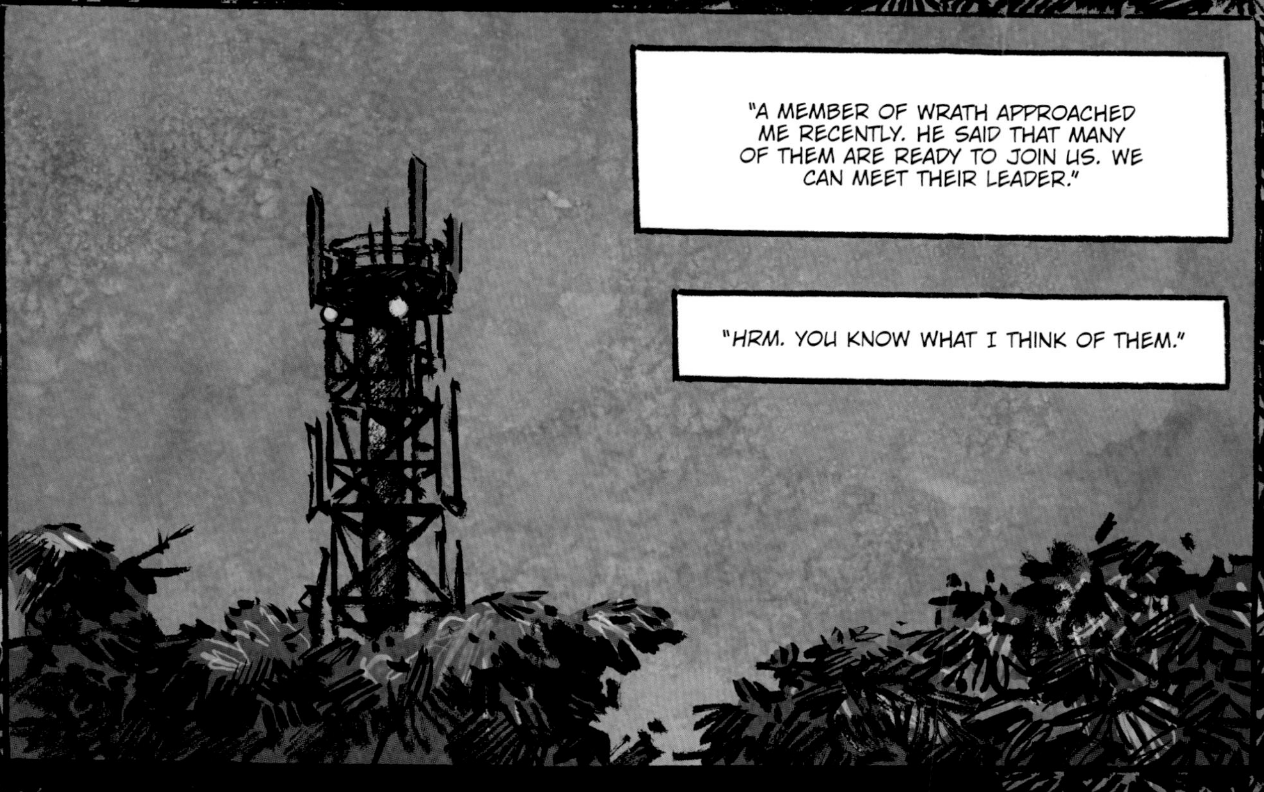
"A MEMBER OF WRATH APPROACHED ME RECENTLY. HE SAID THAT MANY OF THEM ARE READY TO JOIN US. WE CAN MEET THEIR LEADER."
"HRM. YOU KNOW WHAT I THINK OF THEM."

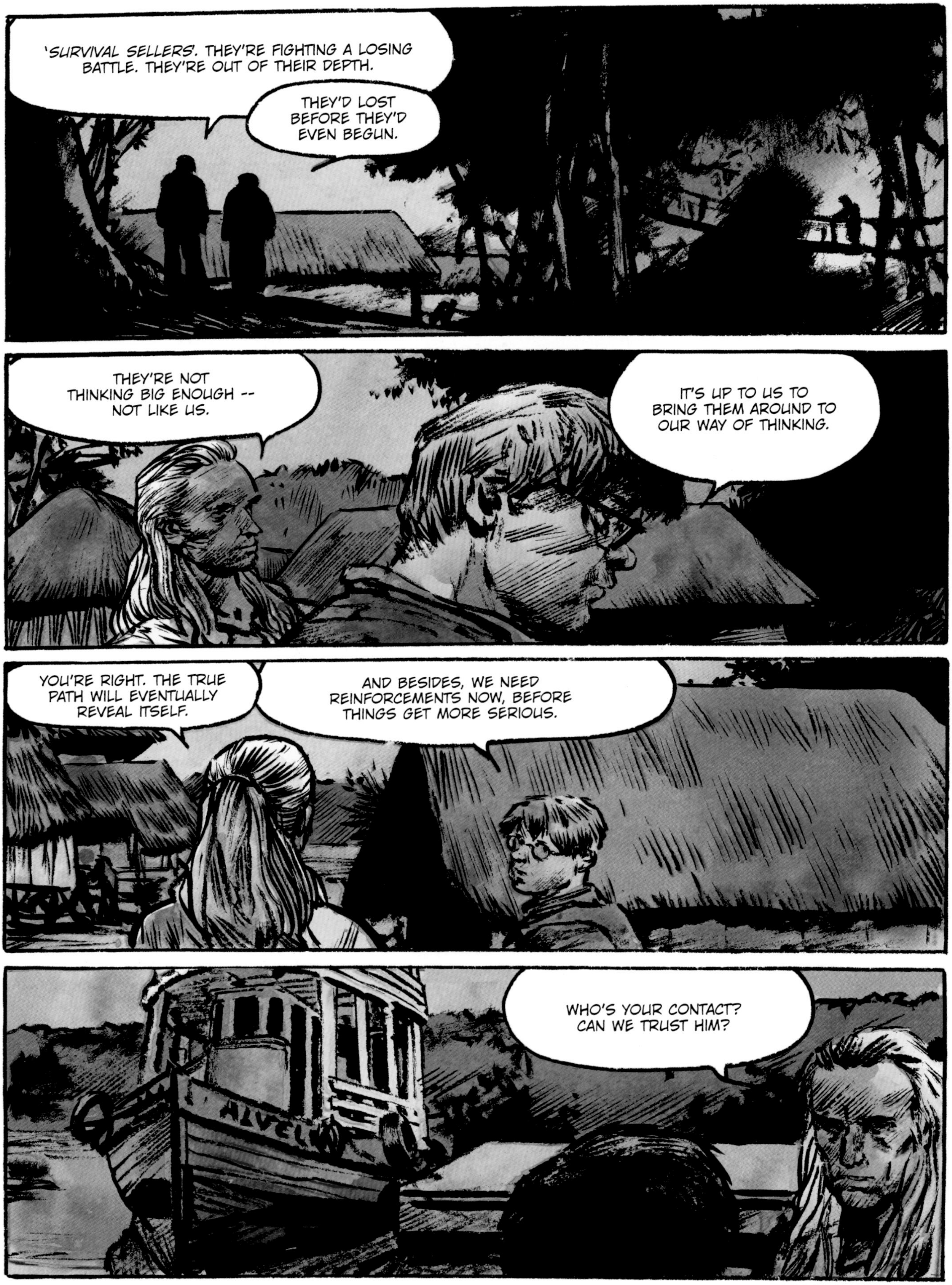
'SURVIVAL SELLERS'. THEY'RE FIGHTING A LOSING BATTLE. THEY'RE OUT OF THEIR DEPTH.
THEY'D LOST BEFORE THEY'D EVEN BEGUN.
THEY'RE NOT THINKING BIG ENOUGH -- NOT LIKE US.
IT'S UP TO US TO BRING THEM AROUND TO OUR WAY OF THINKING.
YOU'RE RIGHT. THE TRUE PATH WILL EVENTUALLY REVEAL ITSELF.
AND BESIDES, WE NEED REINFORCEMENTS NOW, BEFORE THINGS GET MORE SERIOUS.
WHO'S YOUR CONTACT? CAN WE TRUST HIM?

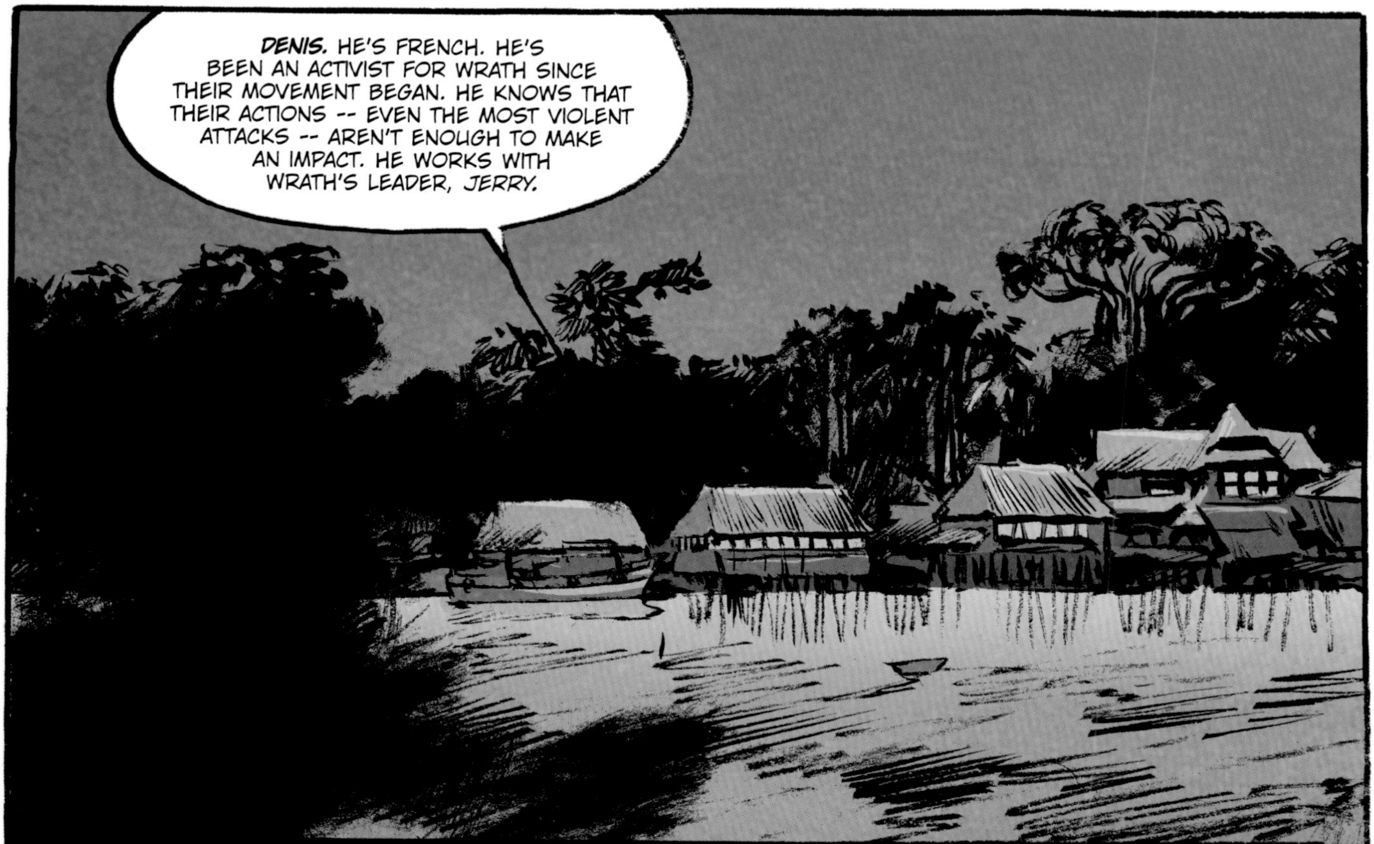
DENIS. HE'S FRENCH. HE'S BEEN AN ACTIVIST FOR WRATH SINCE THEIR MOVEMENT BEGAN. HE KNOWS THAT THEIR ACTIONS -- EVEN THE MOST VIOLENT ATTACKS -- AREN'T ENOUGH TO MAKE AN IMPACT. HE WORKS WITH WRATH'S LEADER, JERRY.

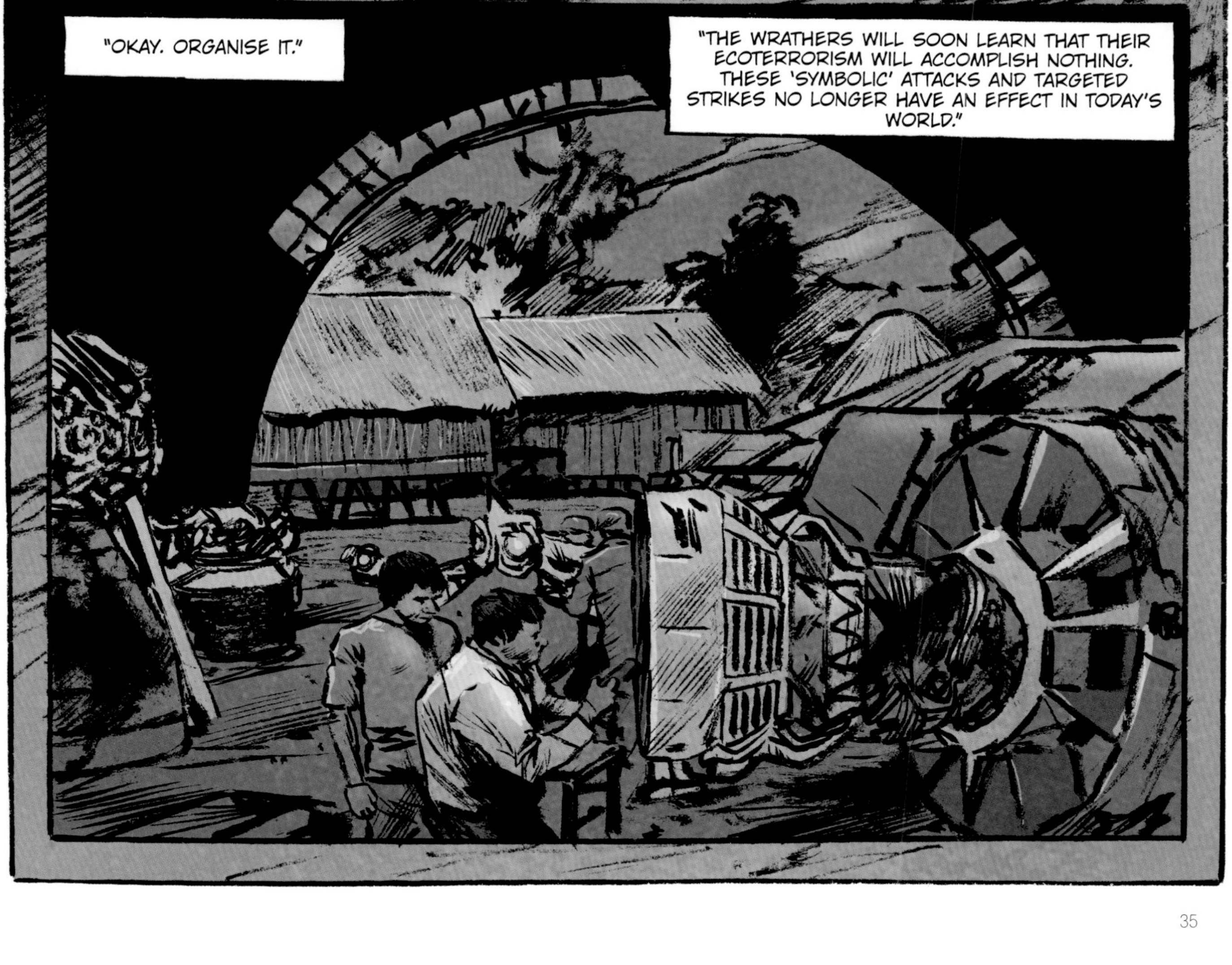
"OKAY. ORGANISE IT."
"THE WRATHERS WILL SOON LEARN THAT THEIR ECOTERRORISM WILL ACCOMPLISH NOTHING. THESE 'SYMBOLIC' ATTACKS AND TARGETED STRIKES NO LONGER HAVE AN EFFECT IN TODAY'S WORLD."

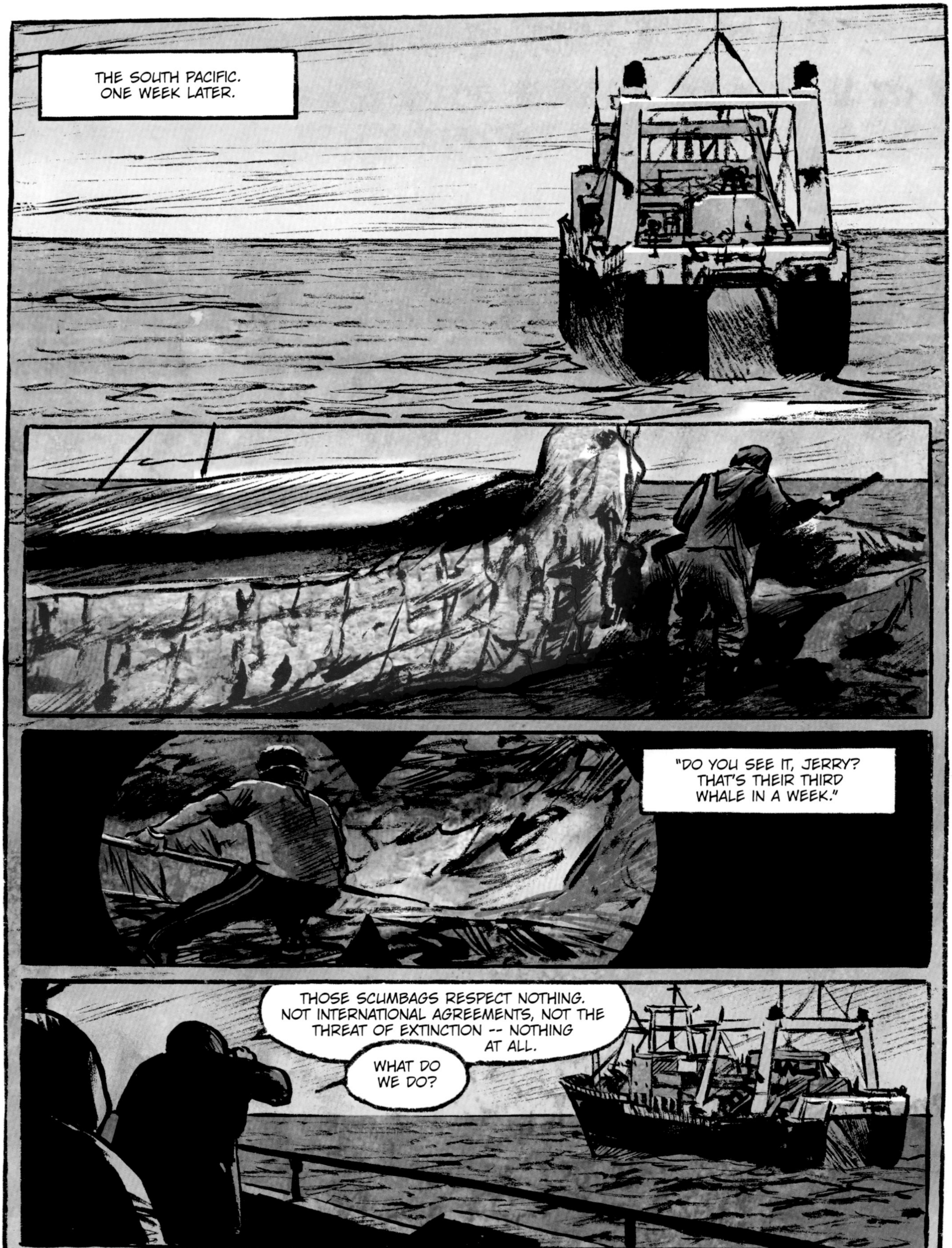
THE SOUTH PACIFIC. ONE WEEK LATER.
"DO YOU SEE IT, JERRY? THAT'S THEIR THIRD WHALE IN A WEEK."
THOSE SCUMBAGS RESPECT NOTHING. NOT INTERNATIONAL AGREEMENTS, NOT THE THREAT OF EXTINCTION -- NOTHING AT ALL.
WHAT DO WE DO?

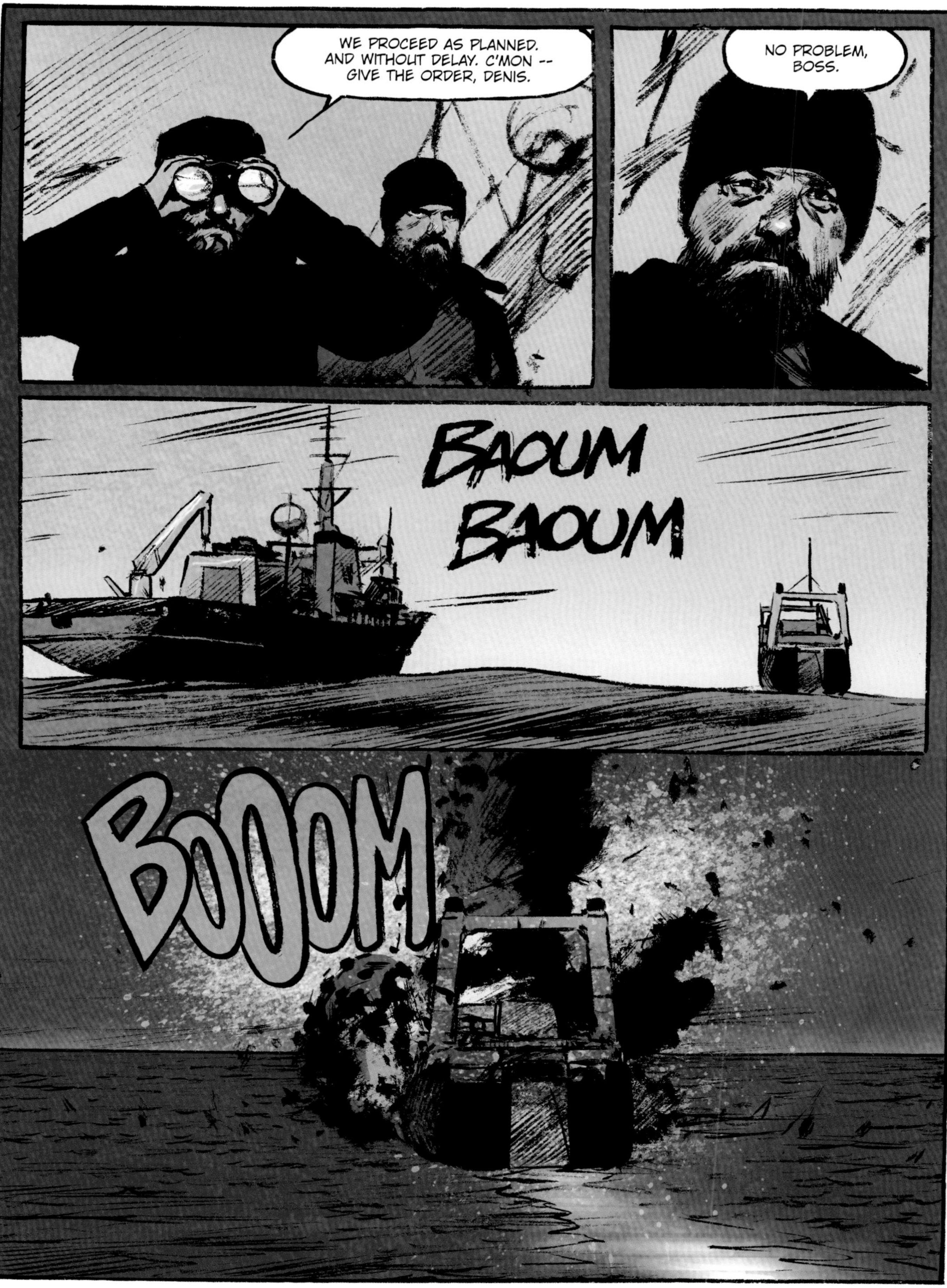
WE PROCEED AS PLANNED. AND WITHOUT DELAY. C'MON -- GIVE THE ORDER, DENIS.
NO PROBLEM, BOSS.
BAOUM
BAOUM
BOOOM

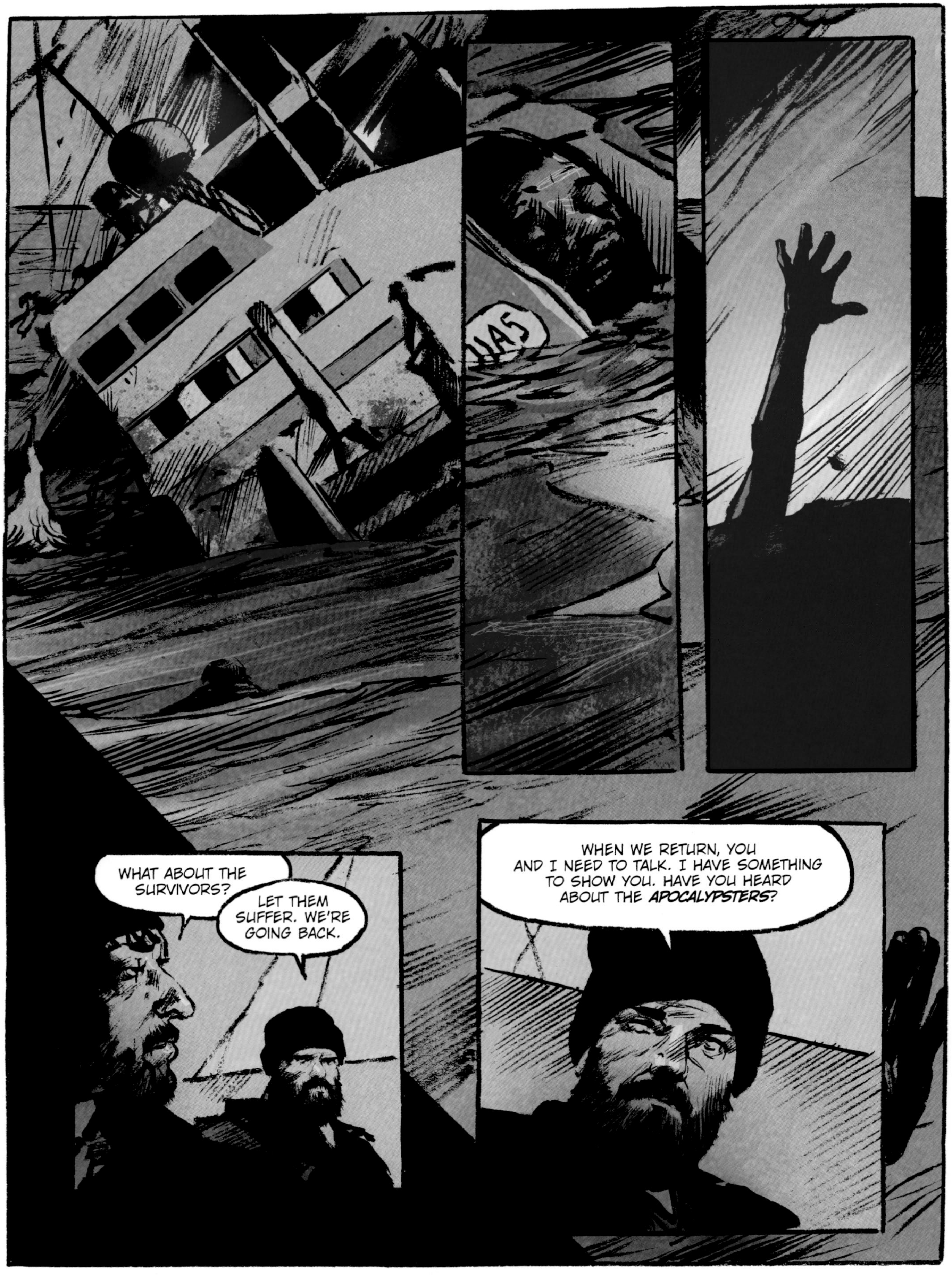
UAS
WHAT ABOUT THE SURVIVORS?
LET THEM SUFFER. WE'RE GOING BACK.
WHEN WE RETURN, YOU AND I NEED TO TALK. I HAVE SOMETHING TO SHOW YOU. HAVE YOU HEARD ABOUT THE *APOCALYPSTERS*?

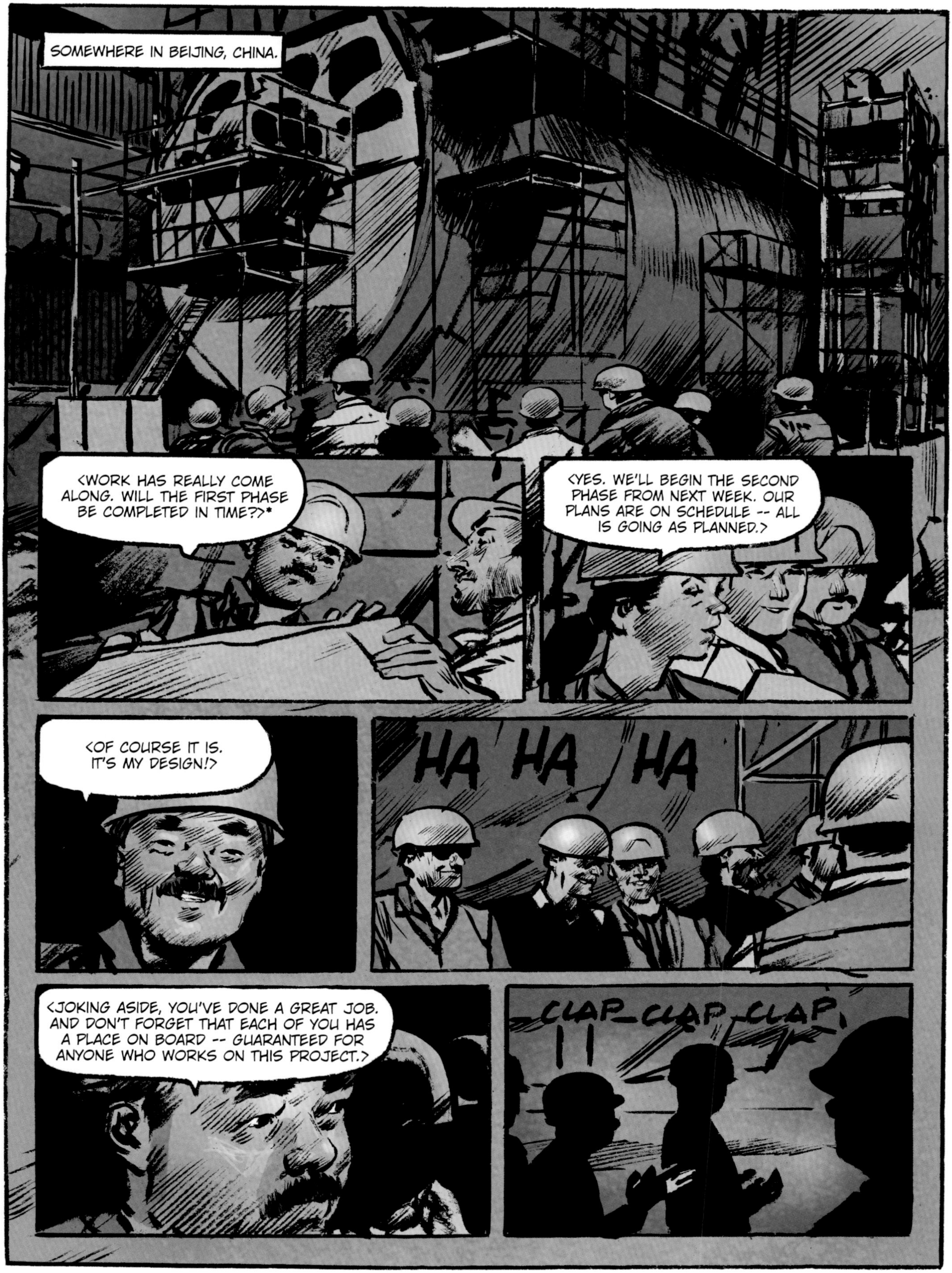
SOMEWHERE IN BEIJING, CHINA.
<WORK HAS REALLY COME ALONG. WILL THE FIRST PHASE BE COMPLETED IN TIME?>*
<YES. WE'LL BEGIN THE SECOND PHASE FROM NEXT WEEK. OUR PLANS ARE ON SCHEDULE -- ALL IS GOING AS PLANNED.>
<OF COURSE IT IS. IT'S MY DESIGN!>
HA HA HA
<JOKING ASIDE, YOU'VE DONE A GREAT JOB. AND DON'T FORGET THAT EACH OF YOU HAS A PLACE ON BOARD -- GUARANTEED FOR ANYONE WHO WORKS ON THIS PROJECT.>
CLAP CLAP CLAP

*TRANSLATED FROM MANDARIN.

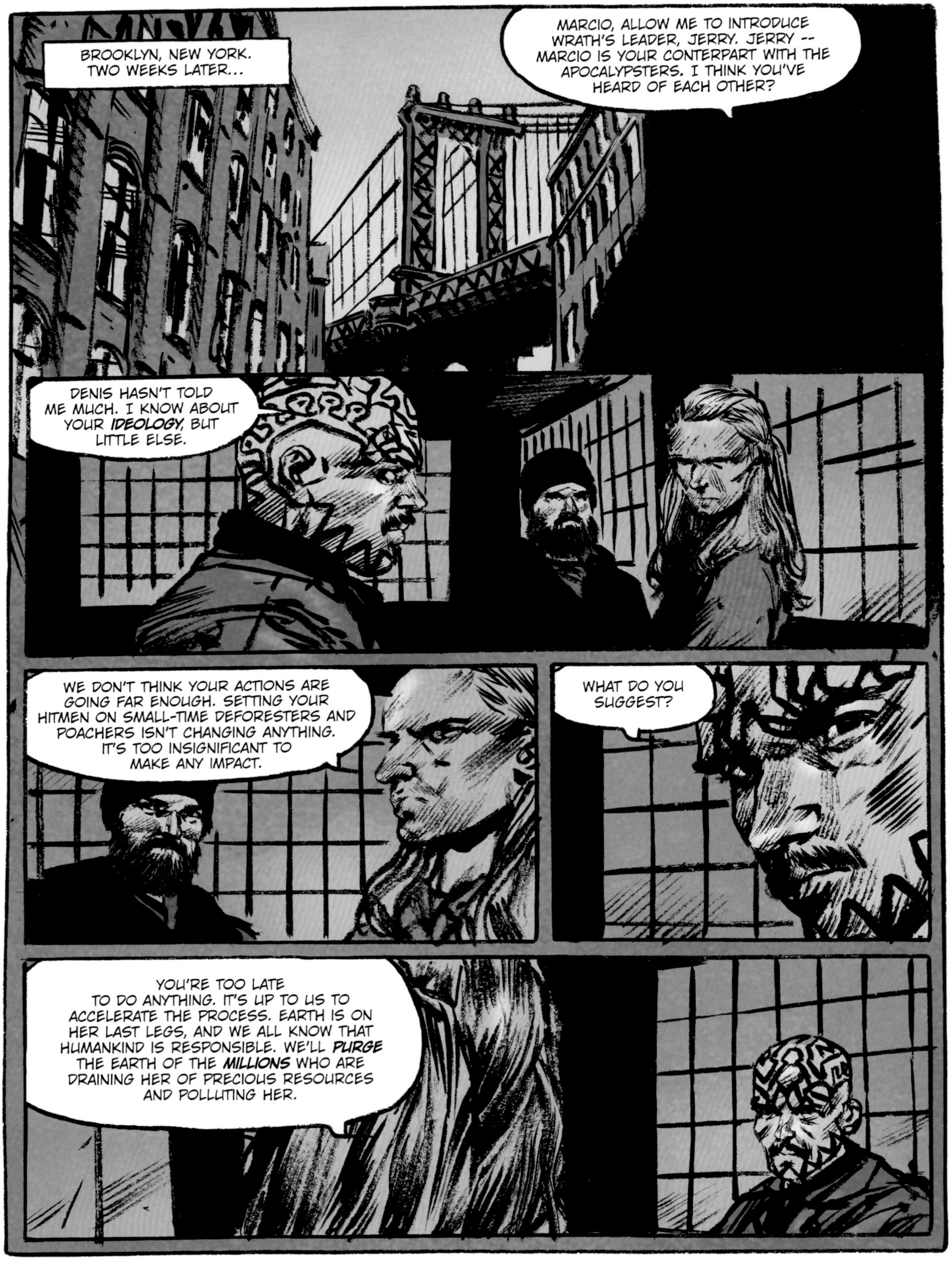
BROOKLYN, NEW YORK. TWO WEEKS LATER...
MARCIO, ALLOW ME TO INTRODUCE WRATH'S LEADER, JERRY. JERRY -- MARCIO IS YOUR CONTERPART WITH THE APOCALYPSTERS. I THINK YOU'VE HEARD OF EACH OTHER?
DENIS HASN'T TOLD ME MUCH. I KNOW ABOUT YOUR *IDEOLOGY*, BUT LITTLE ELSE.
WE DON'T THINK YOUR ACTIONS ARE GOING FAR ENOUGH. SETTING YOUR HITMEN ON SMALL-TIME DEFORESTERS AND POACHERS ISN'T CHANGING ANYTHING. IT'S TOO INSIGNIFICANT TO MAKE ANY IMPACT.
WHAT DO YOU SUGGEST?
YOU'RE TOO LATE TO DO ANYTHING. IT'S UP TO US TO ACCELERATE THE PROCESS. EARTH IS ON HER LAST LEGS, AND WE ALL KNOW THAT HUMANKIND IS RESPONSIBLE. WE'LL *PURGE* THE EARTH OF THE *MILLIONS* WHO ARE DRAINING HER OF PRECIOUS RESOURCES AND POLLUTING HER.

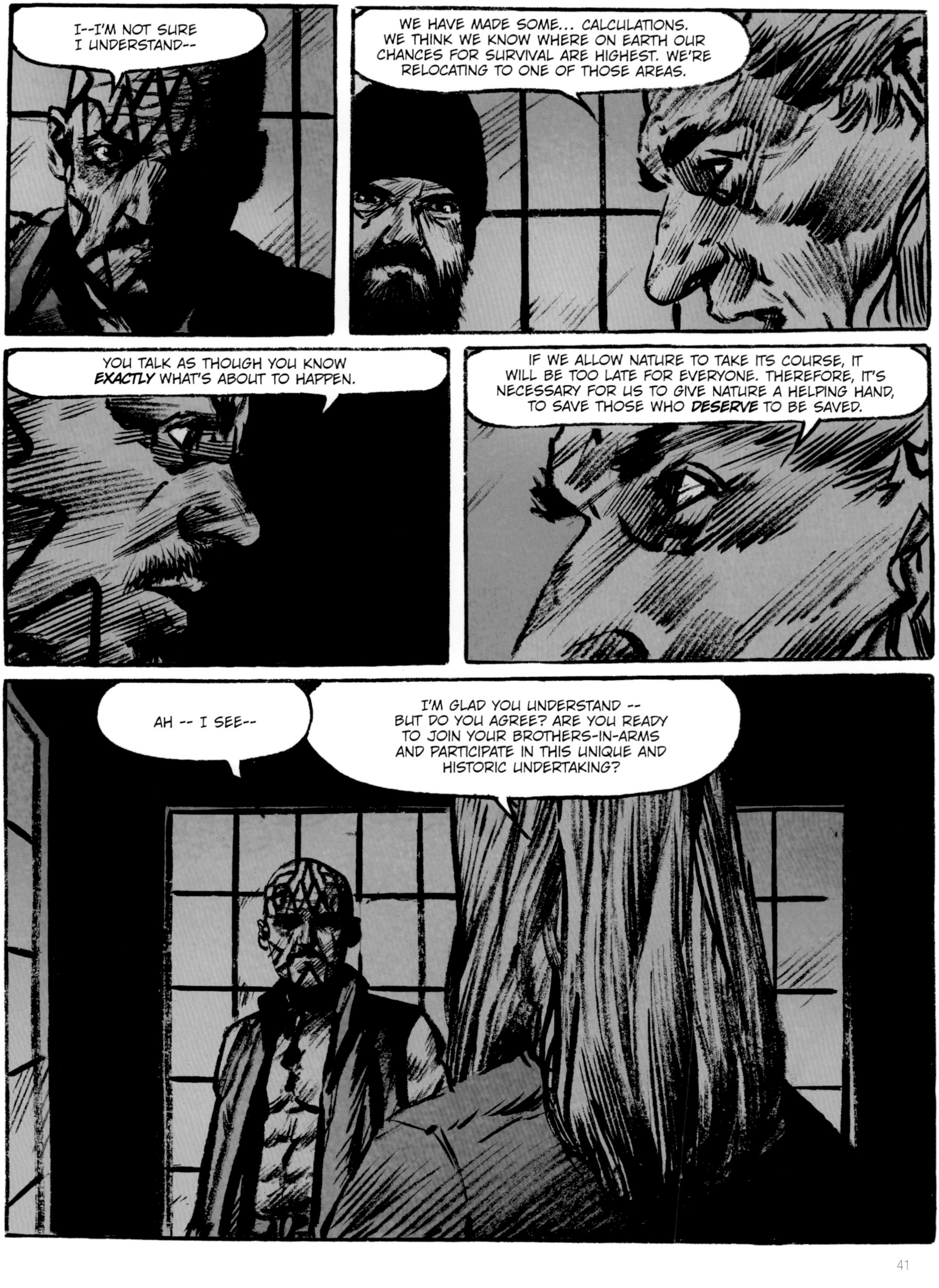
I--I'M NOT SURE I UNDERSTAND--
WE HAVE MADE SOME... CALCULATIONS. WE THINK WE KNOW WHERE ON EARTH OUR CHANCES FOR SURVIVAL ARE HIGHEST. WE'RE RELOCATING TO ONE OF THOSE AREAS.
YOU TALK AS THOUGH YOU KNOW *EXACTLY* WHAT'S ABOUT TO HAPPEN.
IF WE ALLOW NATURE TO TAKE ITS COURSE, IT WILL BE TOO LATE FOR EVERYONE. THEREFORE, IT'S NECESSARY FOR US TO GIVE NATURE A HELPING HAND, TO SAVE THOSE WHO *DESERVE* TO BE SAVED.
AH -- I SEE--
I'M GLAD YOU UNDERSTAND -- BUT DO YOU AGREE? ARE YOU READY TO JOIN YOUR BROTHERS-IN-ARMS AND PARTICIPATE IN THIS UNIQUE AND HISTORIC UNDERTAKING?

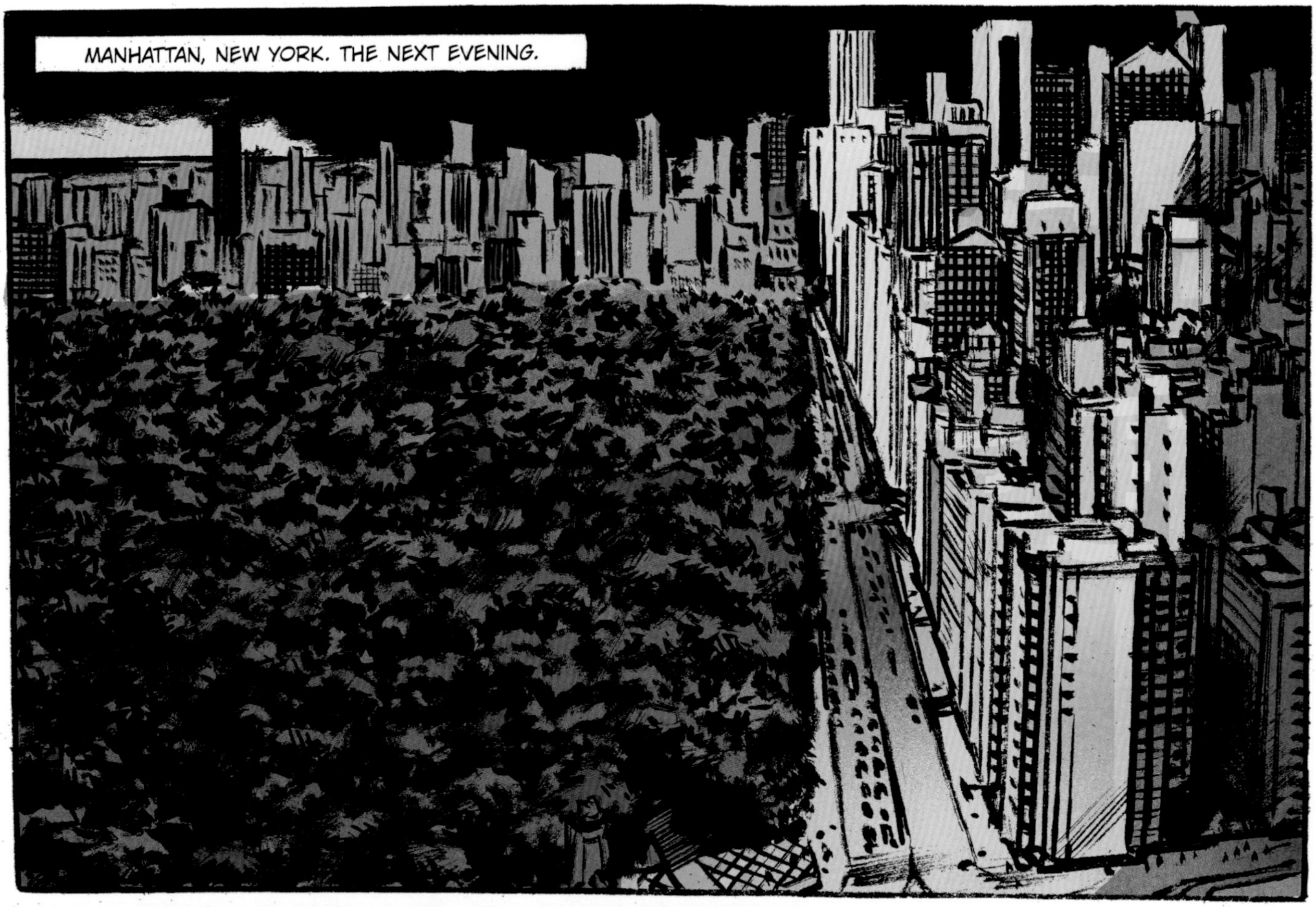
MANHATTAN, NEW YORK. THE NEXT EVENING.

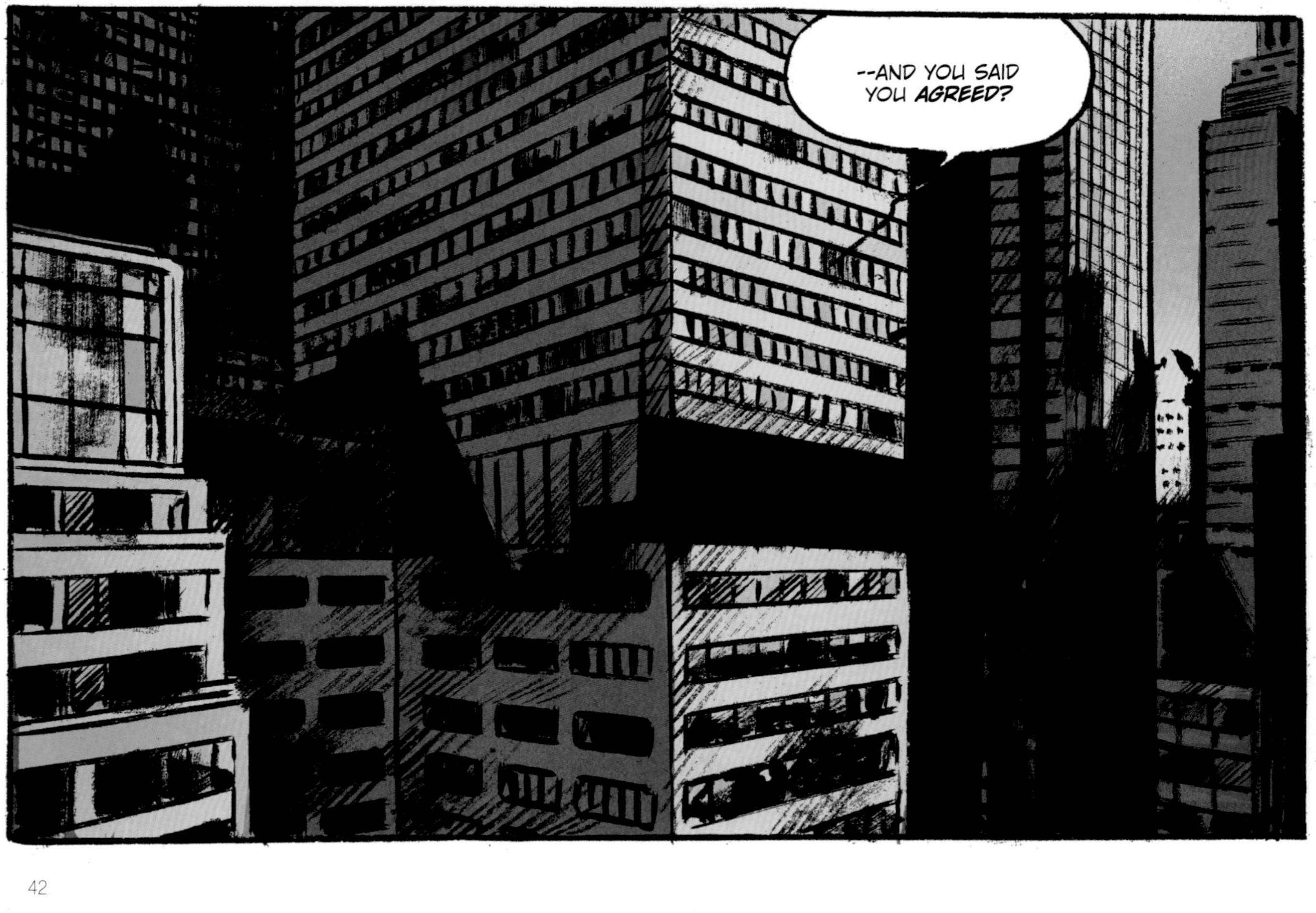
--AND YOU SAID YOU AGREED?

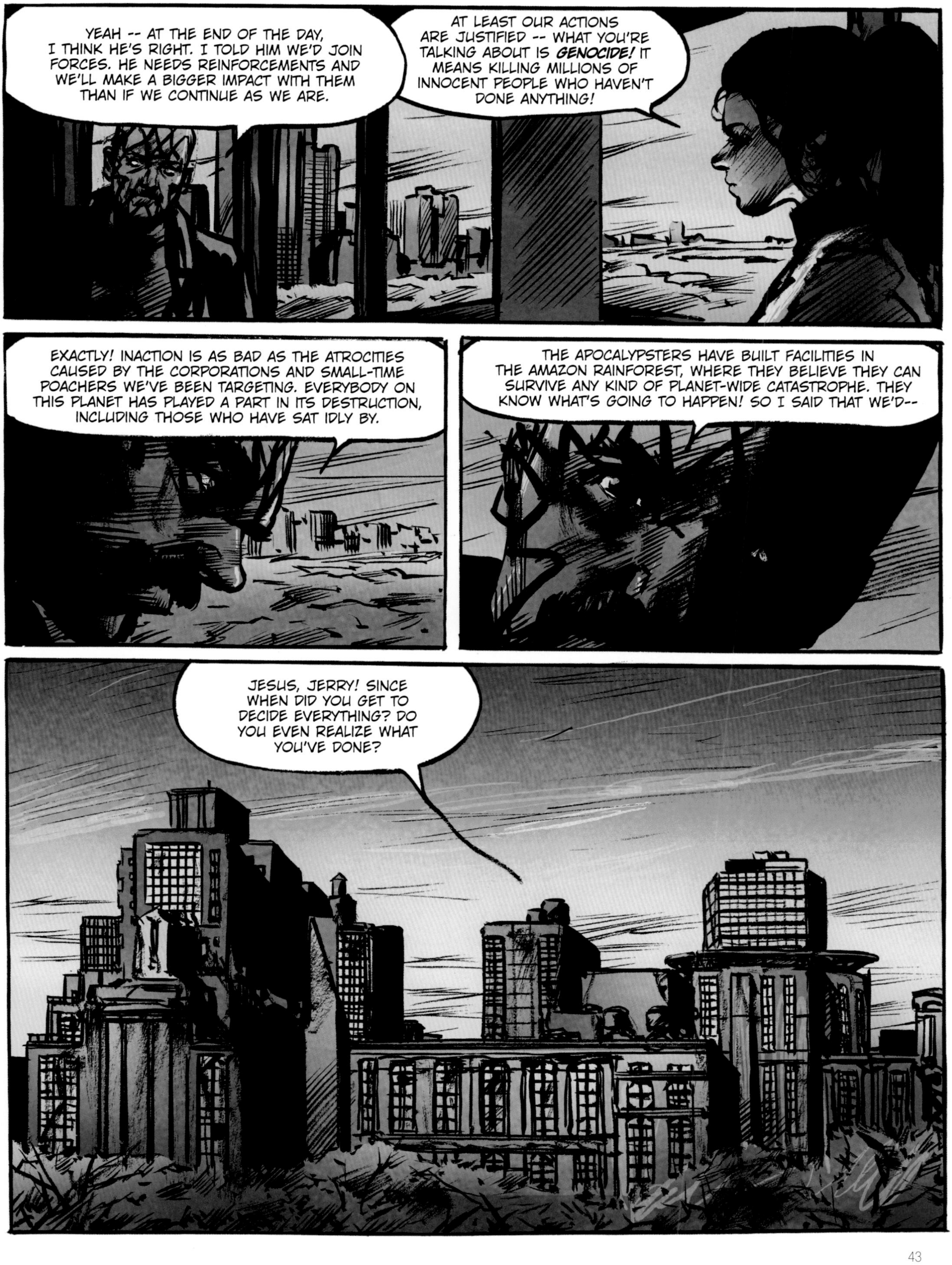
YEAH -- AT THE END OF THE DAY, I THINK HE'S RIGHT. I TOLD HIM WE'D JOIN FORCES. HE NEEDS REINFORCEMENTS AND WE'LL MAKE A BIGGER IMPACT WITH THEM THAN IF WE CONTINUE AS WE ARE.
AT LEAST OUR ACTIONS ARE JUSTIFIED -- WHAT YOU'RE TALKING ABOUT IS ***GENOCIDE!*** IT MEANS KILLING MILLIONS OF INNOCENT PEOPLE WHO HAVEN'T DONE ANYTHING!
EXACTLY! INACTION IS AS BAD AS THE ATROCITIES CAUSED BY THE CORPORATIONS AND SMALL-TIME POACHERS WE'VE BEEN TARGETING. EVERYBODY ON THIS PLANET HAS PLAYED A PART IN ITS DESTRUCTION, INCLUDING THOSE WHO HAVE SAT IDLY BY.
THE APOCALYPSTERS HAVE BUILT FACILITIES IN THE AMAZON RAINFOREST, WHERE THEY BELIEVE THEY CAN SURVIVE ANY KIND OF PLANET-WIDE CATASTROPHE. THEY KNOW WHAT'S GOING TO HAPPEN! SO I SAID THAT WE'D--
JESUS, JERRY! SINCE WHEN DID YOU GET TO DECIDE EVERYTHING? DO YOU EVEN REALIZE WHAT YOU'VE DONE?

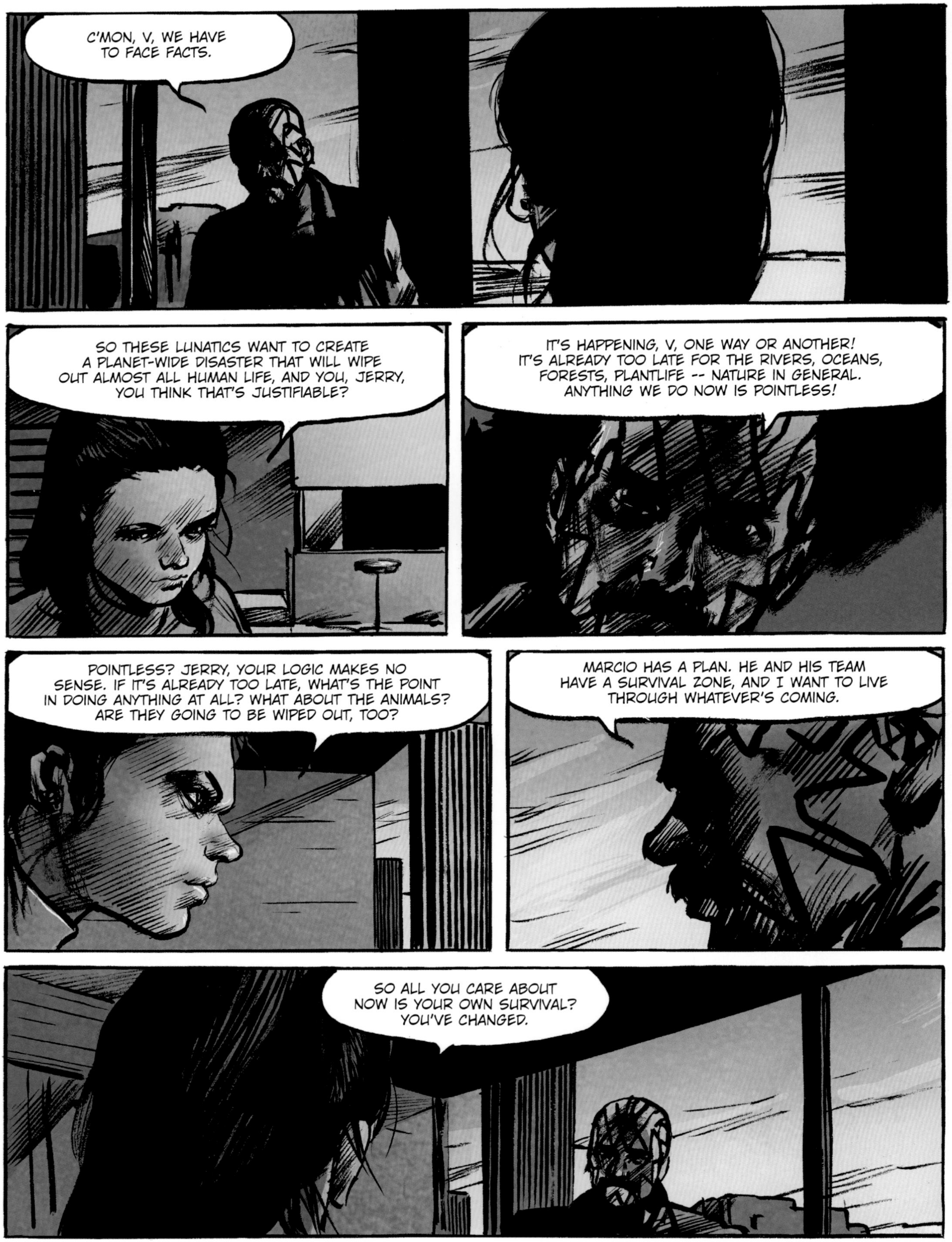

C'MON, V, WE HAVE TO FACE FACTS.
SO THESE LUNATICS WANT TO CREATE A PLANET-WIDE DISASTER THAT WILL WIPE OUT ALMOST ALL HUMAN LIFE, AND YOU, JERRY, YOU THINK THAT'S JUSTIFIABLE?
IT'S HAPPENING, V, ONE WAY OR ANOTHER! IT'S ALREADY TOO LATE FOR THE RIVERS, OCEANS, FORESTS, PLANTLIFE -- NATURE IN GENERAL. ANYTHING WE DO NOW IS POINTLESS!
POINTLESS? JERRY, YOUR LOGIC MAKES NO SENSE. IF IT'S ALREADY TOO LATE, WHAT'S THE POINT IN DOING ANYTHING AT ALL? WHAT ABOUT THE ANIMALS? ARE THEY GOING TO BE WIPED OUT, TOO?
MARCIO HAS A PLAN. HE AND HIS TEAM HAVE A SURVIVAL ZONE, AND I WANT TO LIVE THROUGH WHATEVER'S COMING.
SO ALL YOU CARE ABOUT NOW IS YOUR OWN SURVIVAL? YOU'VE CHANGED.

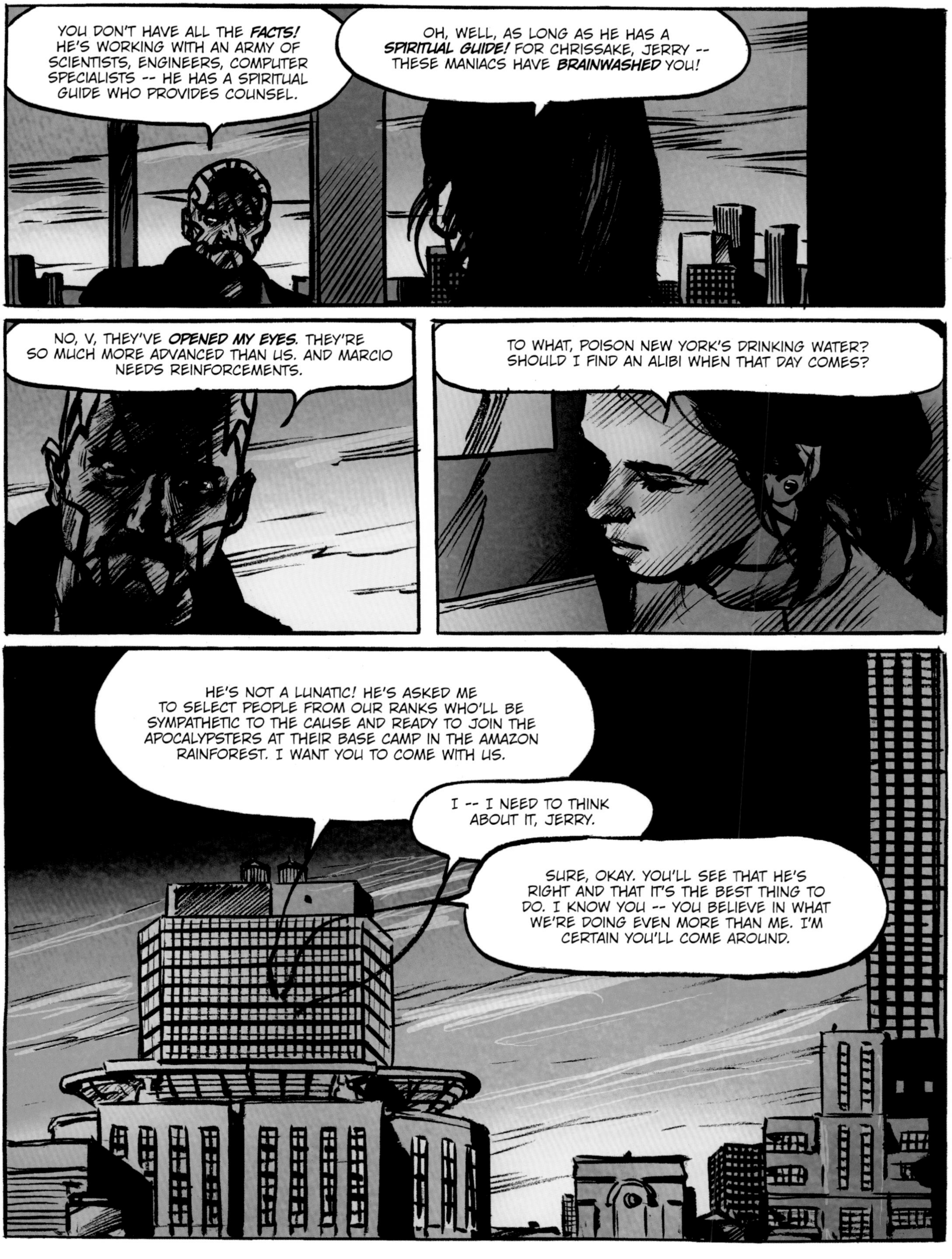
YOU DON'T HAVE ALL THE FACTS! HE'S WORKING WITH AN ARMY OF SCIENTISTS, ENGINEERS, COMPUTER SPECIALISTS -- HE HAS A SPIRITUAL GUIDE WHO PROVIDES COUNSEL.
OH, WELL, AS LONG AS HE HAS A SPIRITUAL GUIDE! FOR CHRISSAKE, JERRY -- THESE MANIACS HAVE BRAINWASHED YOU!
NO, V, THEY'VE OPENED MY EYES. THEY'RE SO MUCH MORE ADVANCED THAN US. AND MARCIO NEEDS REINFORCEMENTS.
TO WHAT, POISON NEW YORK'S DRINKING WATER? SHOULD I FIND AN ALIBI WHEN THAT DAY COMES?
HE'S NOT A LUNATIC! HE'S ASKED ME TO SELECT PEOPLE FROM OUR RANKS WHO'LL BE SYMPATHETIC TO THE CAUSE AND READY TO JOIN THE APOCALYPSTERS AT THEIR BASE CAMP IN THE AMAZON RAINFOREST. I WANT YOU TO COME WITH US.
I -- I NEED TO THINK ABOUT IT, JERRY.
SURE, OKAY. YOU'LL SEE THAT HE'S RIGHT AND THAT IT'S THE BEST THING TO DO. I KNOW YOU -- YOU BELIEVE IN WHAT WE'RE DOING EVEN MORE THAN ME. I'M CERTAIN YOU'LL COME AROUND.

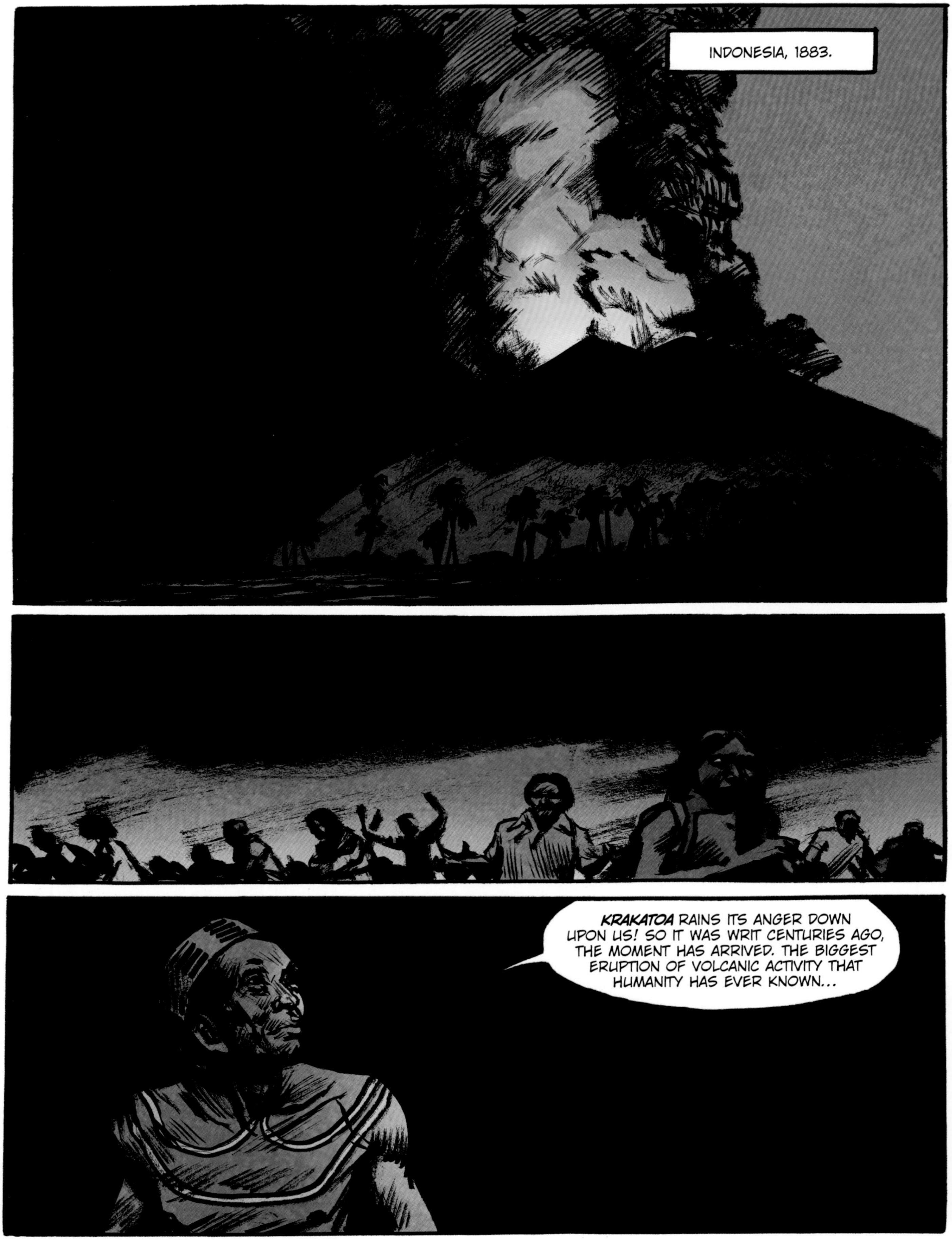
INDONESIA, 1883.
KRAKATOA RAINS ITS ANGER DOWN UPON US! SO IT WAS WRIT CENTURIES AGO, THE MOMENT HAS ARRIVED. THE BIGGEST ERUPTION OF VOLCANIC ACTIVITY THAT HUMANITY HAS EVER KNOWN...

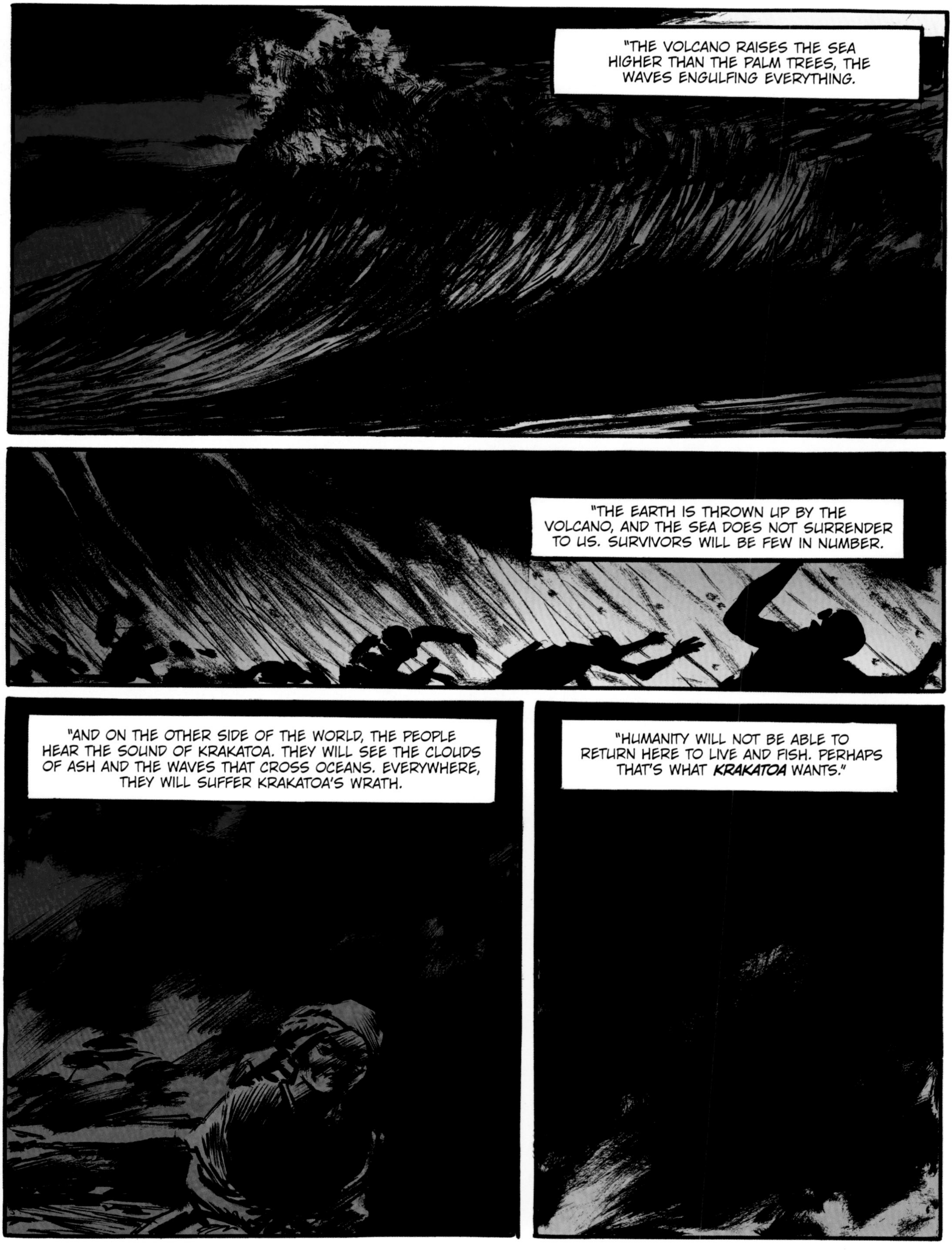
"THE VOLCANO RAISES THE SEA HIGHER THAN THE PALM TREES, THE WAVES ENGULFING EVERYTHING.
"THE EARTH IS THROWN UP BY THE VOLCANO, AND THE SEA DOES NOT SURRENDER TO US. SURVIVORS WILL BE FEW IN NUMBER.
"AND ON THE OTHER SIDE OF THE WORLD, THE PEOPLE HEAR THE SOUND OF KRAKATOA. THEY WILL SEE THE CLOUDS OF ASH AND THE WAVES THAT CROSS OCEANS. EVERYWHERE, THEY WILL SUFFER KRAKATOA'S WRATH.
"HUMANITY WILL NOT BE ABLE TO RETURN HERE TO LIVE AND FISH. PERHAPS THAT'S WHAT ***KRAKATOA*** WANTS."

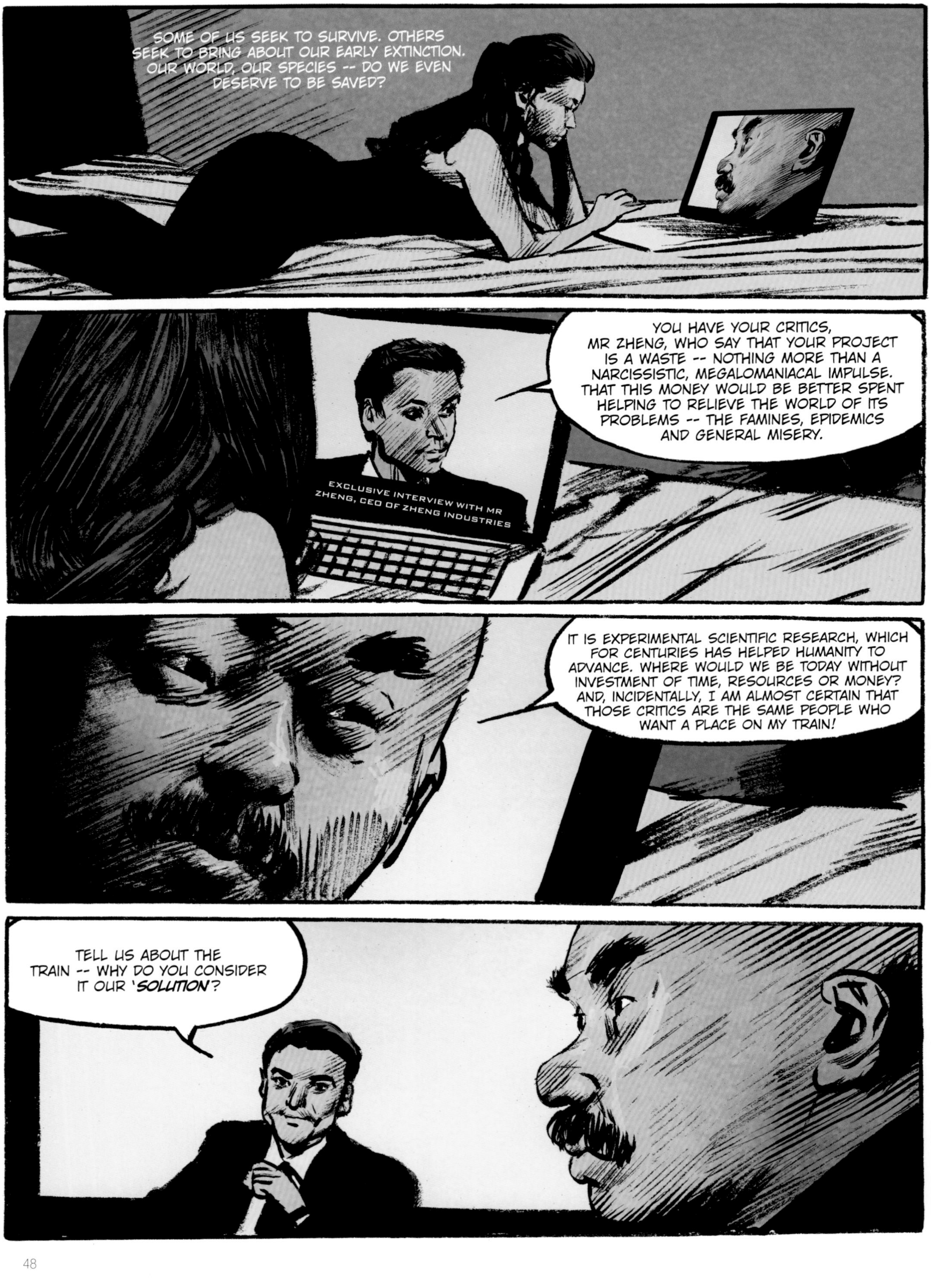
SOME OF US SEEK TO SURVIVE. OTHERS SEEK TO BRING ABOUT OUR EARLY EXTINCTION. OUR WORLD, OUR SPECIES -- DO WE EVEN DESERVE TO BE SAVED?
YOU HAVE YOUR CRITICS, MR ZHENG, WHO SAY THAT YOUR PROJECT IS A WASTE -- NOTHING MORE THAN A NARCISSISTIC, MEGALOMANIACAL IMPULSE. THAT THIS MONEY WOULD BE BETTER SPENT HELPING TO RELIEVE THE WORLD OF ITS PROBLEMS -- THE FAMINES, EPIDEMICS AND GENERAL MISERY.
EXCLUSIVE INTERVIEW WITH MR ZHENG, CEO OF ZHENG INDUSTRIES
IT IS EXPERIMENTAL SCIENTIFIC RESEARCH, WHICH FOR CENTURIES HAS HELPED HUMANITY TO ADVANCE. WHERE WOULD WE BE TODAY WITHOUT INVESTMENT OF TIME, RESOURCES OR MONEY? AND, INCIDENTALLY, I AM ALMOST CERTAIN THAT THOSE CRITICS ARE THE SAME PEOPLE WHO WANT A PLACE ON MY TRAIN!
TELL US ABOUT THE TRAIN -- WHY DO YOU CONSIDER IT OUR '*SOLUTION*'?

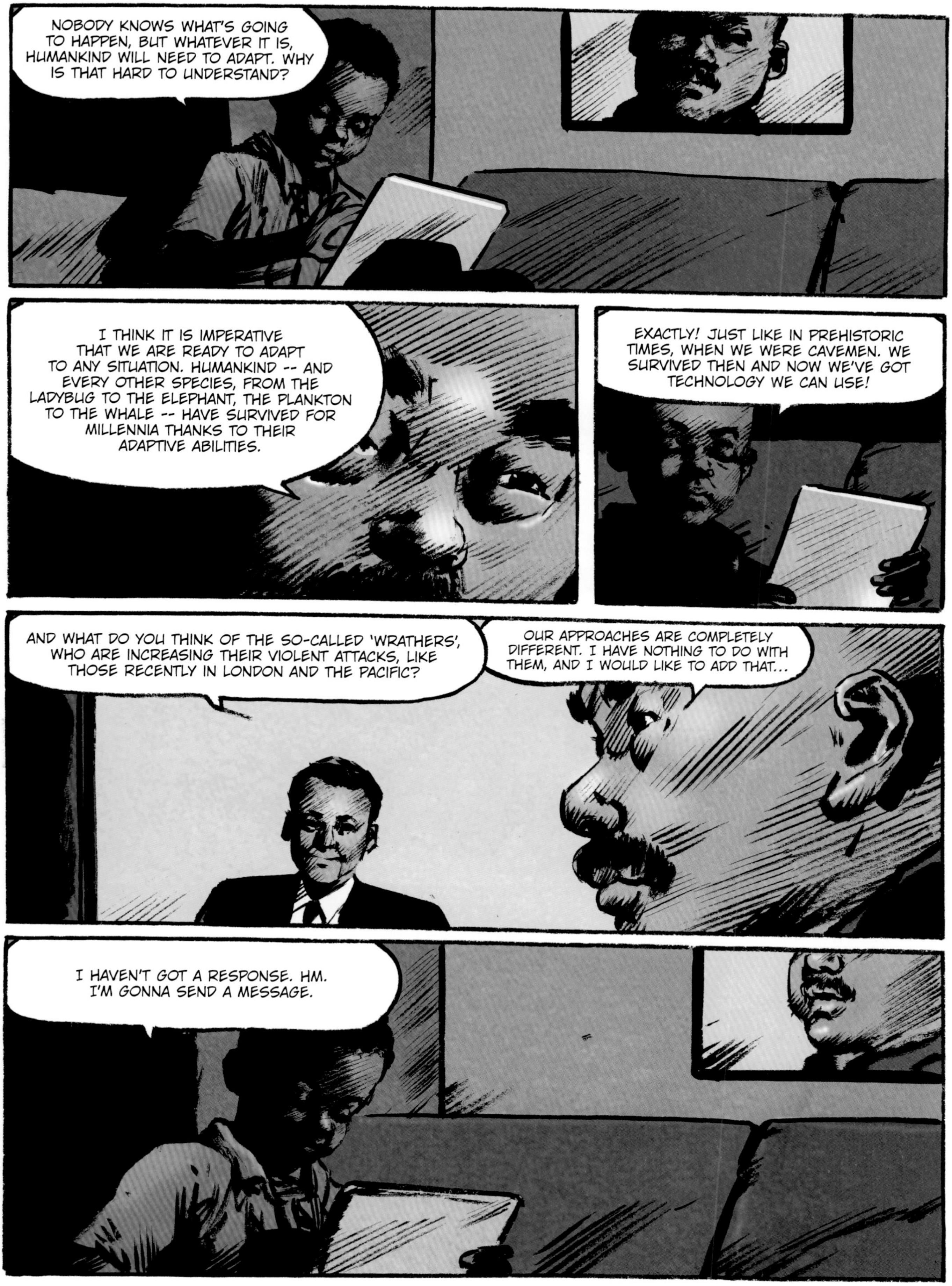
NOBODY KNOWS WHAT'S GOING TO HAPPEN, BUT WHATEVER IT IS, HUMANKIND WILL NEED TO ADAPT. WHY IS THAT HARD TO UNDERSTAND?
I THINK IT IS IMPERATIVE THAT WE ARE READY TO ADAPT TO ANY SITUATION. HUMANKIND -- AND EVERY OTHER SPECIES, FROM THE LADYBUG TO THE ELEPHANT, THE PLANKTON TO THE WHALE -- HAVE SURVIVED FOR MILLENNIA THANKS TO THEIR ADAPTIVE ABILITIES.
EXACTLY! JUST LIKE IN PREHISTORIC TIMES, WHEN WE WERE CAVEMEN. WE SURVIVED THEN AND NOW WE'VE GOT TECHNOLOGY WE CAN USE!
AND WHAT DO YOU THINK OF THE SO-CALLED 'WRATHERS', WHO ARE INCREASING THEIR VIOLENT ATTACKS, LIKE THOSE RECENTLY IN LONDON AND THE PACIFIC?
OUR APPROACHES ARE COMPLETELY DIFFERENT. I HAVE NOTHING TO DO WITH THEM, AND I WOULD LIKE TO ADD THAT...
I HAVEN'T GOT A RESPONSE. HM. I'M GONNA SEND A MESSAGE.

EVERYWHERE, HUMANKIND IS SPREADING DEATH AND DESTRUCTION, TORTURING AND EXTERMINATING, UNTIL THERE'S NOTHING LEFT -- UNTIL EVERYTHING BECOMES STERILE AND UNLIVABLE. MAYBE JERRY AND HIS NEW BUDDIES ARE RIGHT AFTER ALL. BUT ZHENG COULD HAVE IT WRONG BY USING HIS TRAIN TO SAVE THOSE WHO DON'T DESERVE IT.

DOM? IT'S VALENTINA. LISTEN, YOU TOLD ME YOU KNOW THIS ZHENG. COULD YOU PUT ME IN TOUCH WITH HIM? IT'S -- IMPORTANT.

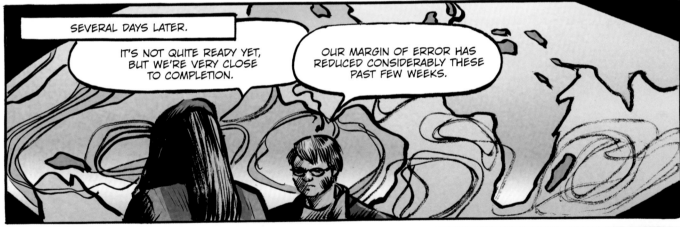

SEVERAL DAYS LATER.

IT'S NOT QUITE READY YET, BUT WE'RE VERY CLOSE TO COMPLETION.

OUR MARGIN OF ERROR HAS REDUCED CONSIDERABLY THESE PAST FEW WEEKS.

IN ANOTHER THREE MONTHS, WE'LL BE READY.

OUR GUIDE AWAITS US, MARCIO.

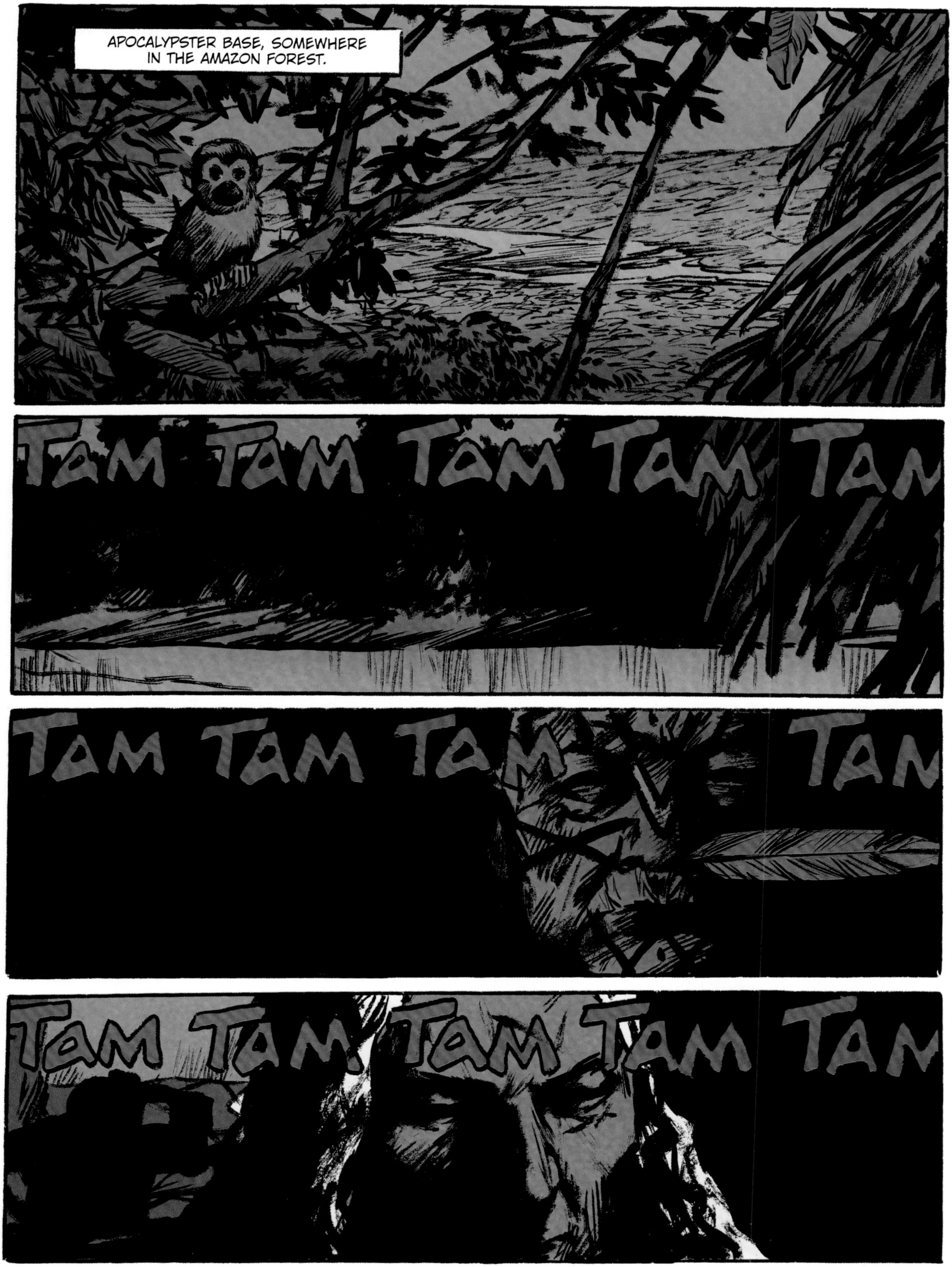
APOCALYPSTER BASE, SOMEWHERE IN THE AMAZON FOREST.
TAM TAM TAM TAM TAN
TAM TAM TAM TAN
TAM TAM TAM TAM TAN

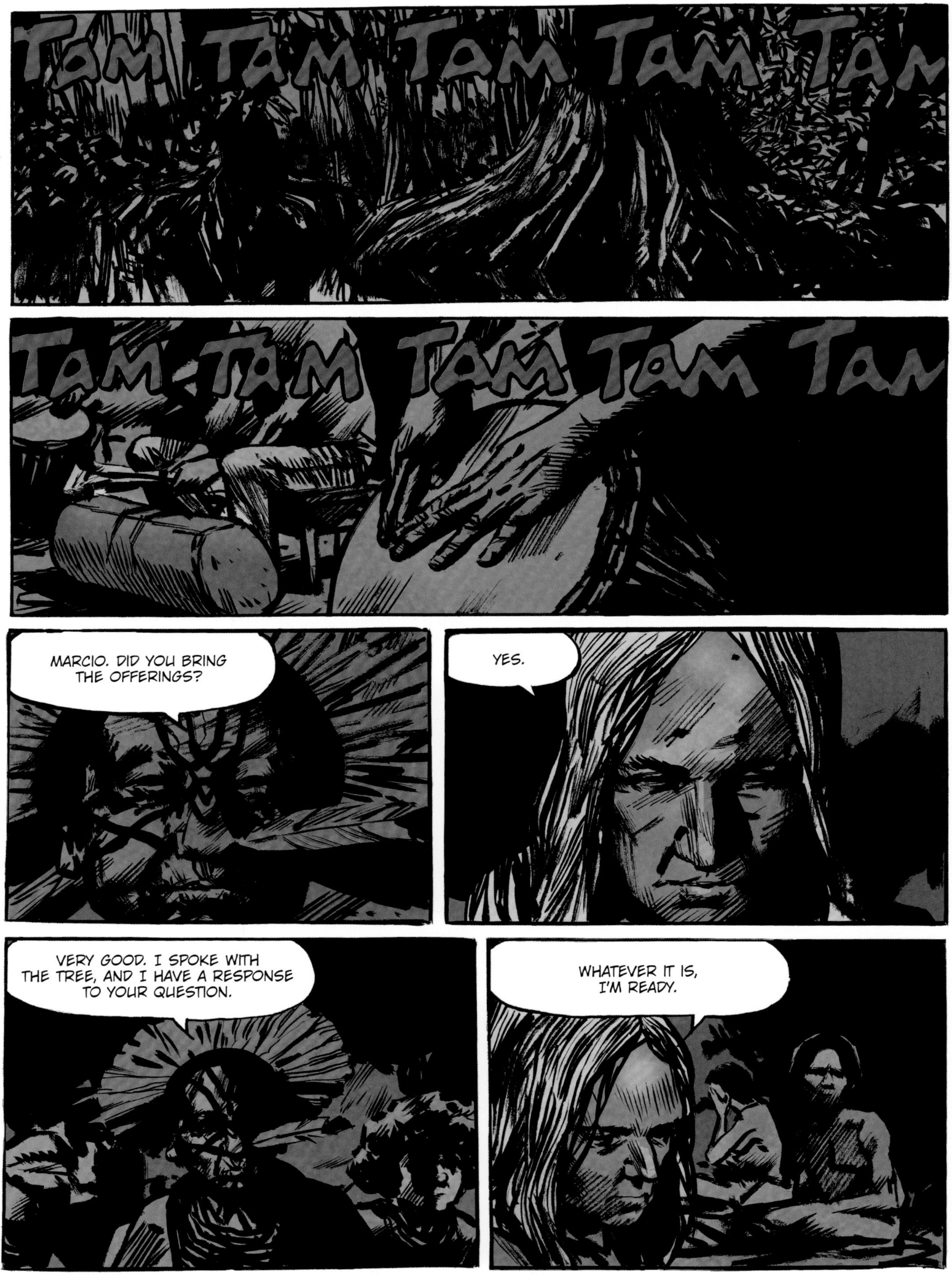
TAM TAM TAM TAM TAM
TAM TAM TAM TAM TAM
MARCIO. DID YOU BRING THE OFFERINGS?
YES.
VERY GOOD. I SPOKE WITH THE TREE, AND I HAVE A RESPONSE TO YOUR QUESTION.
WHATEVER IT IS, I'M READY.

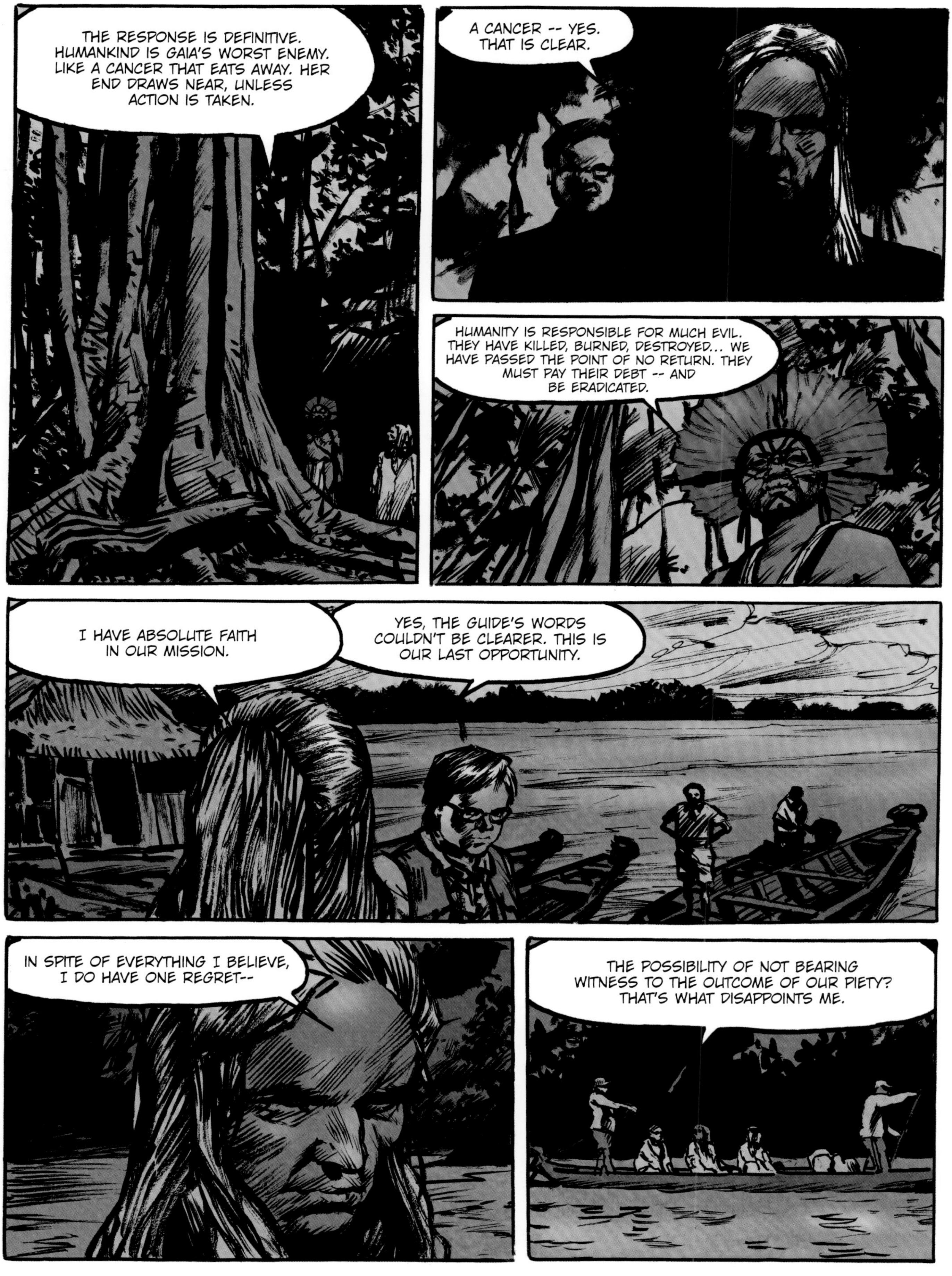
THE RESPONSE IS DEFINITIVE. HUMANKIND IS GAIA'S WORST ENEMY. LIKE A CANCER THAT EATS AWAY. HER END DRAWS NEAR, UNLESS ACTION IS TAKEN.
A CANCER -- YES. THAT IS CLEAR.
HUMANITY IS RESPONSIBLE FOR MUCH EVIL. THEY HAVE KILLED, BURNED, DESTROYED... WE HAVE PASSED THE POINT OF NO RETURN. THEY MUST PAY THEIR DEBT -- AND BE ERADICATED.
I HAVE ABSOLUTE FAITH IN OUR MISSION.
YES, THE GUIDE'S WORDS COULDN'T BE CLEARER. THIS IS OUR LAST OPPORTUNITY.
IN SPITE OF EVERYTHING I BELIEVE, I DO HAVE ONE REGRET--
THE POSSIBILITY OF NOT BEARING WITNESS TO THE OUTCOME OF OUR PIETY? THAT'S WHAT DISAPPOINTS ME.

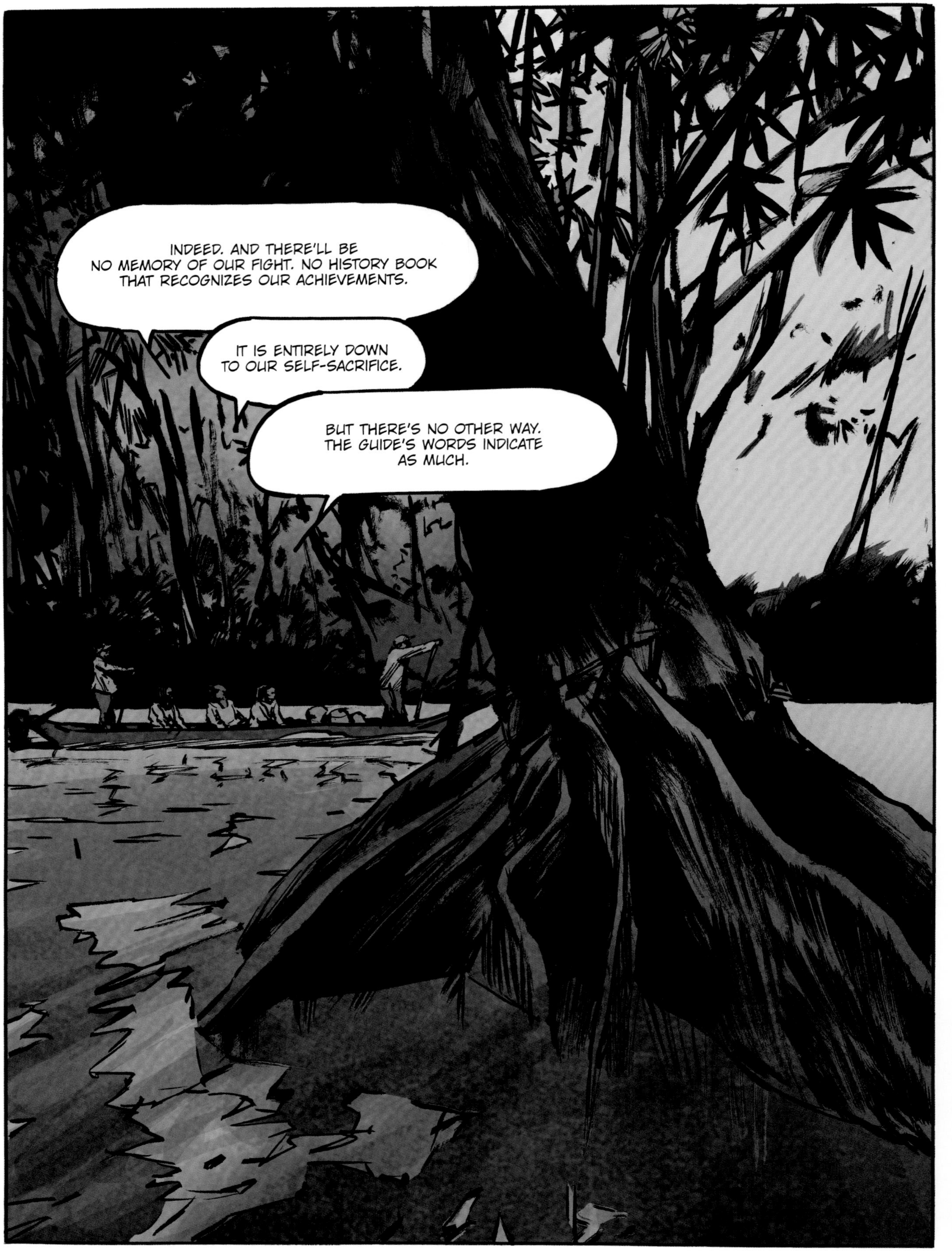
INDEED. AND THERE'LL BE NO MEMORY OF OUR FIGHT. NO HISTORY BOOK THAT RECOGNIZES OUR ACHIEVEMENTS.
IT IS ENTIRELY DOWN TO OUR SELF-SACRIFICE.
BUT THERE'S NO OTHER WAY. THE GUIDE'S WORDS INDICATE AS MUCH.

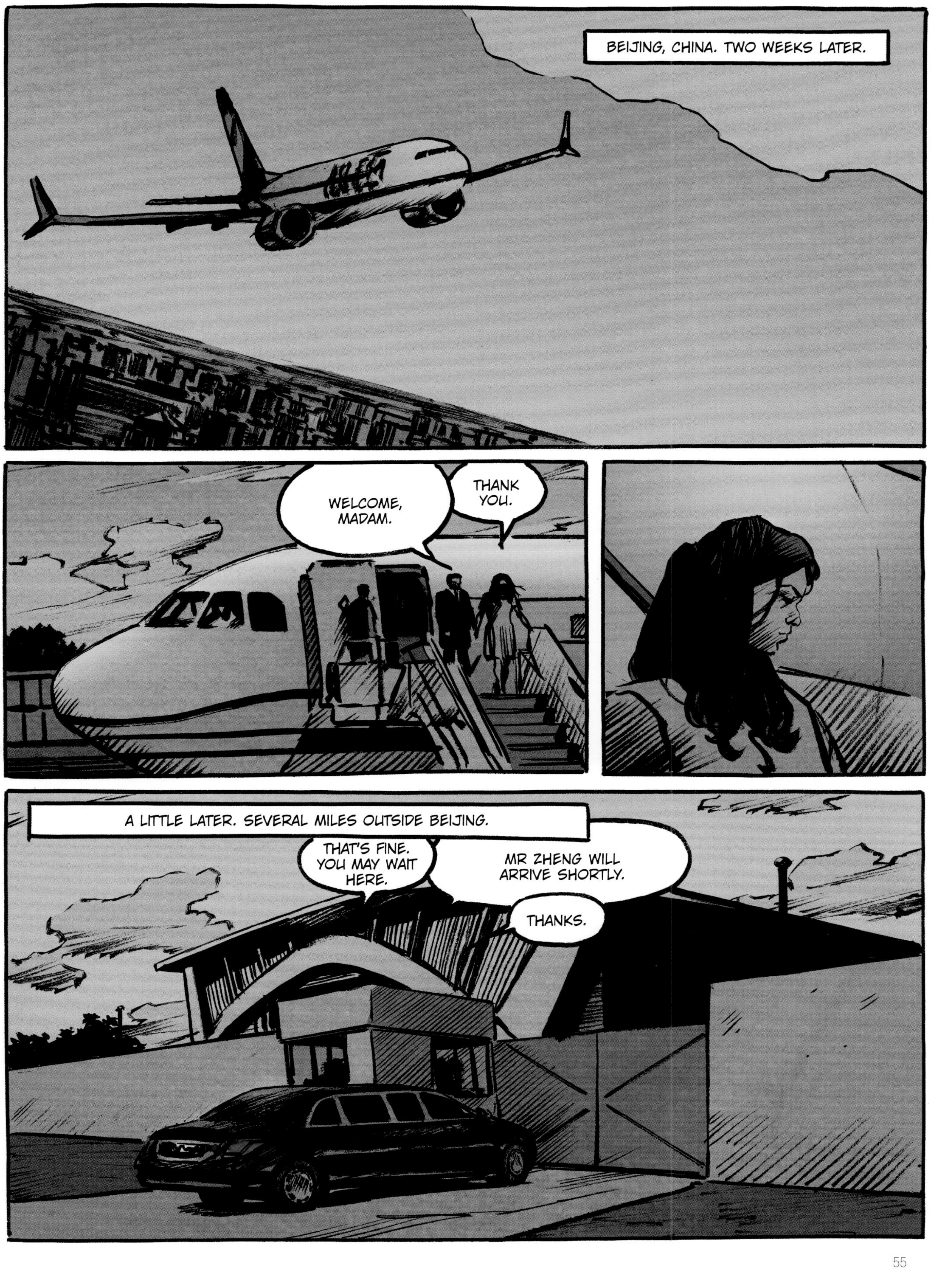

BEIJING, CHINA. TWO WEEKS LATER.
WELCOME, MADAM.
THANK YOU.
A LITTLE LATER. SEVERAL MILES OUTSIDE BEIJING.
MR ZHENG WILL ARRIVE SHORTLY.
THAT'S FINE. YOU MAY WAIT HERE.
THANKS.

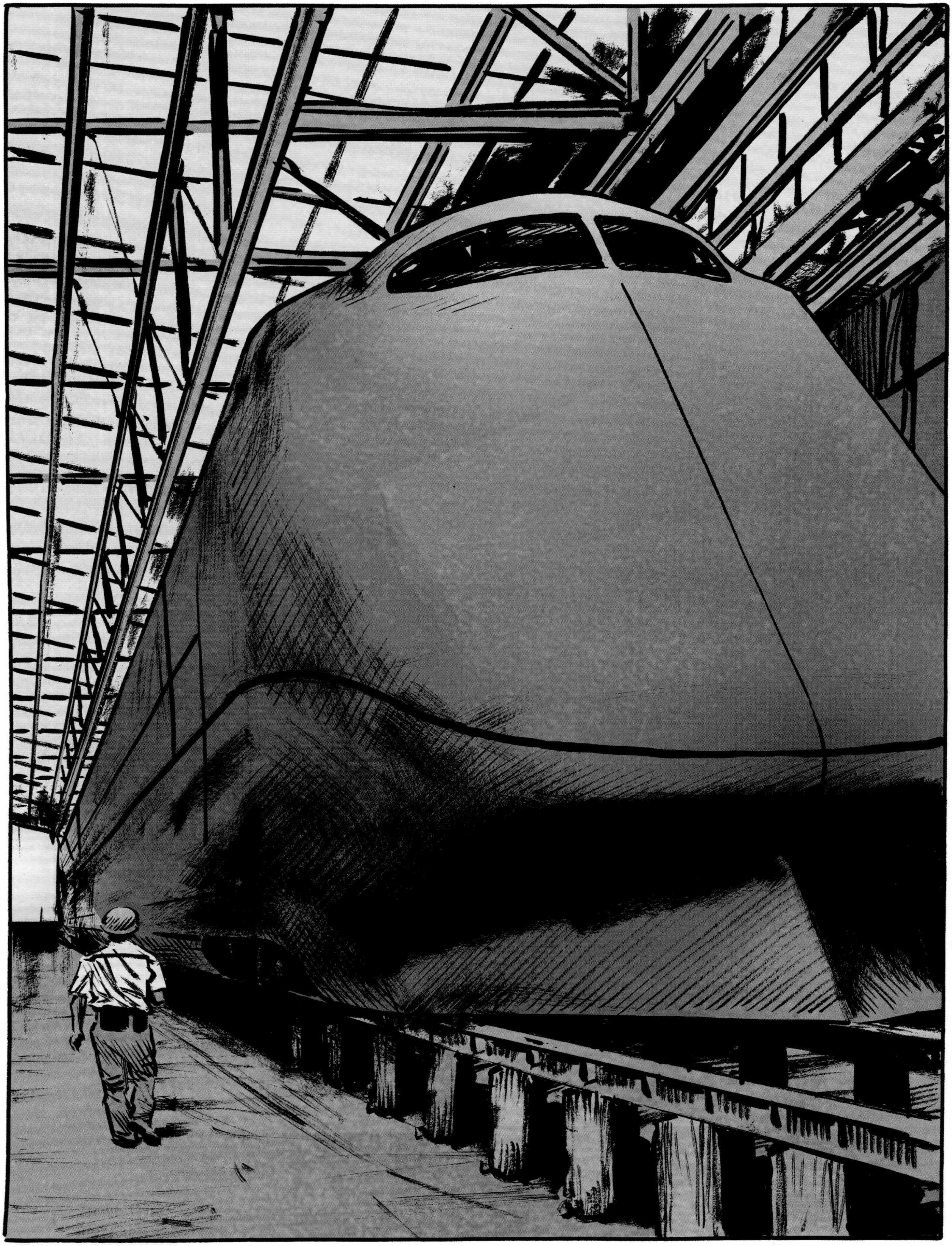

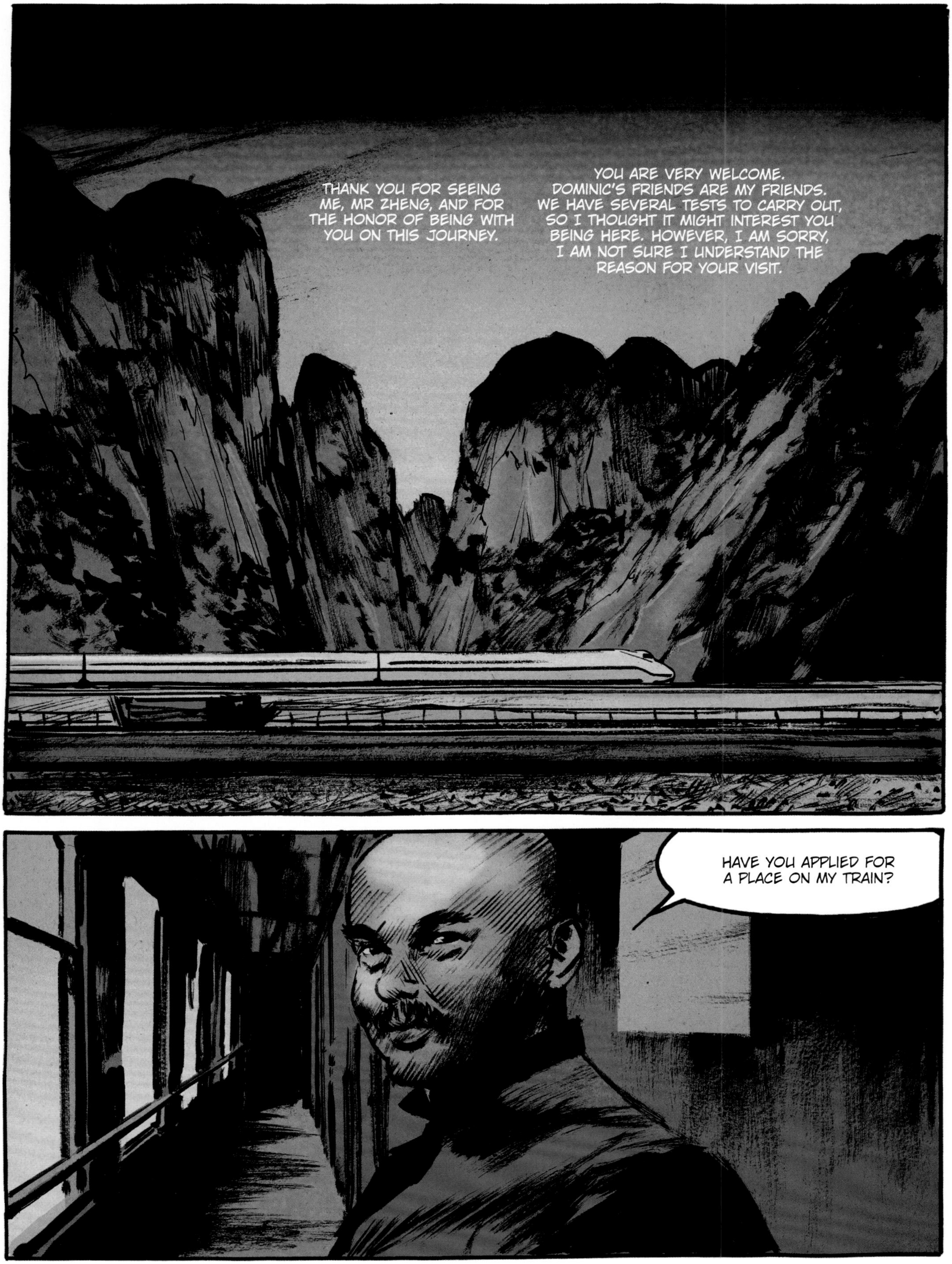
THANK YOU FOR SEEING ME, MR ZHENG, AND FOR THE HONOR OF BEING WITH YOU ON THIS JOURNEY.
YOU ARE VERY WELCOME. DOMINIC'S FRIENDS ARE MY FRIENDS. WE HAVE SEVERAL TESTS TO CARRY OUT, SO I THOUGHT IT MIGHT INTEREST YOU BEING HERE. HOWEVER, I AM SORRY, I AM NOT SURE I UNDERSTAND THE REASON FOR YOUR VISIT.
HAVE YOU APPLIED FOR A PLACE ON MY TRAIN?

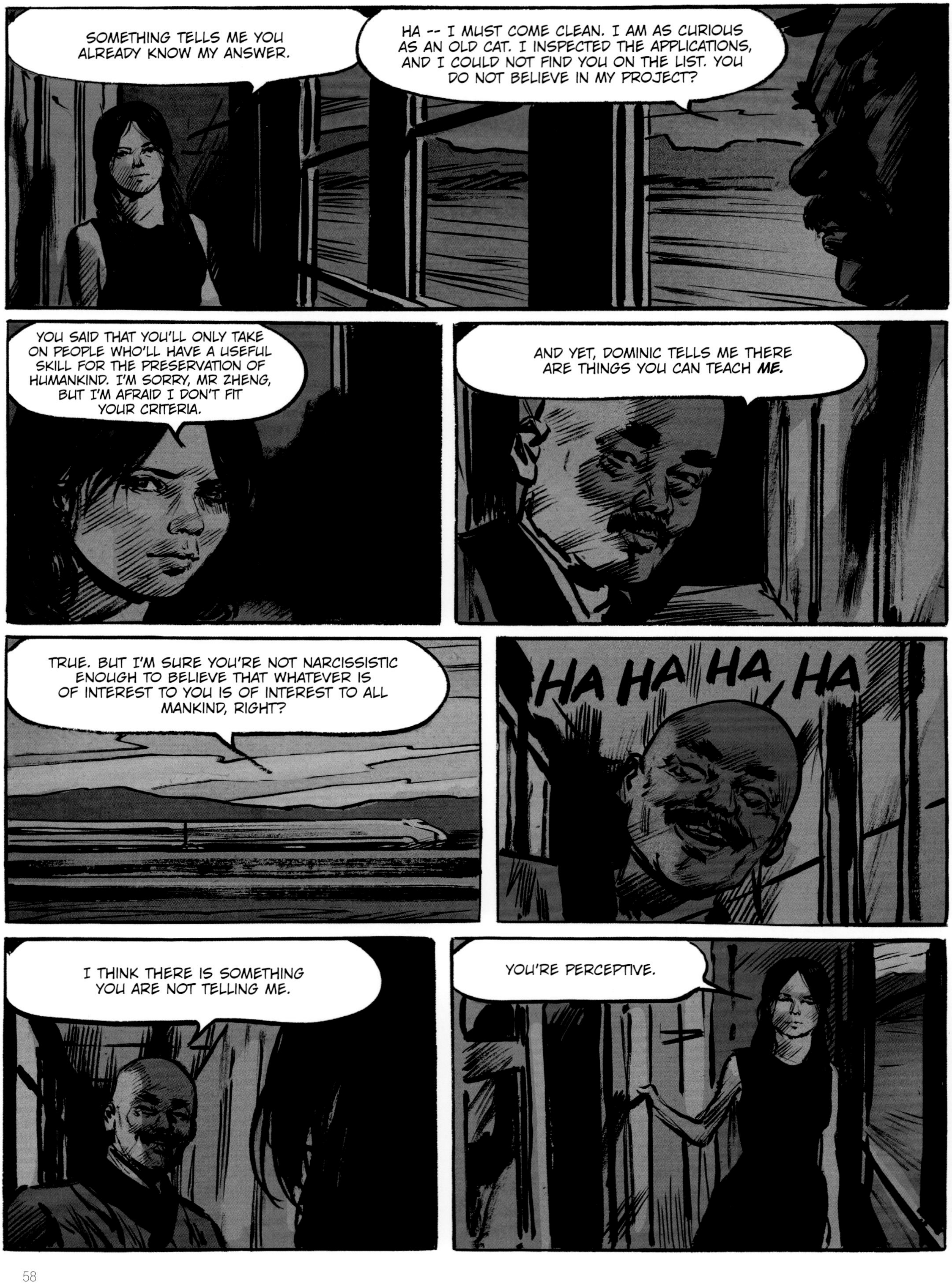
SOMETHING TELLS ME YOU ALREADY KNOW MY ANSWER.
HA -- I MUST COME CLEAN. I AM AS CURIOUS AS AN OLD CAT. I INSPECTED THE APPLICATIONS, AND I COULD NOT FIND YOU ON THE LIST. YOU DO NOT BELIEVE IN MY PROJECT?
YOU SAID THAT YOU'LL ONLY TAKE ON PEOPLE WHO'LL HAVE A USEFUL SKILL FOR THE PRESERVATION OF HUMANKIND. I'M SORRY, MR ZHENG, BUT I'M AFRAID I DON'T FIT YOUR CRITERIA.
AND YET, DOMINIC TELLS ME THERE ARE THINGS YOU CAN TEACH ***ME.***
TRUE. BUT I'M SURE YOU'RE NOT NARCISSISTIC ENOUGH TO BELIEVE THAT WHATEVER IS OF INTEREST TO YOU IS OF INTEREST TO ALL MANKIND, RIGHT?
HA HA HA HA
I THINK THERE IS SOMETHING YOU ARE NOT TELLING ME.
YOU'RE PERCEPTIVE.

I AM INTERESTED IN PEOPLE. I LIKE TO TRY AND UNDERSTAND THEM. AND UNLIKE ALL THE OTHERS WHO ARE DESPERATE TO GET ON BOARD THIS TRAIN, THIS IS NOT A PLACE YOU WANT TO BE.

CORRECT?

YOU ARE DECIDING IF YOU CAN TRUST ME.

HMM, NOT JUST THAT. I HAVE TO ADMIT THAT I FIND YOU INTRIGUING. YOU HAVE A SINCERE AIR ABOUT YOU WHEN YOU TALK ABOUT HOW PEOPLE INTEREST YOU.

WHY WOULD I NOT BE?

SINCERE? OR INTERESTED IN PEOPLE?

BOTH.

THESE ARE THE THINGS WE HAVE LOST FROM OUR WORLD NOWADAYS.

FOLLOW ME. I AM GOING TO SHOW YOU SOME OF THIS MACHINE'S WORKING PARTS.

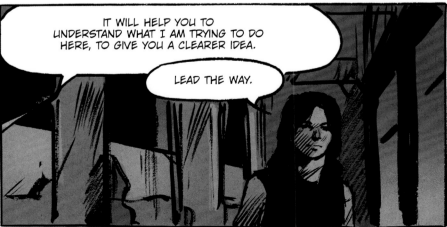

IT WILL HELP YOU TO UNDERSTAND WHAT I AM TRYING TO DO HERE, TO GIVE YOU A CLEARER IDEA.

LEAD THE WAY.

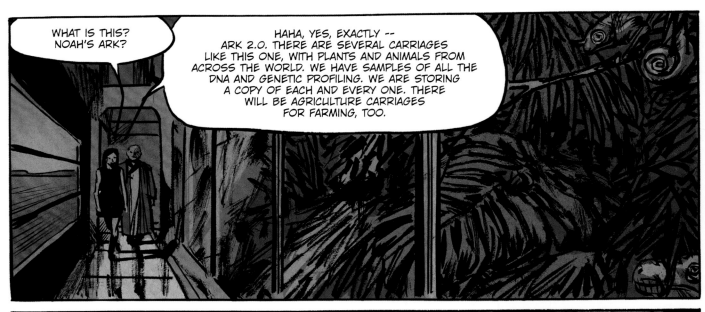

WHAT IS THIS? NOAH'S ARK?

HAHA, YES, EXACTLY -- ARK 2.0. THERE ARE SEVERAL CARRIAGES LIKE THIS ONE, WITH PLANTS AND ANIMALS FROM ACROSS THE WORLD. WE HAVE SAMPLES OF ALL THE DNA AND GENETIC PROFILING. WE ARE STORING A COPY OF EACH AND EVERY ONE. THERE WILL BE AGRICULTURE CARRIAGES FOR FARMING, TOO.

AFTER THE NATURAL COMES THE SPIRITUAL. IN HERE WE KEEP DIGITAL RECORDS OF ALL THE WORLD'S MAJOR WORKS -- PICTURES, MUSIC, LITERATURE, PATENTS, HISTORICAL RECORDS, INVENTIONS...

HUMANITY'S COLLECTIVE MEMORY, IN OTHER WORDS?

YOU COULD CALL IT THAT, I SUPPOSE, YES.

IT IS MY PERSONAL COLLECTION. WE'VE THOUGHT ABOUT HOW TO ARCHIVE AND PROTECT IT.

YOU THINK OF EVERYTHING.

WE CAN NEVER THINK OF EVERYTHING. BUT WE TRY.

AGAIN WITH THE MODESTY.

HAHAHA!

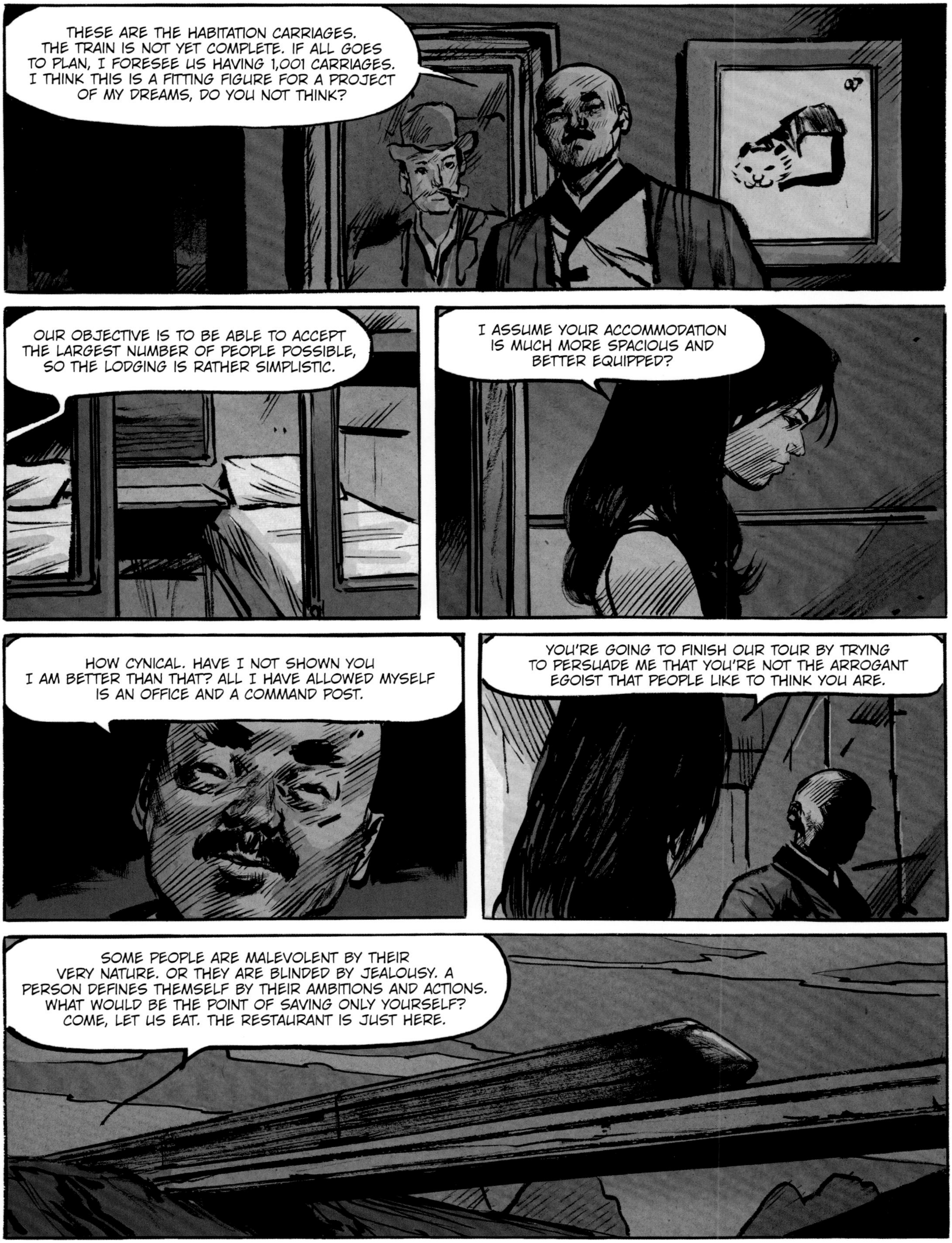

THESE ARE THE HABITATION CARRIAGES. THE TRAIN IS NOT YET COMPLETE. IF ALL GOES TO PLAN, I FORESEE US HAVING 1,001 CARRIAGES. I THINK THIS IS A FITTING FIGURE FOR A PROJECT OF MY DREAMS, DO YOU NOT THINK?
OUR OBJECTIVE IS TO BE ABLE TO ACCEPT THE LARGEST NUMBER OF PEOPLE POSSIBLE, SO THE LODGING IS RATHER SIMPLISTIC.
I ASSUME YOUR ACCOMMODATION IS MUCH MORE SPACIOUS AND BETTER EQUIPPED?
HOW CYNICAL. HAVE I NOT SHOWN YOU I AM BETTER THAN THAT? ALL I HAVE ALLOWED MYSELF IS AN OFFICE AND A COMMAND POST.
YOU'RE GOING TO FINISH OUR TOUR BY TRYING TO PERSUADE ME THAT YOU'RE NOT THE ARROGANT EGOIST THAT PEOPLE LIKE TO THINK YOU ARE.
SOME PEOPLE ARE MALEVOLENT BY THEIR VERY NATURE. OR THEY ARE BLINDED BY JEALOUSY. A PERSON DEFINES THEMSELF BY THEIR AMBITIONS AND ACTIONS. WHAT WOULD BE THE POINT OF SAVING ONLY YOURSELF? COME, LET US EAT. THE RESTAURANT IS JUST HERE.

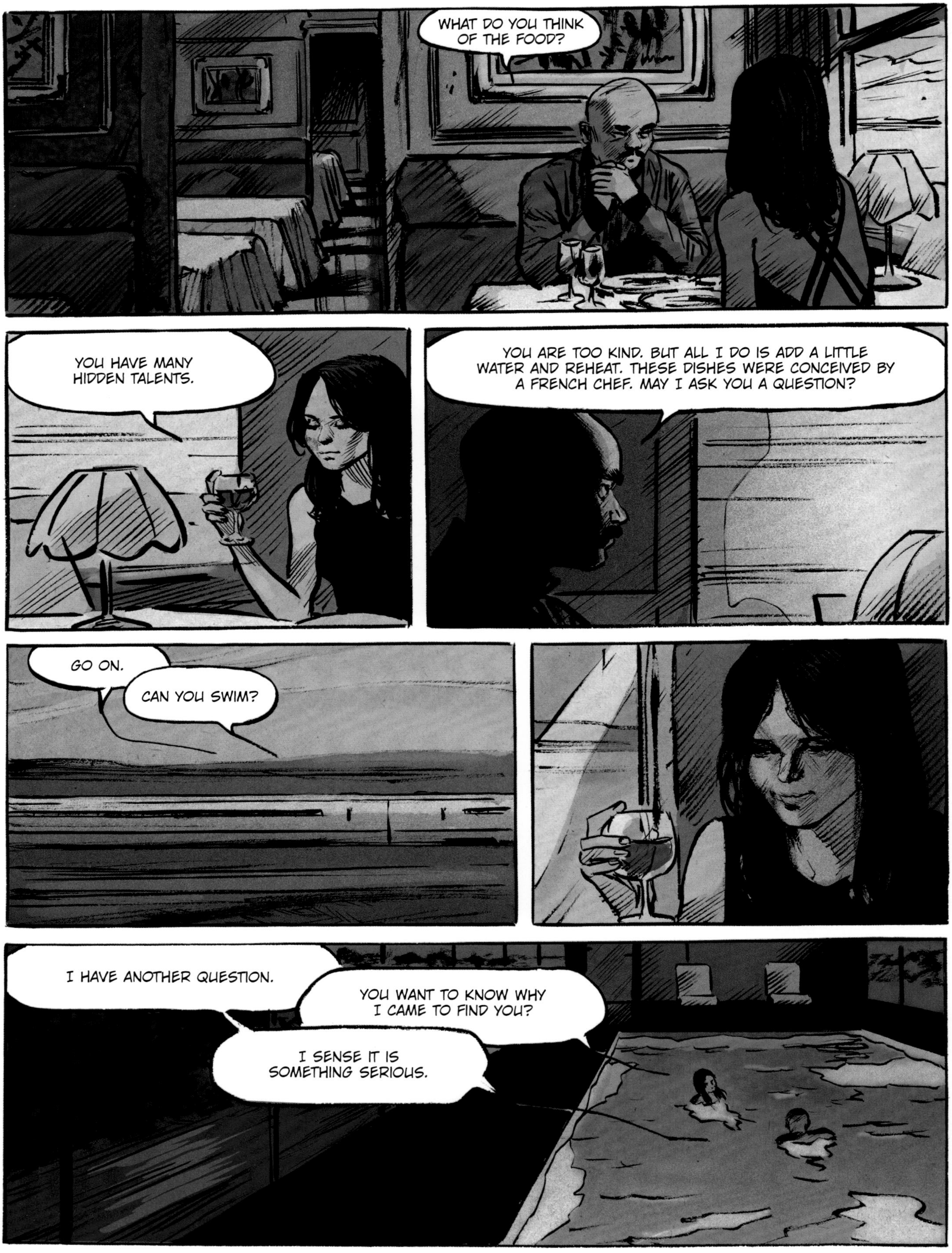
WHAT DO YOU THINK OF THE FOOD?
YOU HAVE MANY HIDDEN TALENTS.
YOU ARE TOO KIND. BUT ALL I DO IS ADD A LITTLE WATER AND REHEAT. THESE DISHES WERE CONCEIVED BY A FRENCH CHEF. MAY I ASK YOU A QUESTION?
GO ON.
CAN YOU SWIM?
I HAVE ANOTHER QUESTION.
YOU WANT TO KNOW WHY I CAME TO FIND YOU?
I SENSE IT IS SOMETHING SERIOUS.

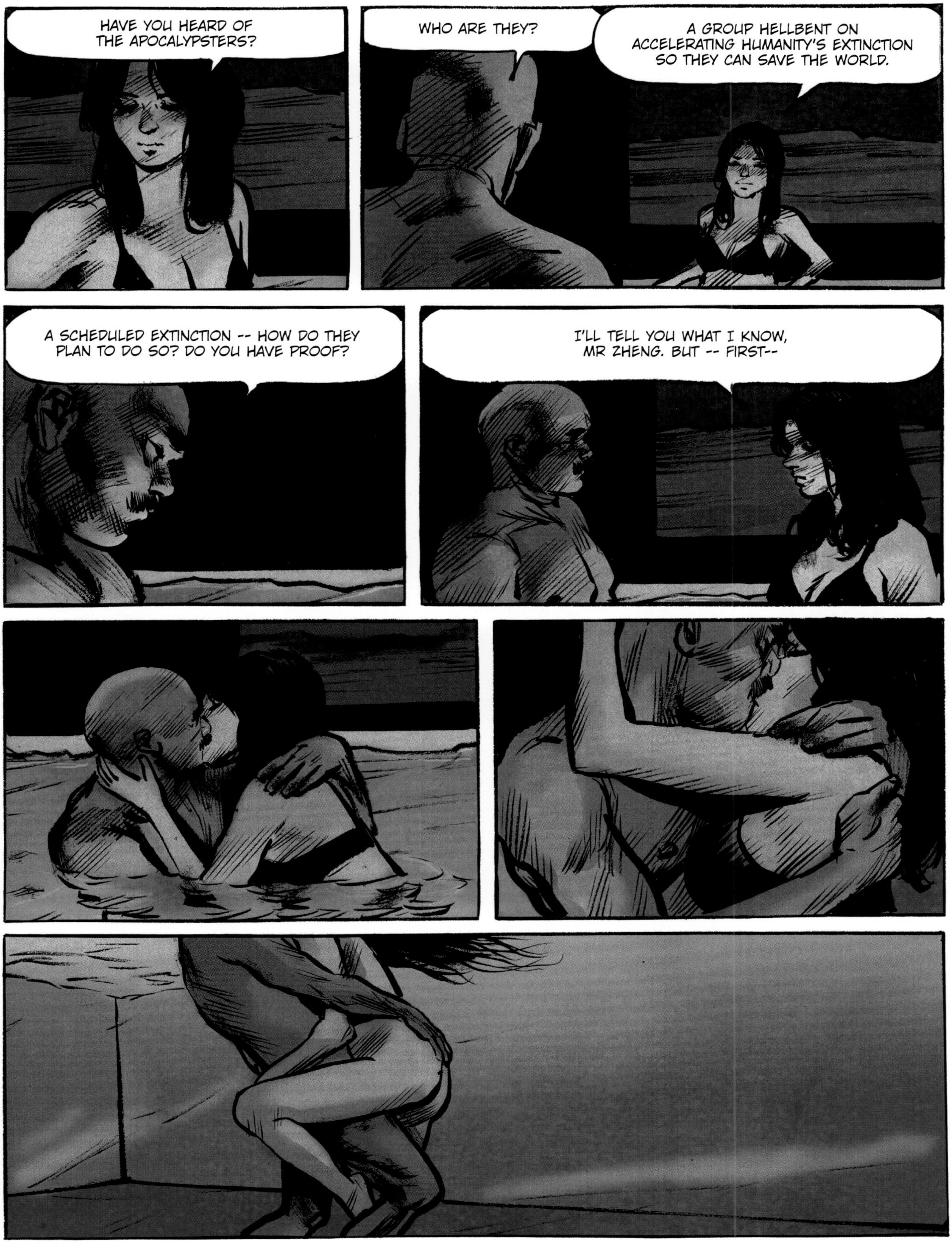
HAVE YOU HEARD OF THE APOCALYPSTERS?
WHO ARE THEY?
A GROUP HELLBENT ON ACCELERATING HUMANITY'S EXTINCTION SO THEY CAN SAVE THE WORLD.
A SCHEDULED EXTINCTION -- HOW DO THEY PLAN TO DO SO? DO YOU HAVE PROOF?
I'LL TELL YOU WHAT I KNOW, MR ZHENG. BUT -- FIRST--

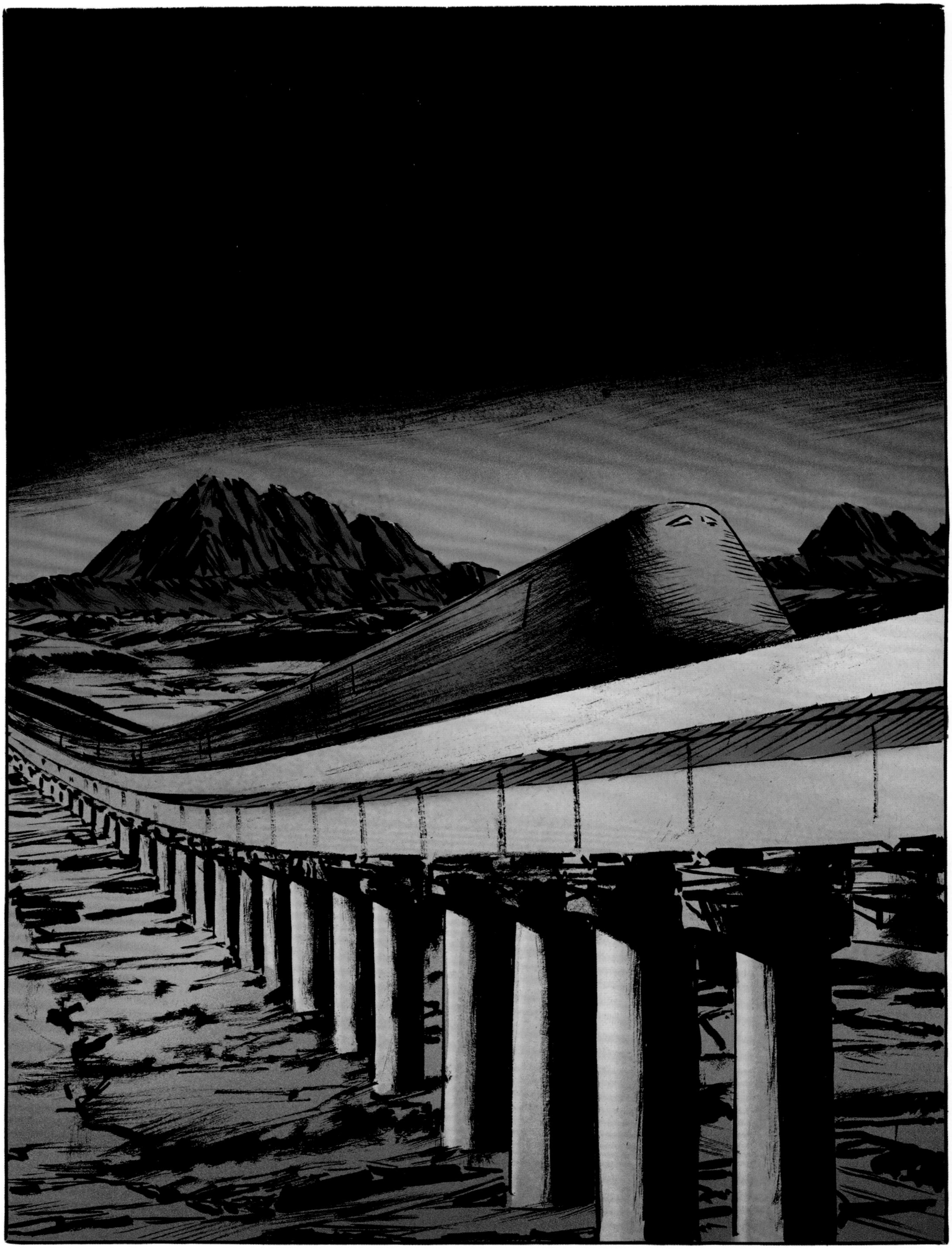

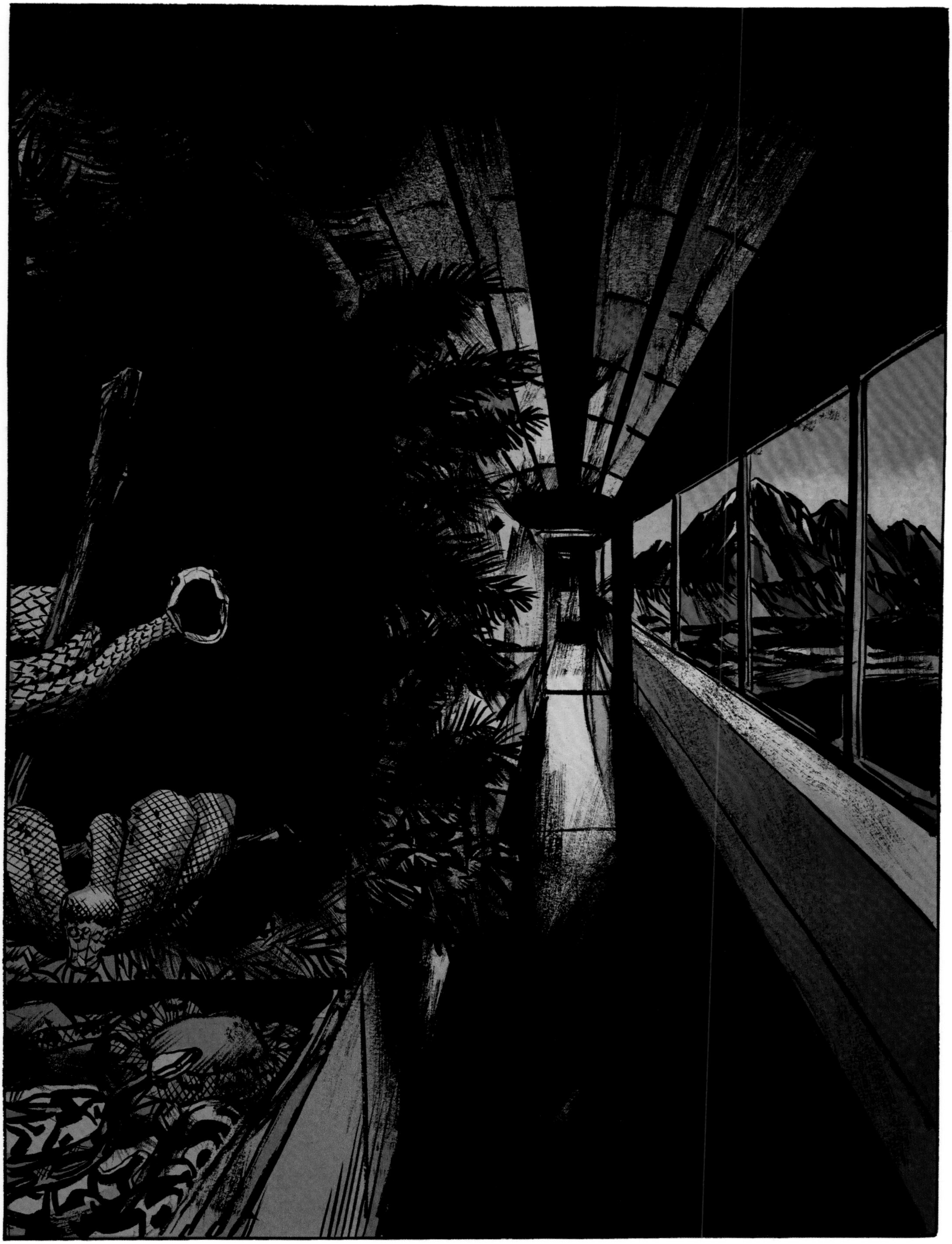

WE ARE GOING TO INITIATE SOME NEW RECRUITS -- A MAN AND A WOMAN. RADICALISTS WHO WANT TO COMMIT MORE TO OUR CAUSE.

WE'D LIKE YOU TO TEST THEM.

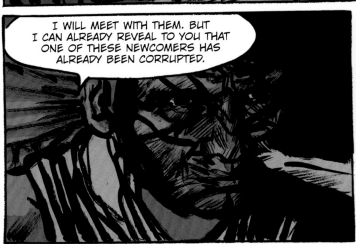

I WILL MEET WITH THEM. BUT I CAN ALREADY REVEAL TO YOU THAT ONE OF THESE NEWCOMERS HAS ALREADY BEEN CORRUPTED.

CORRUPTED? HOW?

VIGILANCE MUST BE UPHELD. MORE AND MORE PEOPLE ARE JOINING OUR CAUSE. THIS PLACE MUST REMAIN HIDDEN. DANGER PREYS ON US. IT IS CLOSING IN. ONE DAY, A TRAITOR WILL COME.

AND ONE OF THESE TWO NEW RECRUITS WILL BE THE TRAITOR?

THAT'S WHAT I BELIEVE. I WILL KNOW WHEN I SEE THEM.

VERY WELL. WHEN THEY ARRIVE, WE WILL BRING THEM TO YOU.

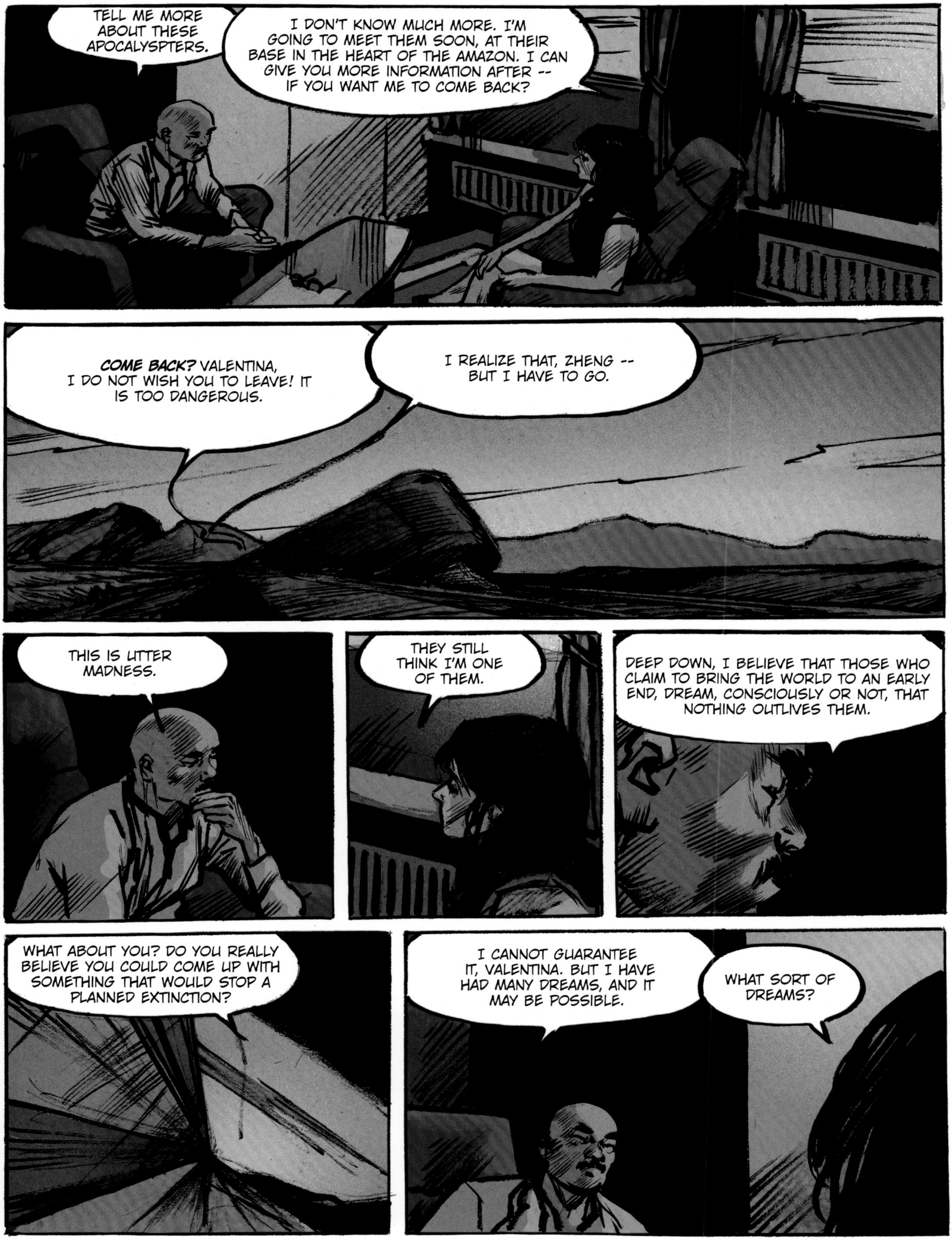
TELL ME MORE ABOUT THESE APOCALYSPTERS.
I DON'T KNOW MUCH MORE. I'M GOING TO MEET THEM SOON, AT THEIR BASE IN THE HEART OF THE AMAZON. I CAN GIVE YOU MORE INFORMATION AFTER -- IF YOU WANT ME TO COME BACK?
COME BACK? VALENTINA, I DO NOT WISH YOU TO LEAVE! IT IS TOO DANGEROUS.
I REALIZE THAT, ZHENG -- BUT I HAVE TO GO.
THIS IS UTTER MADNESS.
THEY STILL THINK I'M ONE OF THEM.
DEEP DOWN, I BELIEVE THAT THOSE WHO CLAIM TO BRING THE WORLD TO AN EARLY END, DREAM, CONSCIOUSLY OR NOT, THAT NOTHING OUTLIVES THEM.
WHAT ABOUT YOU? DO YOU REALLY BELIEVE YOU COULD COME UP WITH SOMETHING THAT WOULD STOP A PLANNED EXTINCTION?
I CANNOT GUARANTEE IT, VALENTINA. BUT I HAVE HAD MANY DREAMS, AND IT MAY BE POSSIBLE.
WHAT SORT OF DREAMS?

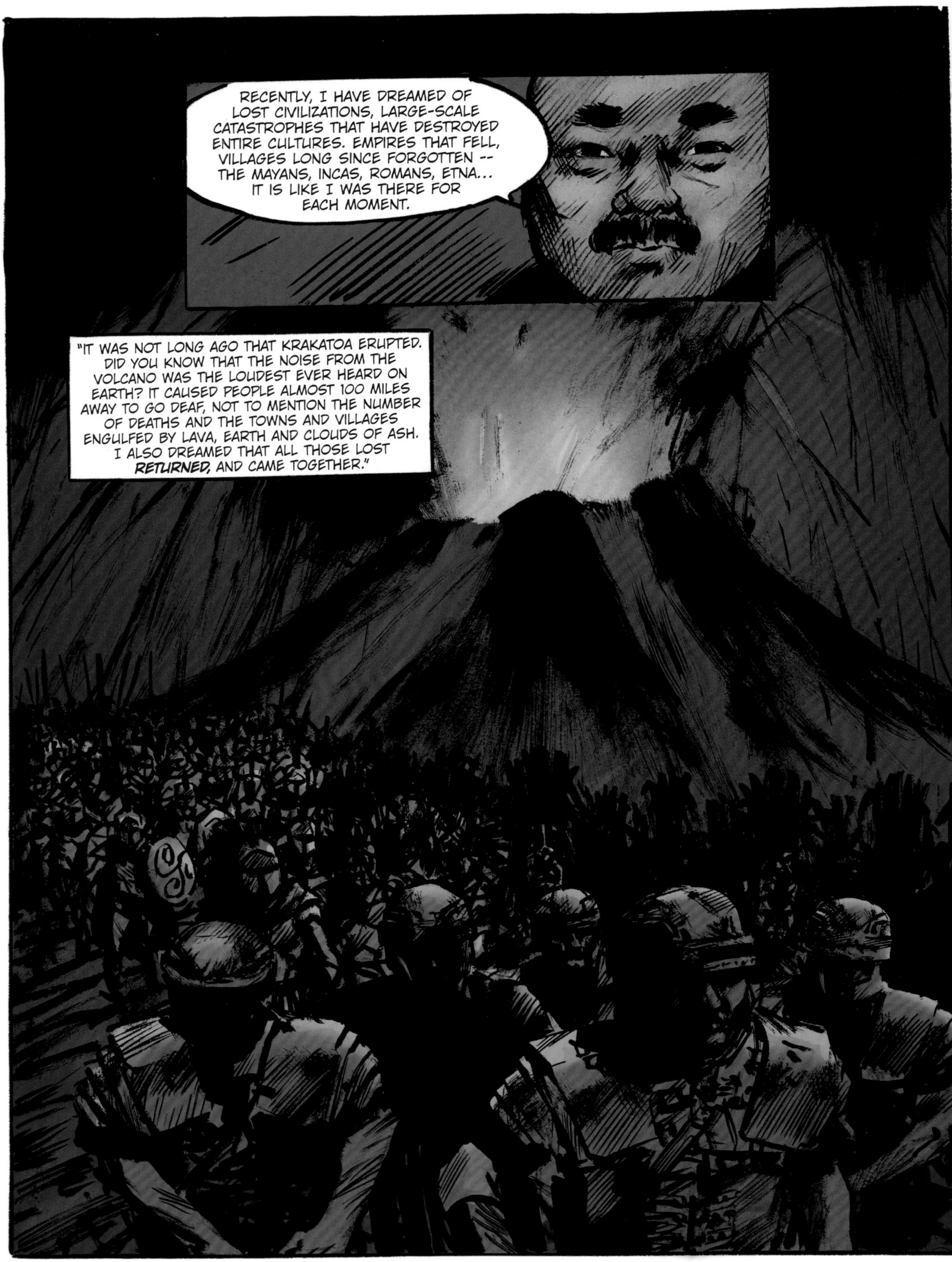
RECENTLY, I HAVE DREAMED OF LOST CIVILIZATIONS, LARGE-SCALE CATASTROPHES THAT HAVE DESTROYED ENTIRE CULTURES. EMPIRES THAT FELL, VILLAGES LONG SINCE FORGOTTEN -- THE MAYANS, INCAS, ROMANS, ETNA... IT IS LIKE I WAS THERE FOR EACH MOMENT.
"IT WAS NOT LONG AGO THAT KRAKATOA ERUPTED. DID YOU KNOW THAT THE NOISE FROM THE VOLCANO WAS THE LOUDEST EVER HEARD ON EARTH? IT CAUSED PEOPLE ALMOST 100 MILES AWAY TO GO DEAF, NOT TO MENTION THE NUMBER OF DEATHS AND THE TOWNS AND VILLAGES ENGULFED BY LAVA, EARTH AND CLOUDS OF ASH. I ALSO DREAMED THAT ALL THOSE LOST ***RETURNED,*** AND CAME TOGETHER."

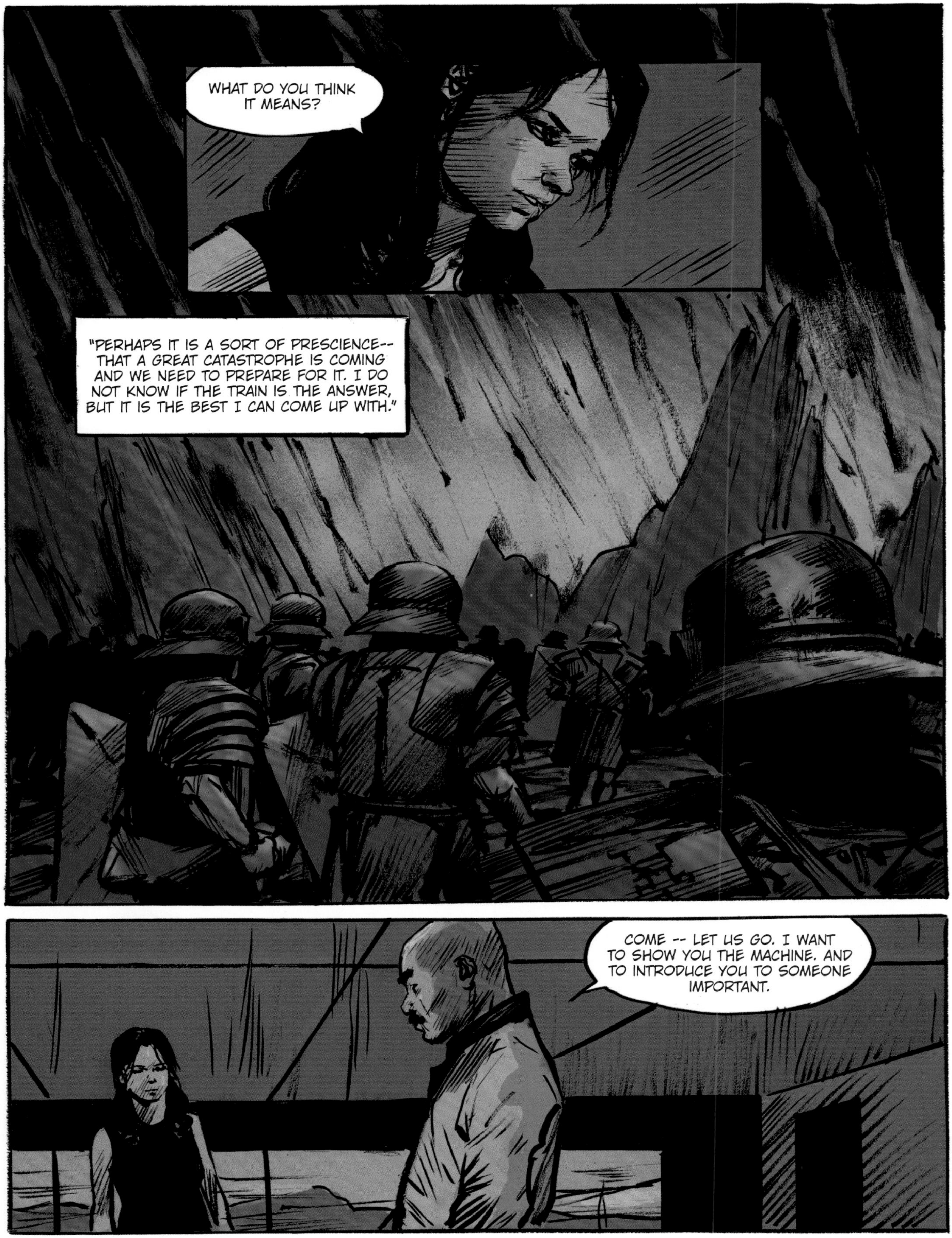
WHAT DO YOU THINK IT MEANS?
"PERHAPS IT IS A SORT OF PRESCIENCE-- THAT A GREAT CATASTROPHE IS COMING AND WE NEED TO PREPARE FOR IT. I DO NOT KNOW IF THE TRAIN IS THE ANSWER, BUT IT IS THE BEST I CAN COME UP WITH."
COME -- LET US GO. I WANT TO SHOW YOU THE MACHINE. AND TO INTRODUCE YOU TO SOMEONE IMPORTANT.

VALENTINA, MAY I INTRODUCE YOU TO FORRESTER, THE MAN BEHIND THE CURTAIN.

IT'S A PLEASURE TO MEET YOU, MR FORRESTER.

YOU CAN DROP THE "MISTER", IT'S JUST FORRESTER. PLEASURE.

THE AIM OF THIS JOURNEY IS TO TEST THE LAST OF OUR TEETHING PROBLEMS. ARE WE READY, FORRESTER?

YES, WE'VE FIXED THE PROBLEM WE WERE HAVING WITH AUTOMATIC ADJUSTMENT TO THE RAILS ON DIFFERENT NETWORKS. I CAN CONFIRM THAT WE'RE GOOD TO GO.

YOU SEE, VALENTINA -- FORRESTER IS THE MAN WITHOUT WHOM NOTHING WOULD HAPPEN! HE HAS HELPED ME TO ADAPT THE TRAIN TO MY PERPETUAL PROPULSION ENGINE.

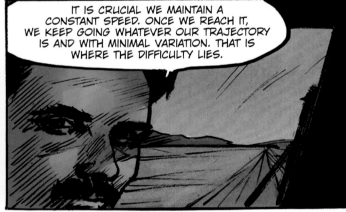

IT IS CRUCIAL WE MAINTAIN A CONSTANT SPEED. ONCE WE REACH IT, WE KEEP GOING WHATEVER OUR TRAJECTORY IS AND WITH MINIMAL VARIATION. THAT IS WHERE THE DIFFICULTY LIES.

SPARE ME THE DETAILS. I'M NOT APPLYING FOR AN ENGINEERING POSITION...

HAHAHA!

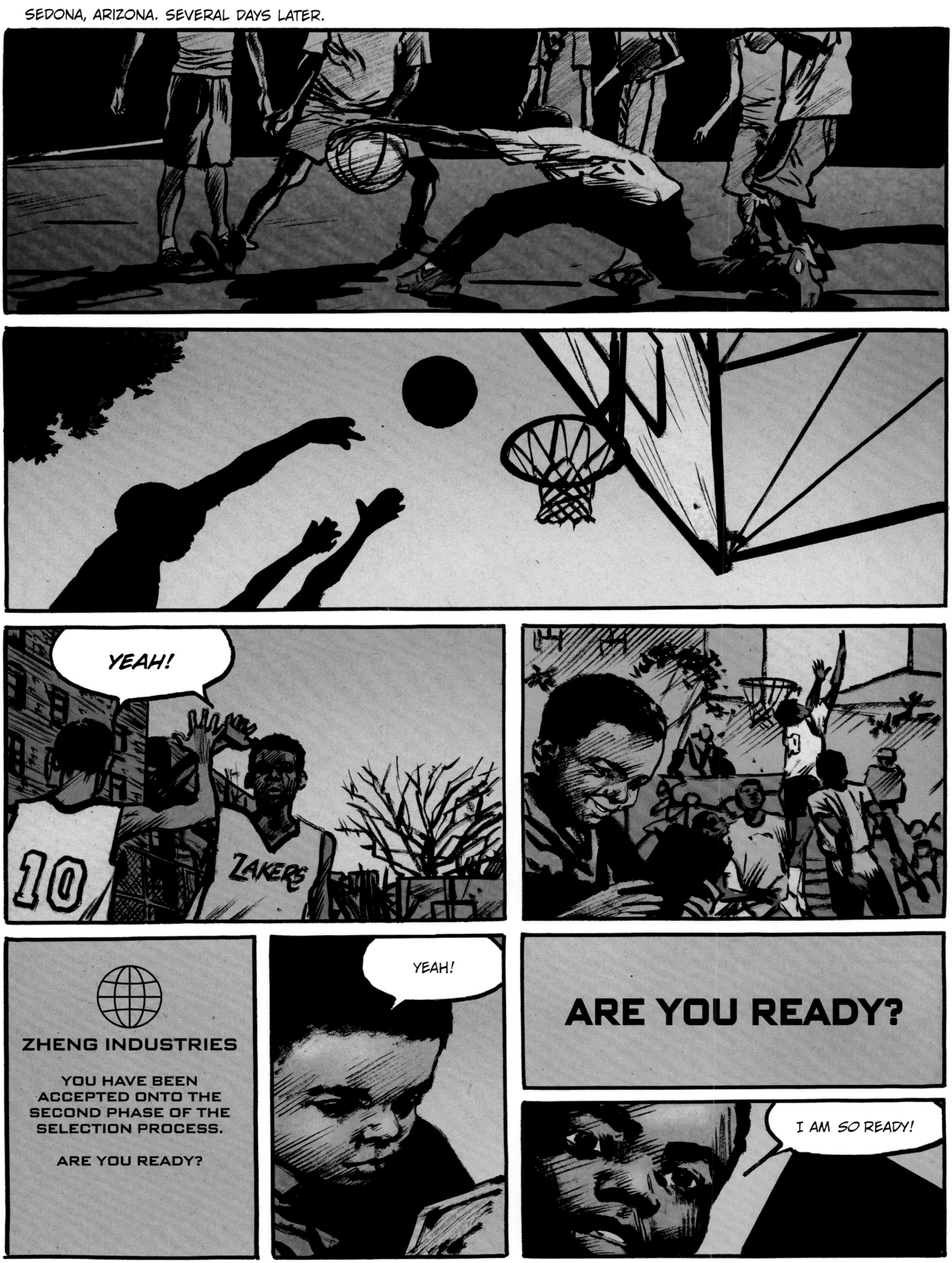
SEDONA, ARIZONA. SEVERAL DAYS LATER.
YEAH!
10
ZAKERS
ZHENG INDUSTRIES
YOU HAVE BEEN ACCEPTED ONTO THE SECOND PHASE OF THE SELECTION PROCESS.
ARE YOU READY?
YEAH!
ARE YOU READY?
I AM SO READY!

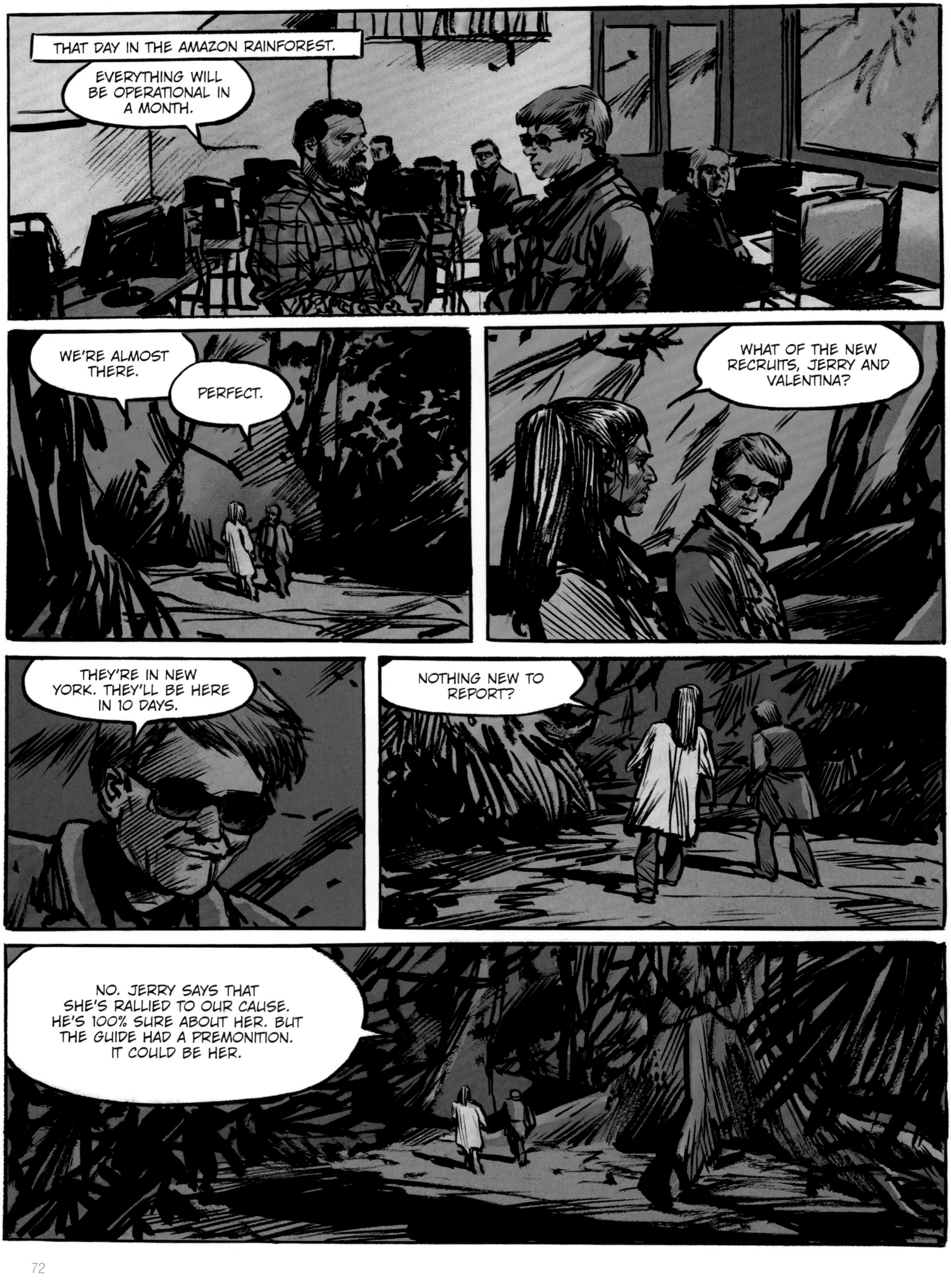
THAT DAY IN THE AMAZON RAINFOREST.
EVERYTHING WILL BE OPERATIONAL IN A MONTH.
WE'RE ALMOST THERE.
PERFECT.
WHAT OF THE NEW RECRUITS, JERRY AND VALENTINA?
THEY'RE IN NEW YORK. THEY'LL BE HERE IN 10 DAYS.
NOTHING NEW TO REPORT?
NO. JERRY SAYS THAT SHE'S RALLIED TO OUR CAUSE. HE'S 100% SURE ABOUT HER. BUT THE GUIDE HAD A PREMONITION. IT COULD BE HER.

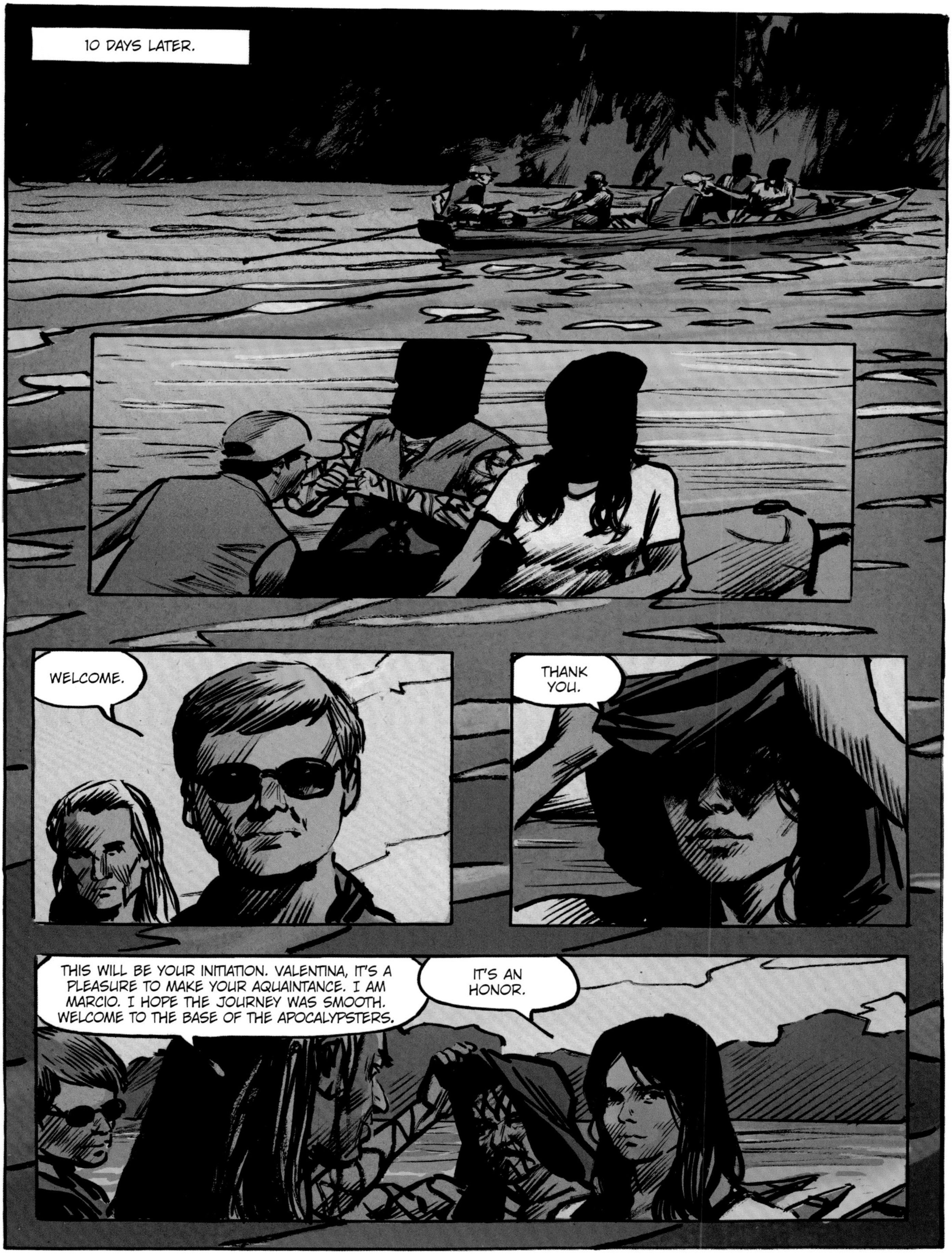
10 DAYS LATER.
WELCOME.
THANK YOU.
THIS WILL BE YOUR INITIATION. VALENTINA, IT'S A PLEASURE TO MAKE YOUR AQUAINTANCE. I AM MARCIO. I HOPE THE JOURNEY WAS SMOOTH. WELCOME TO THE BASE OF THE APOCALYPSTERS.
IT'S AN HONOR.

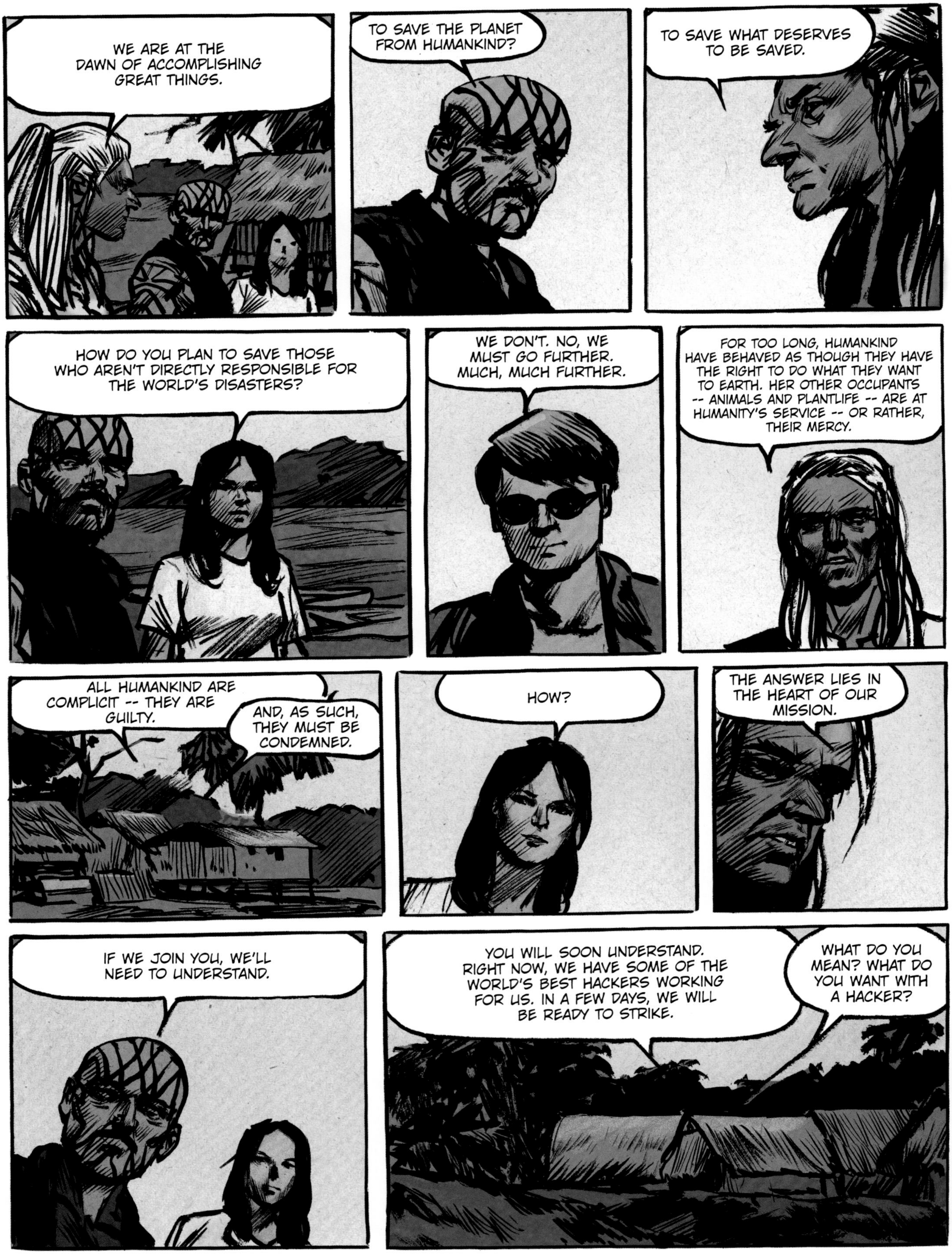
WE ARE AT THE DAWN OF ACCOMPLISHING GREAT THINGS.
TO SAVE THE PLANET FROM HUMANKIND?
TO SAVE WHAT DESERVES TO BE SAVED.
HOW DO YOU PLAN TO SAVE THOSE WHO AREN'T DIRECTLY RESPONSIBLE FOR THE WORLD'S DISASTERS?
WE DON'T. NO, WE MUST GO FURTHER. MUCH, MUCH FURTHER.
FOR TOO LONG, HUMANKIND HAVE BEHAVED AS THOUGH THEY HAVE THE RIGHT TO DO WHAT THEY WANT TO EARTH. HER OTHER OCCUPANTS -- ANIMALS AND PLANTLIFE -- ARE AT HUMANITY'S SERVICE -- OR RATHER, THEIR MERCY.
ALL HUMANKIND ARE COMPLICIT -- THEY ARE GUILTY.
AND, AS SUCH, THEY MUST BE CONDEMNED.
HOW?
THE ANSWER LIES IN THE HEART OF OUR MISSION.
IF WE JOIN YOU, WE'LL NEED TO UNDERSTAND.
YOU WILL SOON UNDERSTAND. RIGHT NOW, WE HAVE SOME OF THE WORLD'S BEST HACKERS WORKING FOR US. IN A FEW DAYS, WE WILL BE READY TO STRIKE.
WHAT DO YOU MEAN? WHAT DO YOU WANT WITH A HACKER?

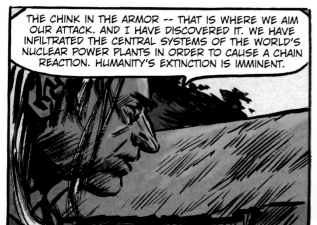

THE CHINK IN THE ARMOR -- THAT IS WHERE WE AIM OUR ATTACK. AND I HAVE DISCOVERED IT. WE HAVE INFILTRATED THE CENTRAL SYSTEMS OF THE WORLD'S NUCLEAR POWER PLANTS IN ORDER TO CAUSE A CHAIN REACTION. HUMANITY'S EXTINCTION IS IMMINENT.

WHAT WE WANT TO KNOW IS -- ARE YOU WITH US? DO YOU WANT TO BE A PART OF WHAT WE'RE TRYING TO ACHIEVE?

YEAH. I'M IN.

GREAT. THERE'S JUST ONE MORE FORMALITY.

WHAT'S THAT?

TO MEET THE GUIDE. HIS INSIGHT IS UNERRING. HE READS ONE'S HEART AND SOUL. HE KNOWS THE SECRET LANGUAGE OF THE EARTH, THE TREES, THE ANIMALS... YOU WILL SEE HIM, AND ONLY AFTER WILL YOU BE ACCEPTED.

AND IF HE DECIDES THAT WE CAN'T JOIN YOU?

LOOK, THERE'S NO REASON TO WORRY. IF YOU'RE HERE, IT'S BECAUSE YOU'VE MADE A CHOICE. YOU'LL HAVE A ROLE TO PLAY, DURING AND AFTER THE EXTINCTION.

HE IS READY. HE IS WAITING FOR YOU. DRINK THIS BEFORE YOU MEET WITH HIM.

WHAT IS IT?

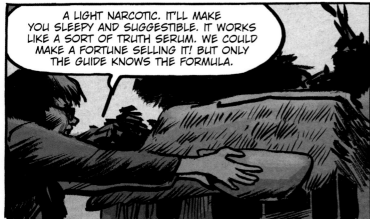

A LIGHT NARCOTIC. IT'LL MAKE YOU SLEEPY AND SUGGESTIBLE. IT WORKS LIKE A SORT OF TRUTH SERUM. WE COULD MAKE A FORTUNE SELLING IT! BUT ONLY THE GUIDE KNOWS THE FORMULA.

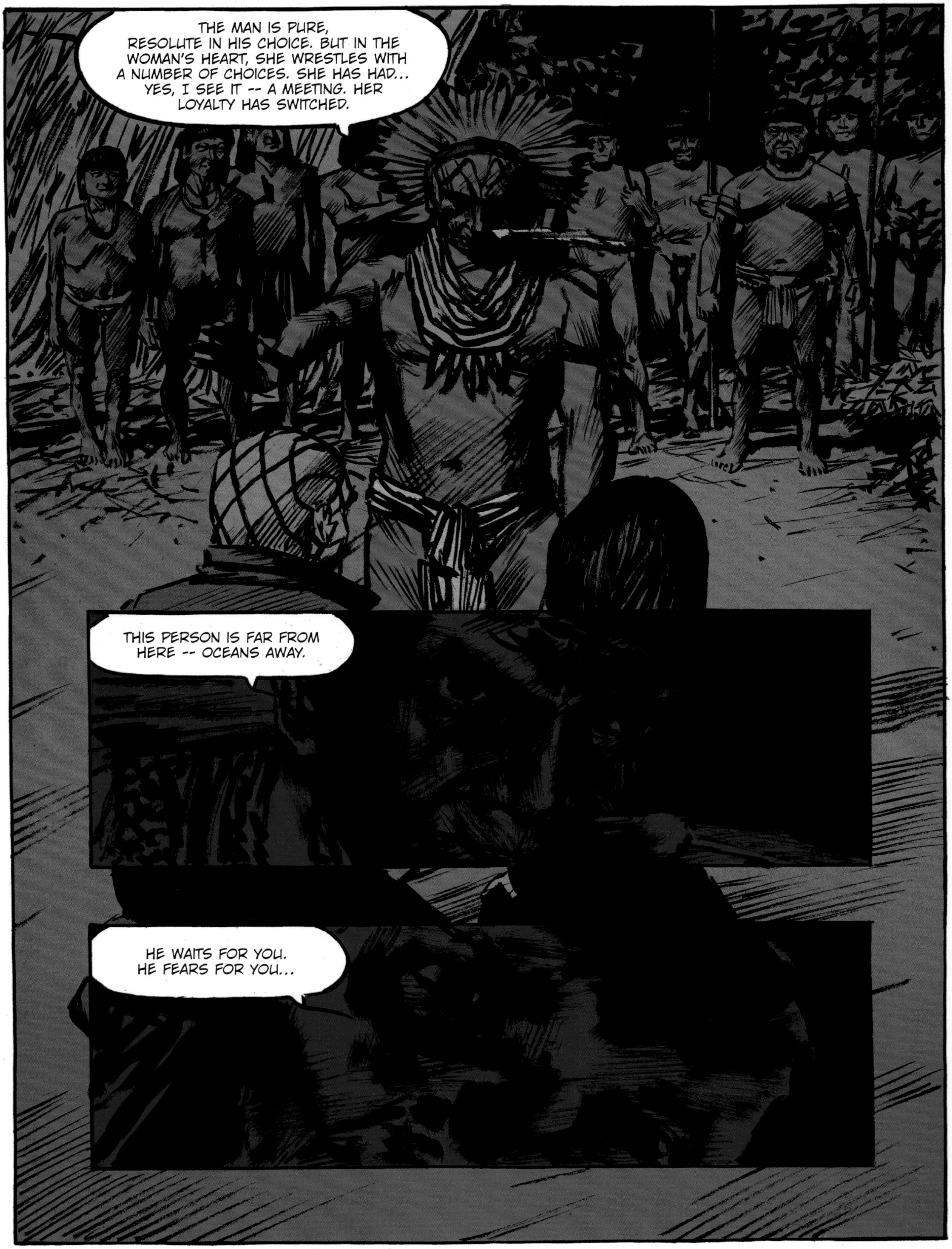
THE MAN IS PURE, RESOLUTE IN HIS CHOICE. BUT IN THE WOMAN'S HEART, SHE WRESTLES WITH A NUMBER OF CHOICES. SHE HAS HAD... YES, I SEE IT -- A MEETING. HER LOYALTY HAS SWITCHED.
THIS PERSON IS FAR FROM HERE -- OCEANS AWAY.
HE WAITS FOR YOU. HE FEARS FOR YOU...

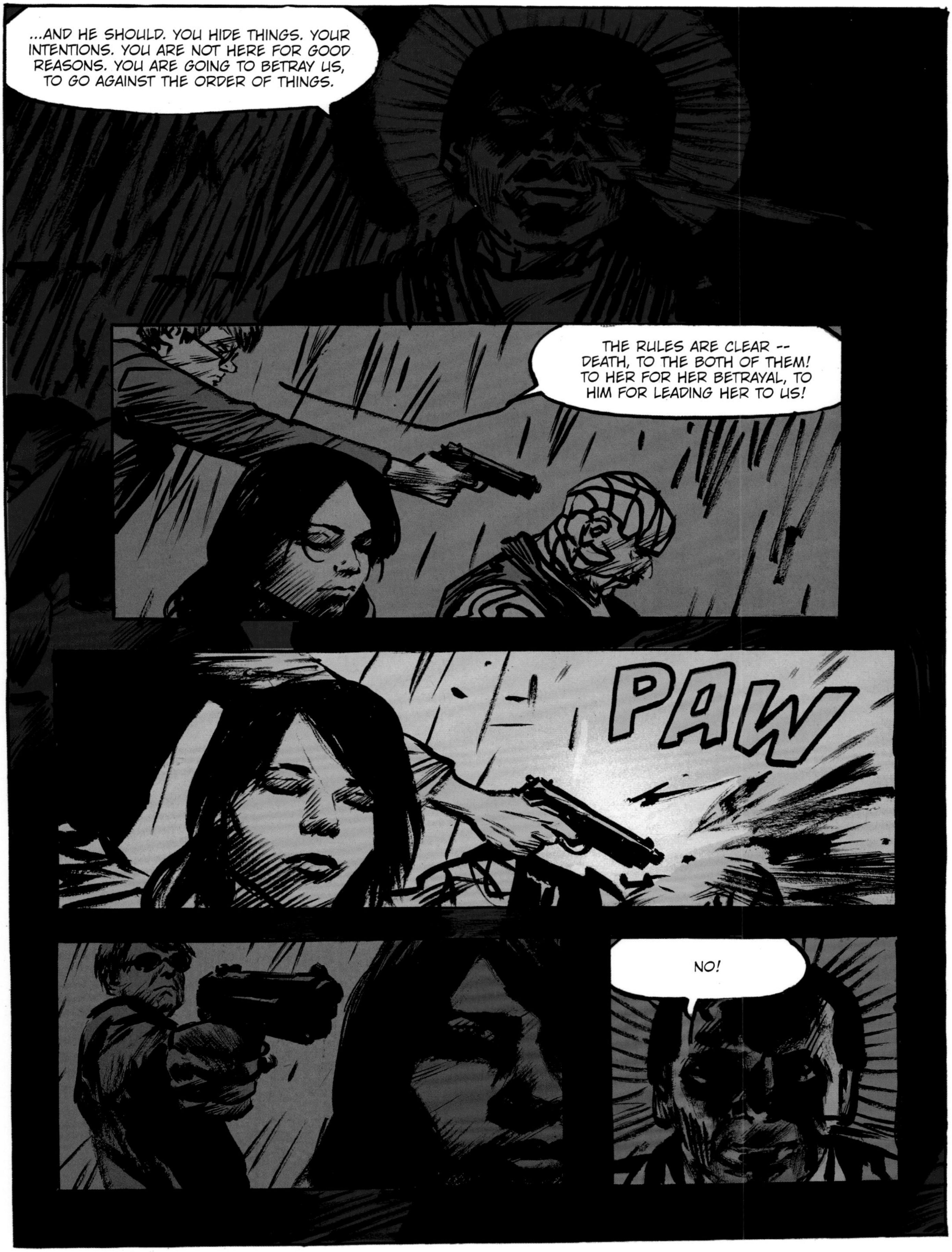
...AND HE SHOULD. YOU HIDE THINGS. YOUR INTENTIONS. YOU ARE NOT HERE FOR GOOD REASONS. YOU ARE GOING TO BETRAY US, TO GO AGAINST THE ORDER OF THINGS.
THE RULES ARE CLEAR -- DEATH, TO THE BOTH OF THEM! TO HER FOR HER BETRAYAL, TO HIM FOR LEADING HER TO US!
PAW
NO!

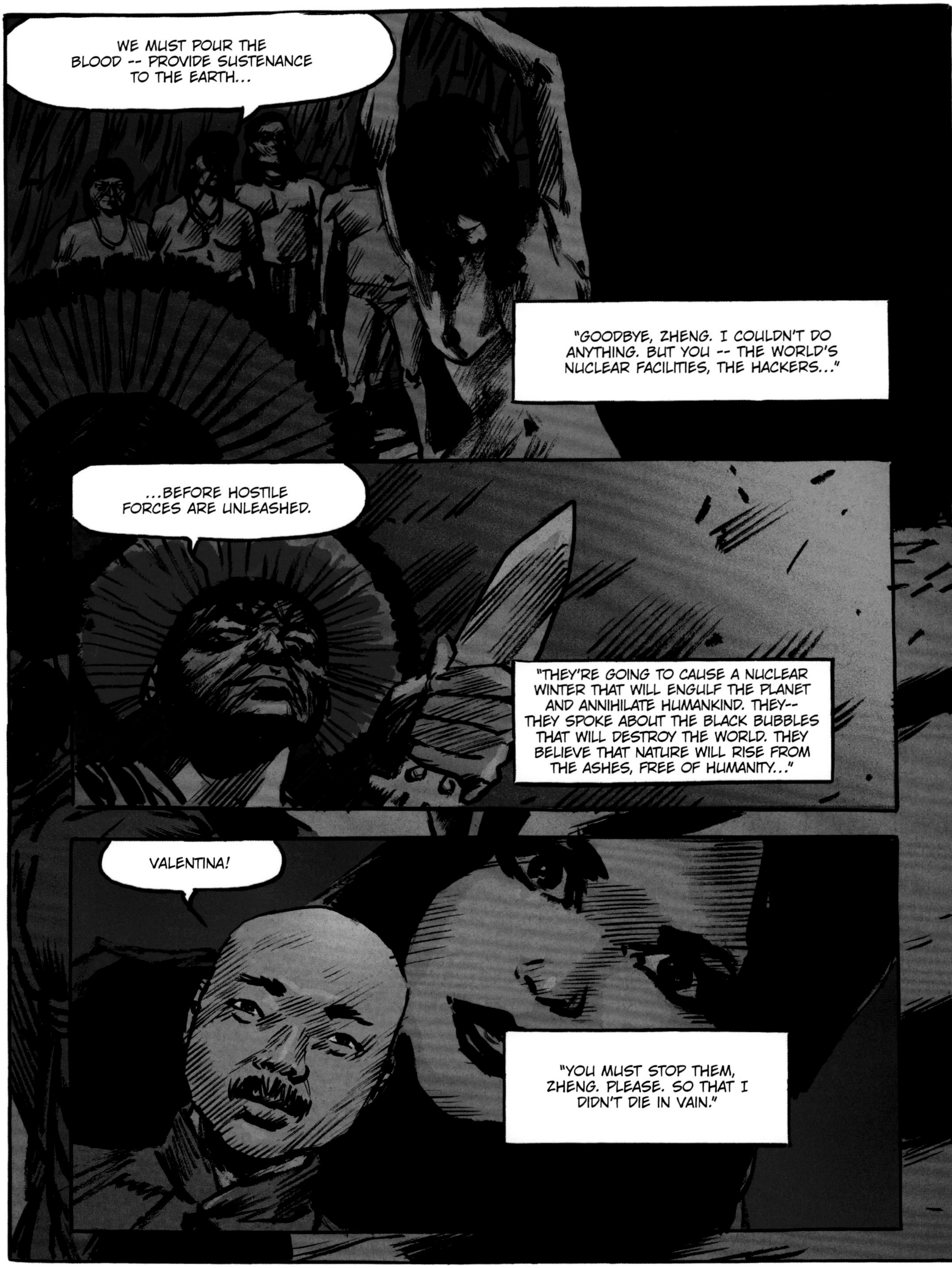
WE MUST POUR THE BLOOD -- PROVIDE SUSTENANCE TO THE EARTH...
"GOODBYE, ZHENG. I COULDN'T DO ANYTHING. BUT YOU -- THE WORLD'S NUCLEAR FACILITIES, THE HACKERS..."
...BEFORE HOSTILE FORCES ARE UNLEASHED.
"THEY'RE GOING TO CAUSE A NUCLEAR WINTER THAT WILL ENGULF THE PLANET AND ANNIHILATE HUMANKIND. THEY-- THEY SPOKE ABOUT THE BLACK BUBBLES THAT WILL DESTROY THE WORLD. THEY BELIEVE THAT NATURE WILL RISE FROM THE ASHES, FREE OF HUMANITY..."
VALENTINA!
"YOU MUST STOP THEM, ZHENG. PLEASE. SO THAT I DIDN'T DIE IN VAIN."

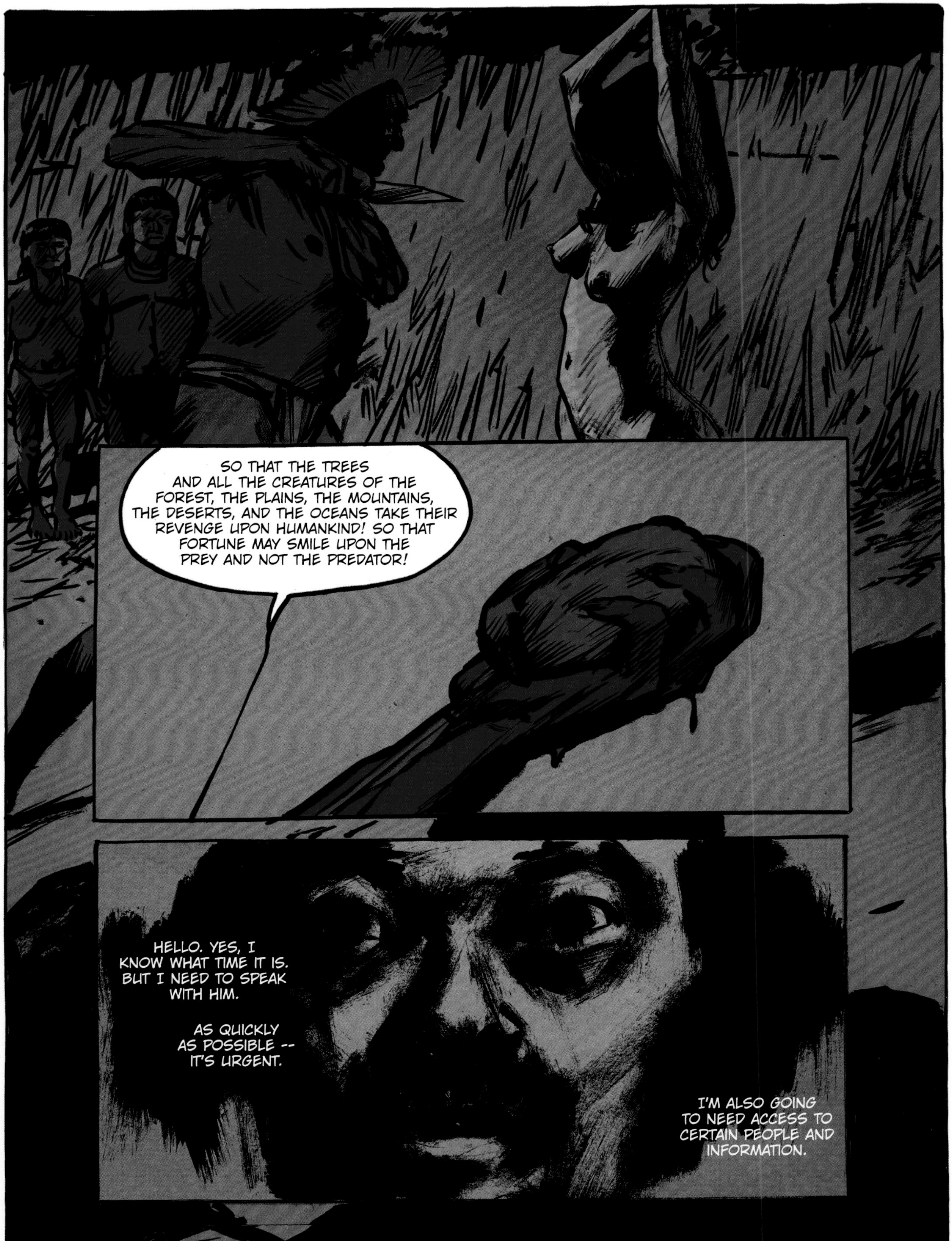
SO THAT THE TREES AND ALL THE CREATURES OF THE FOREST, THE PLAINS, THE MOUNTAINS, THE DESERTS, AND THE OCEANS TAKE THEIR REVENGE UPON HUMANKIND! SO THAT FORTUNE MAY SMILE UPON THE PREY AND NOT THE PREDATOR!
HELLO. YES, I KNOW WHAT TIME IT IS. BUT I NEED TO SPEAK WITH HIM.
AS QUICKLY AS POSSIBLE -- IT'S URGENT.
I'M ALSO GOING TO NEED ACCESS TO CERTAIN PEOPLE AND INFORMATION.

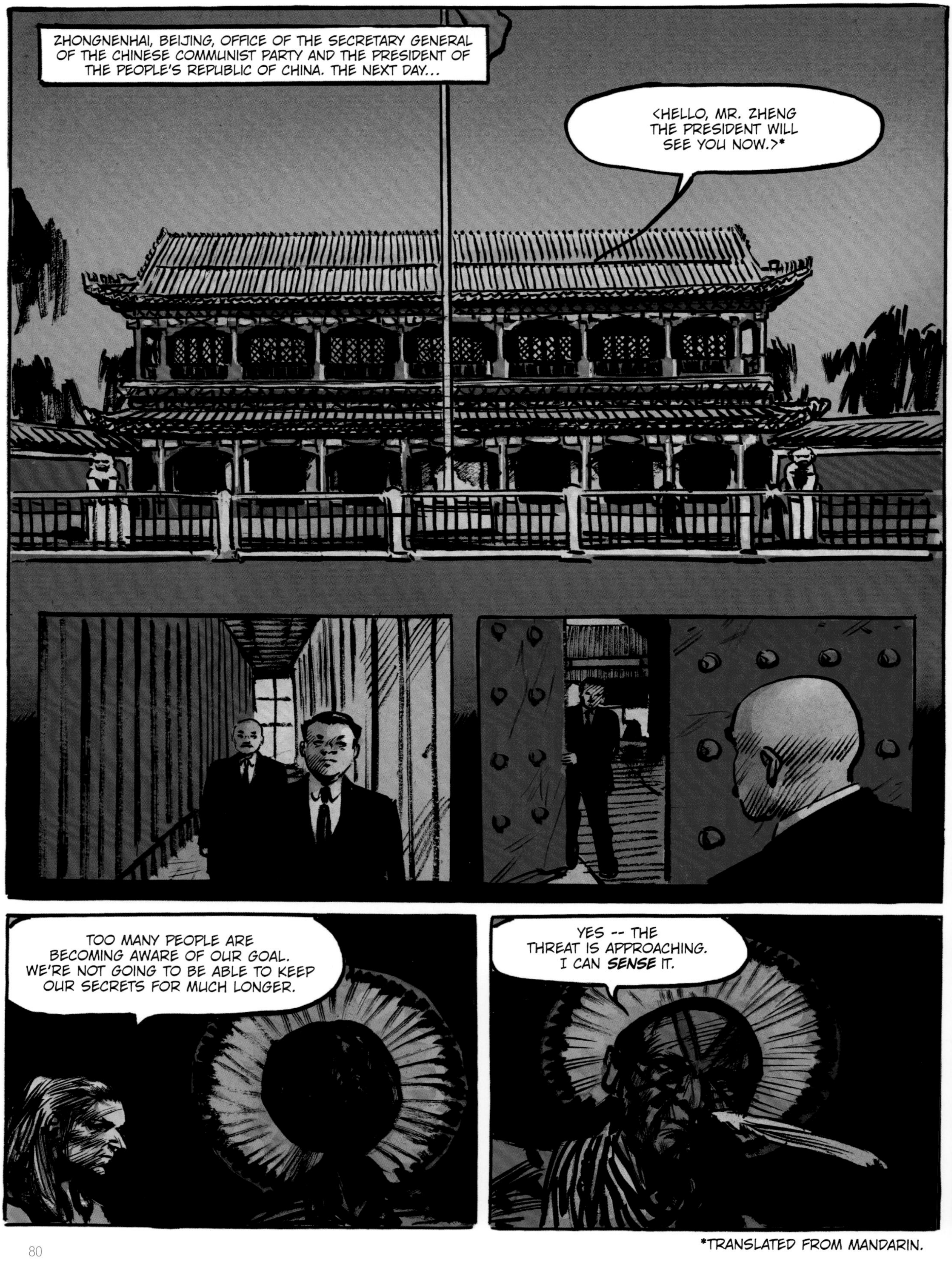
ZHONGNENHAI, BEIJING, OFFICE OF THE SECRETARY GENERAL OF THE CHINESE COMMUNIST PARTY AND THE PRESIDENT OF THE PEOPLE'S REPUBLIC OF CHINA. THE NEXT DAY...
<HELLO, MR. ZHENG THE PRESIDENT WILL SEE YOU NOW.>*
TOO MANY PEOPLE ARE BECOMING AWARE OF OUR GOAL. WE'RE NOT GOING TO BE ABLE TO KEEP OUR SECRETS FOR MUCH LONGER.
YES -- THE THREAT IS APPROACHING. I CAN **SENSE** IT.

*TRANSLATED FROM MANDARIN.

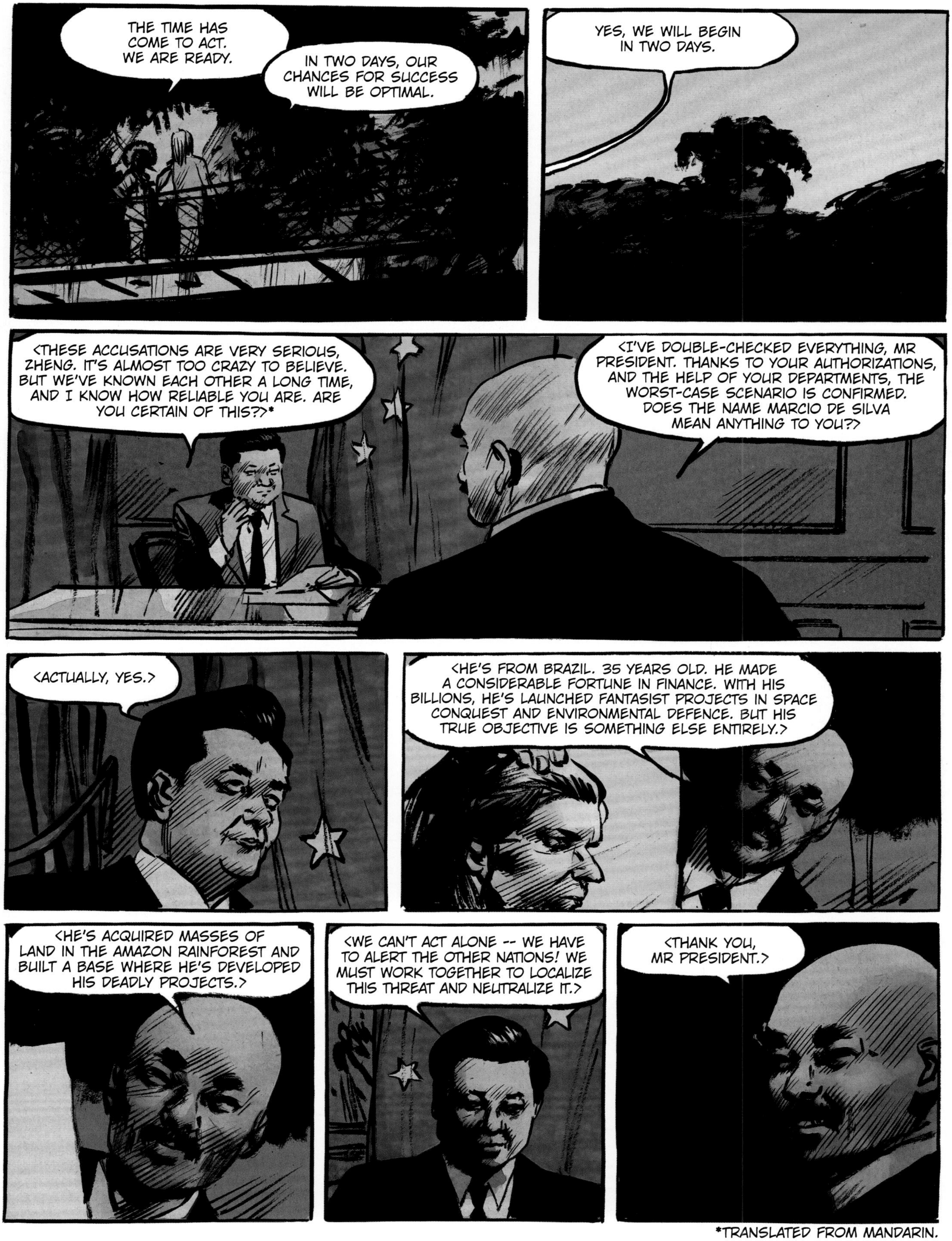
THE TIME HAS COME TO ACT. WE ARE READY.
IN TWO DAYS, OUR CHANCES FOR SUCCESS WILL BE OPTIMAL.
YES, WE WILL BEGIN IN TWO DAYS.
<THESE ACCUSATIONS ARE VERY SERIOUS, ZHENG. IT'S ALMOST TOO CRAZY TO BELIEVE. BUT WE'VE KNOWN EACH OTHER A LONG TIME, AND I KNOW HOW RELIABLE YOU ARE. ARE YOU CERTAIN OF THIS?>*
<I'VE DOUBLE-CHECKED EVERYTHING, MR PRESIDENT. THANKS TO YOUR AUTHORIZATIONS, AND THE HELP OF YOUR DEPARTMENTS, THE WORST-CASE SCENARIO IS CONFIRMED. DOES THE NAME MARCIO DE SILVA MEAN ANYTHING TO YOU?>
<ACTUALLY, YES.>
<HE'S FROM BRAZIL. 35 YEARS OLD. HE MADE A CONSIDERABLE FORTUNE IN FINANCE. WITH HIS BILLIONS, HE'S LAUNCHED FANTASIST PROJECTS IN SPACE CONQUEST AND ENVIRONMENTAL DEFENCE. BUT HIS TRUE OBJECTIVE IS SOMETHING ELSE ENTIRELY.>
<HE'S ACQUIRED MASSES OF LAND IN THE AMAZON RAINFOREST AND BUILT A BASE WHERE HE'S DEVELOPED HIS DEADLY PROJECTS.>
<WE CAN'T ACT ALONE -- WE HAVE TO ALERT THE OTHER NATIONS! WE MUST WORK TOGETHER TO LOCALIZE THIS THREAT AND NEUTRALIZE IT.>
<THANK YOU, MR PRESIDENT.>

*TRANSLATED FROM MANDARIN.

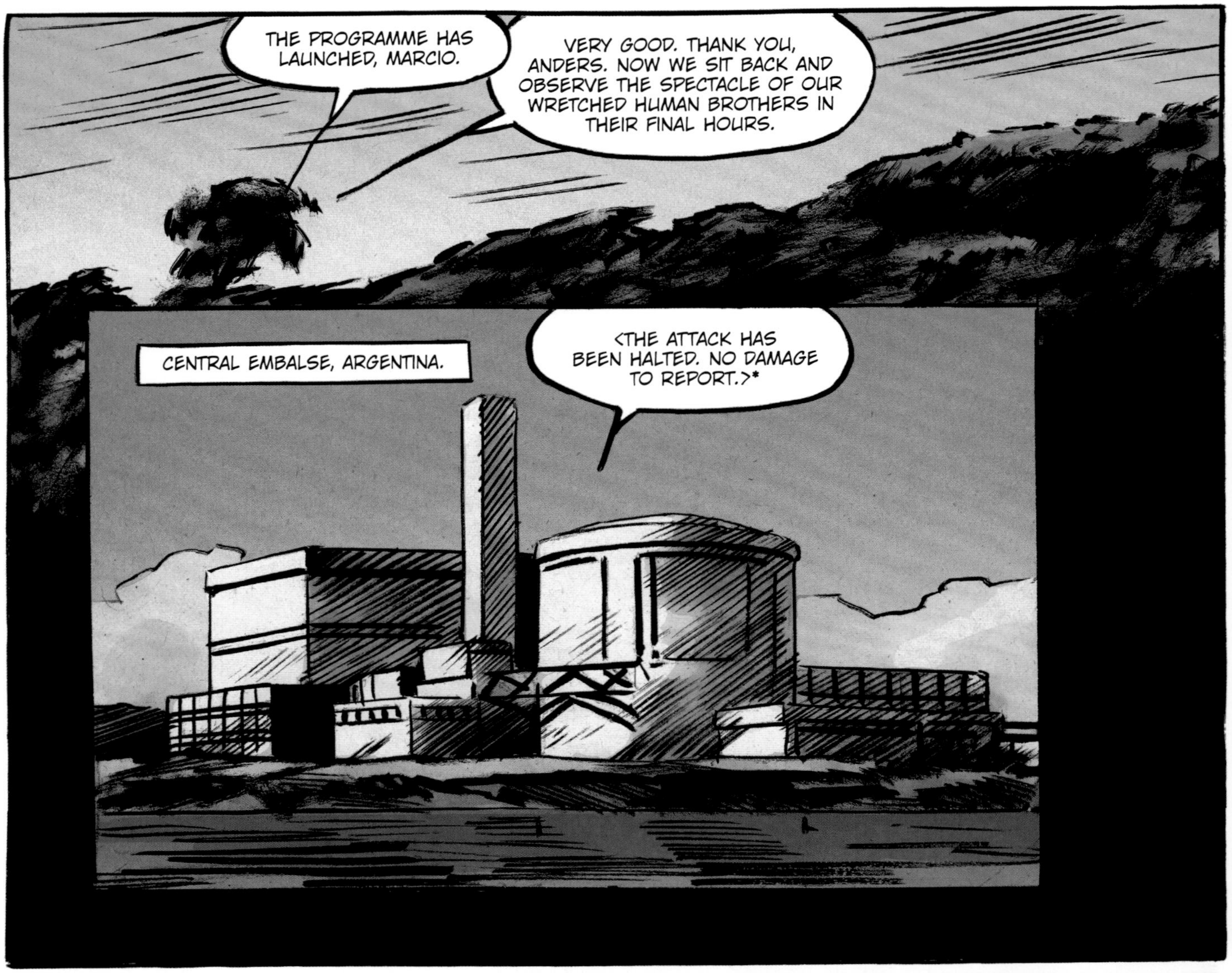
THE PROGRAMME HAS LAUNCHED, MARCIO.
VERY GOOD. THANK YOU, ANDERS. NOW WE SIT BACK AND OBSERVE THE SPECTACLE OF OUR WRETCHED HUMAN BROTHERS IN THEIR FINAL HOURS.
CENTRAL EMBALSE, ARGENTINA.
<THE ATTACK HAS BEEN HALTED. NO DAMAGE TO REPORT.>*

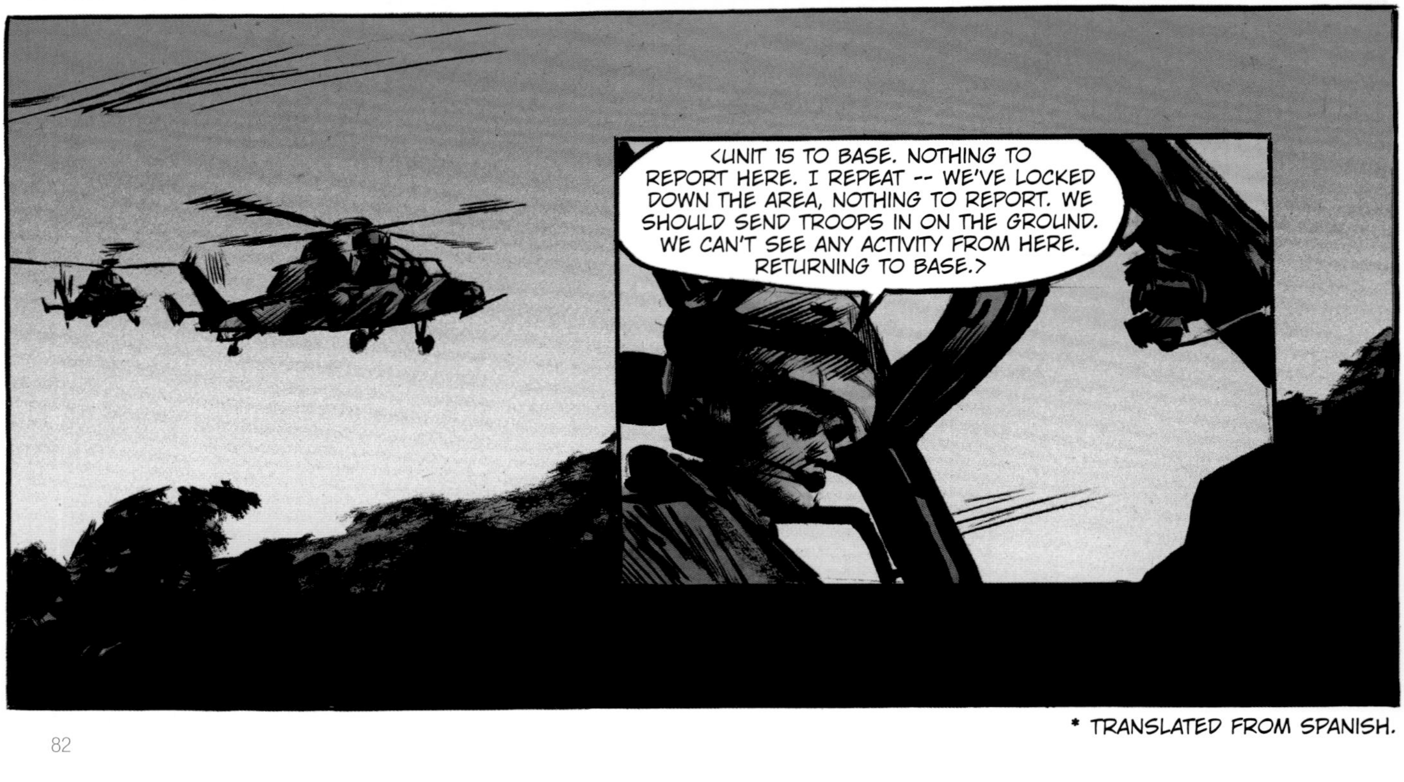
<UNIT 15 TO BASE. NOTHING TO REPORT HERE. I REPEAT -- WE'VE LOCKED DOWN THE AREA, NOTHING TO REPORT. WE SHOULD SEND TROOPS IN ON THE GROUND. WE CAN'T SEE ANY ACTIVITY FROM HERE. RETURNING TO BASE.>

* TRANSLATED FROM SPANISH.

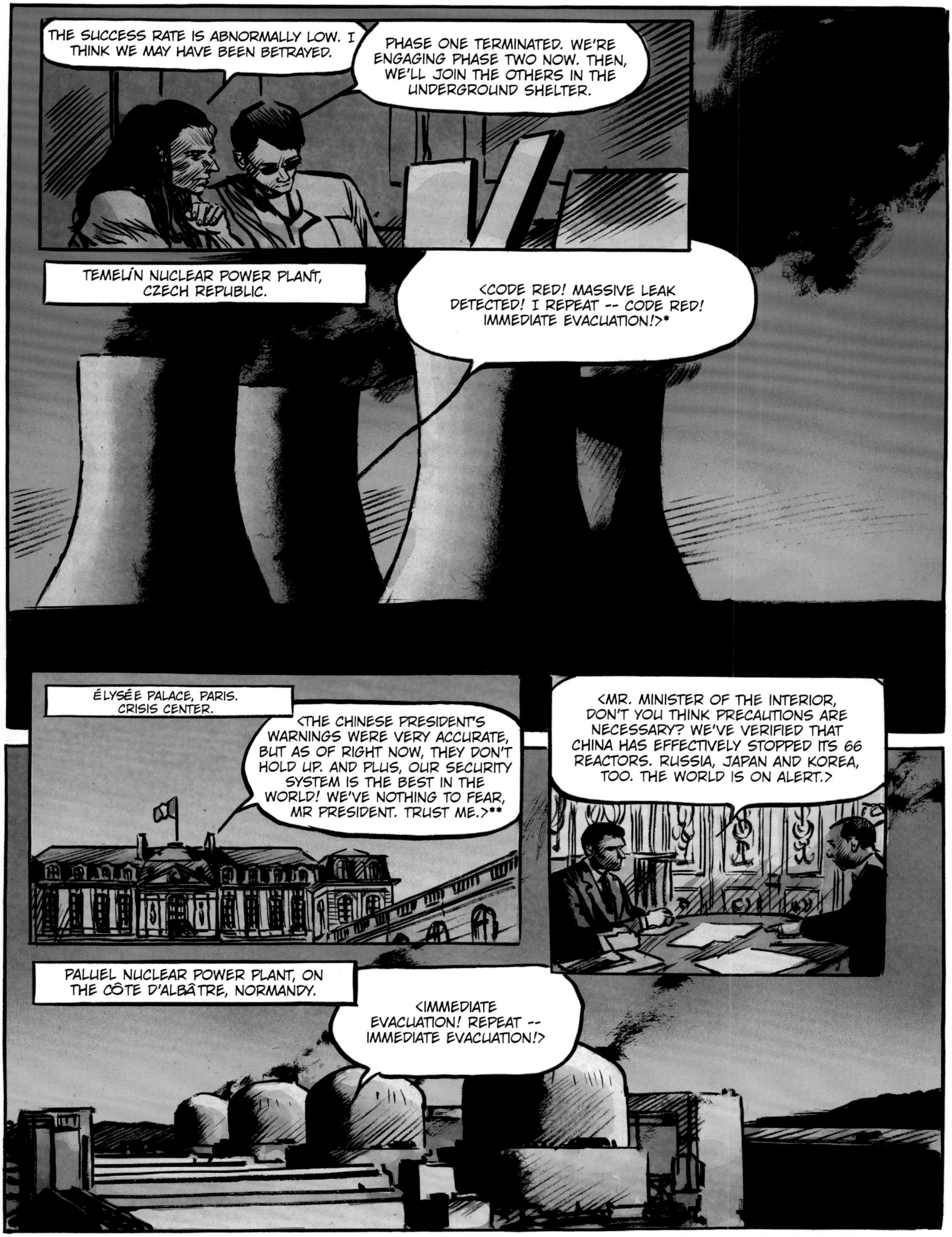
THE SUCCESS RATE IS ABNORMALLY LOW. I THINK WE MAY HAVE BEEN BETRAYED.
PHASE ONE TERMINATED. WE'RE ENGAGING PHASE TWO NOW. THEN, WE'LL JOIN THE OTHERS IN THE UNDERGROUND SHELTER.
TEMELÍN NUCLEAR POWER PLANT, CZECH REPUBLIC.
<CODE RED! MASSIVE LEAK DETECTED! I REPEAT -- CODE RED! IMMEDIATE EVACUATION!>*
ÉLYSÉE PALACE, PARIS. CRISIS CENTER.
<THE CHINESE PRESIDENT'S WARNINGS WERE VERY ACCURATE, BUT AS OF RIGHT NOW, THEY DON'T HOLD UP. AND PLUS, OUR SECURITY SYSTEM IS THE BEST IN THE WORLD! WE'VE NOTHING TO FEAR, MR PRESIDENT. TRUST ME.>**
<MR. MINISTER OF THE INTERIOR, DON'T YOU THINK PRECAUTIONS ARE NECESSARY? WE'VE VERIFIED THAT CHINA HAS EFFECTIVELY STOPPED ITS 66 REACTORS. RUSSIA, JAPAN AND KOREA, TOO. THE WORLD IS ON ALERT.>
PALUEL NUCLEAR POWER PLANT, ON THE CÔTE D'ALBÂTRE, NORMANDY.
<IMMEDIATE EVACUATION! REPEAT -- IMMEDIATE EVACUATION!>

*TRANSLATED FROM CZECH.
**TRANSLATED FROM FRENCH.

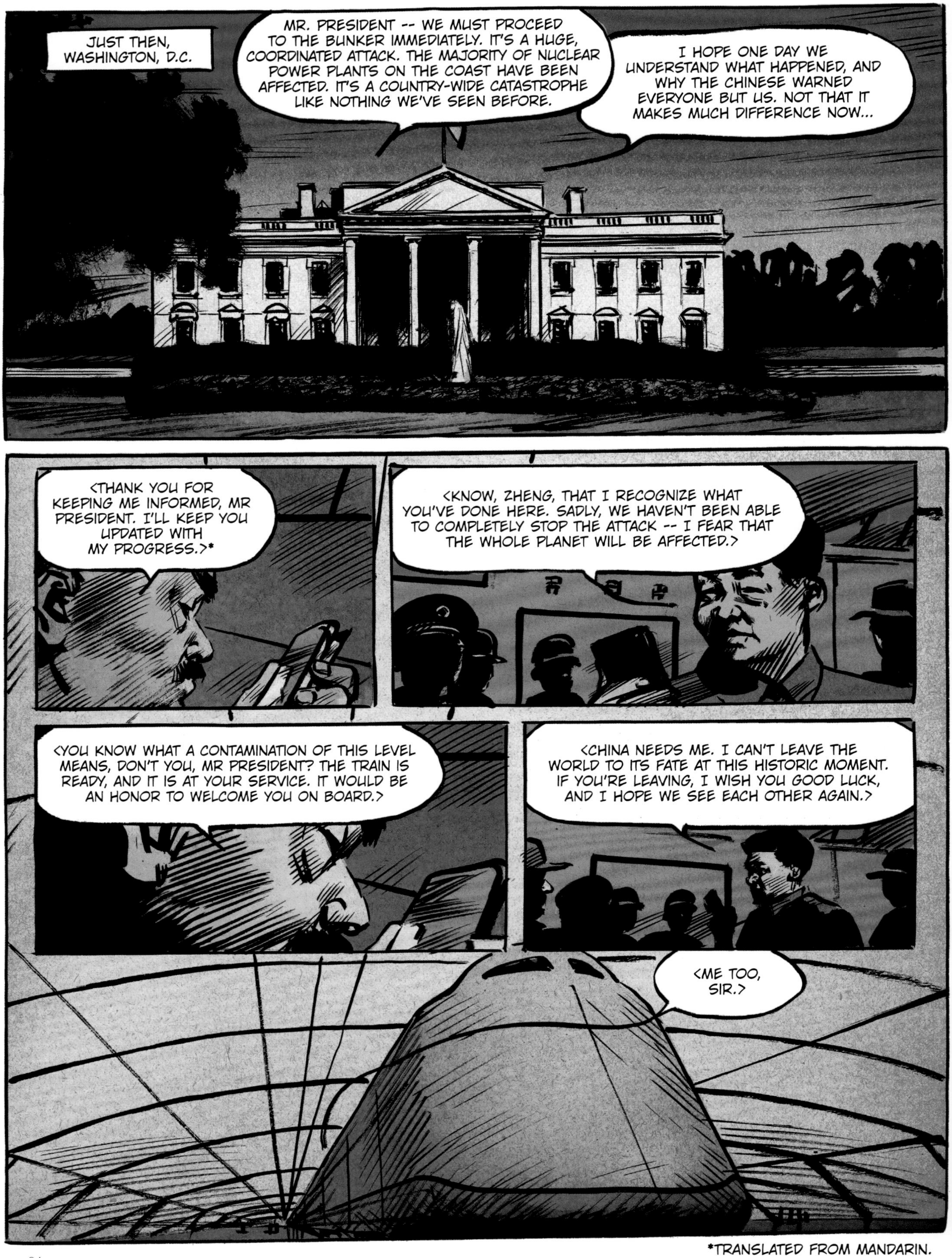
JUST THEN, WASHINGTON, D.C.
MR. PRESIDENT -- WE MUST PROCEED TO THE BUNKER IMMEDIATELY. IT'S A HUGE, COORDINATED ATTACK. THE MAJORITY OF NUCLEAR POWER PLANTS ON THE COAST HAVE BEEN AFFECTED. IT'S A COUNTRY-WIDE CATASTROPHE LIKE NOTHING WE'VE SEEN BEFORE.
I HOPE ONE DAY WE UNDERSTAND WHAT HAPPENED, AND WHY THE CHINESE WARNED EVERYONE BUT US. NOT THAT IT MAKES MUCH DIFFERENCE NOW...
<THANK YOU FOR KEEPING ME INFORMED, MR PRESIDENT. I'LL KEEP YOU UPDATED WITH MY PROGRESS.>*
<KNOW, ZHENG, THAT I RECOGNIZE WHAT YOU'VE DONE HERE. SADLY, WE HAVEN'T BEEN ABLE TO COMPLETELY STOP THE ATTACK -- I FEAR THAT THE WHOLE PLANET WILL BE AFFECTED.>
<YOU KNOW WHAT A CONTAMINATION OF THIS LEVEL MEANS, DON'T YOU, MR PRESIDENT? THE TRAIN IS READY, AND IT IS AT YOUR SERVICE. IT WOULD BE AN HONOR TO WELCOME YOU ON BOARD.>
<CHINA NEEDS ME. I CAN'T LEAVE THE WORLD TO ITS FATE AT THIS HISTORIC MOMENT. IF YOU'RE LEAVING, I WISH YOU GOOD LUCK, AND I HOPE WE SEE EACH OTHER AGAIN.>
<ME TOO, SIR.>

*TRANSLATED FROM MANDARIN.

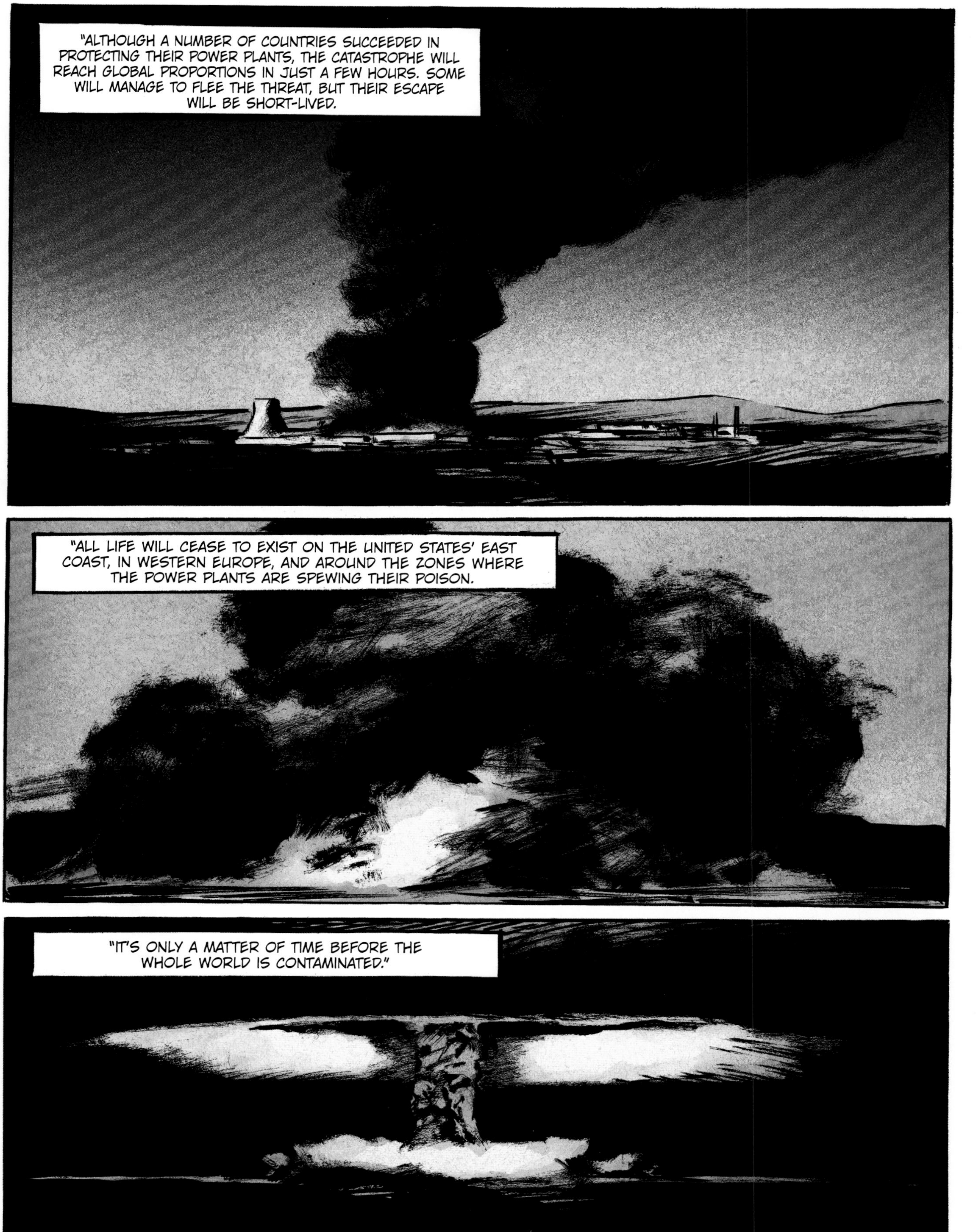
"ALTHOUGH A NUMBER OF COUNTRIES SUCCEEDED IN PROTECTING THEIR POWER PLANTS, THE CATASTROPHE WILL REACH GLOBAL PROPORTIONS IN JUST A FEW HOURS. SOME WILL MANAGE TO FLEE THE THREAT, BUT THEIR ESCAPE WILL BE SHORT-LIVED.
"ALL LIFE WILL CEASE TO EXIST ON THE UNITED STATES' EAST COAST, IN WESTERN EUROPE, AND AROUND THE ZONES WHERE THE POWER PLANTS ARE SPEWING THEIR POISON.
"IT'S ONLY A MATTER OF TIME BEFORE THE WHOLE WORLD IS CONTAMINATED."

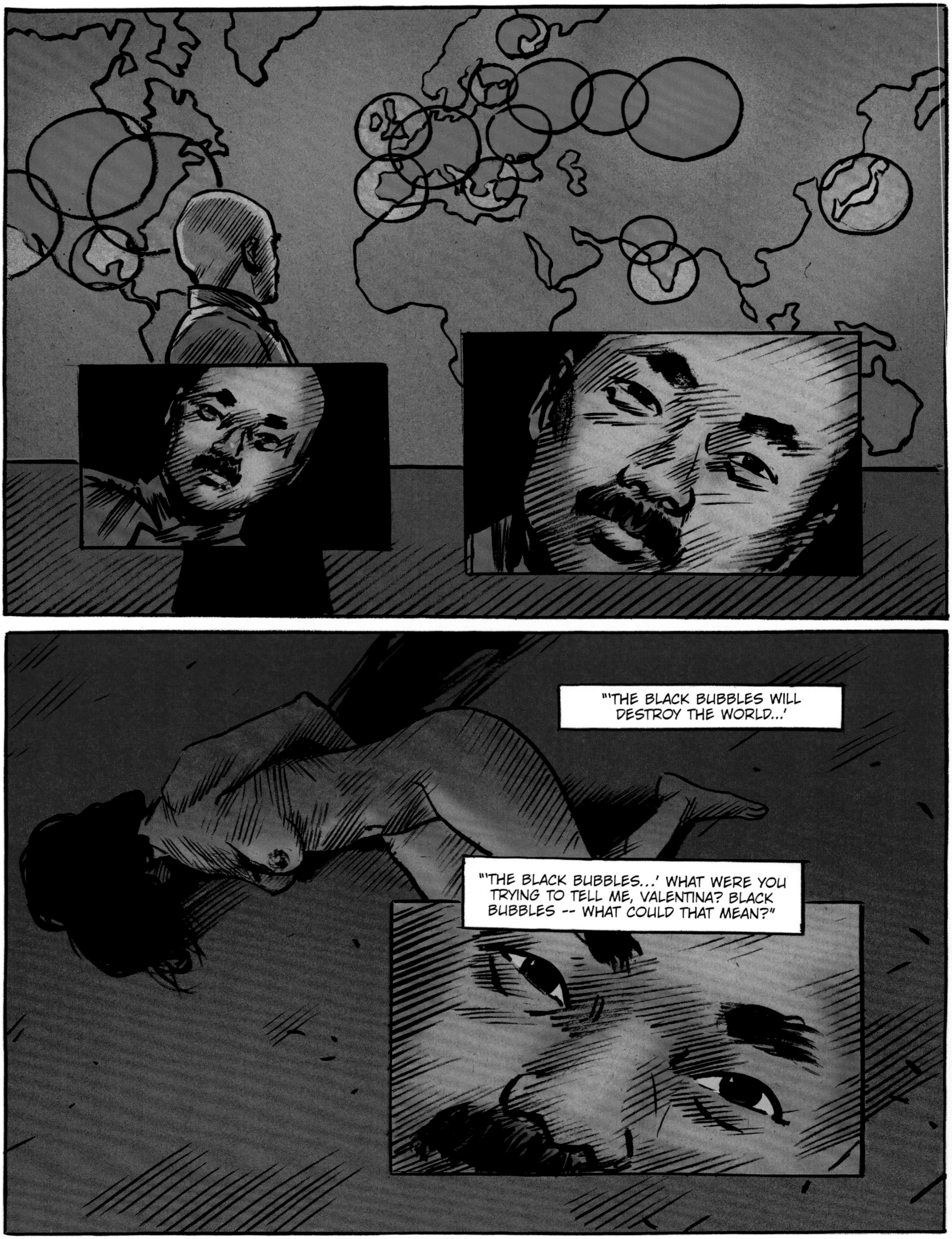
"'THE BLACK BUBBLES WILL DESTROY THE WORLD...'
"'THE BLACK BUBBLES...' WHAT WERE YOU TRYING TO TELL ME, VALENTINA? BLACK BUBBLES -- WHAT COULD THAT MEAN?"

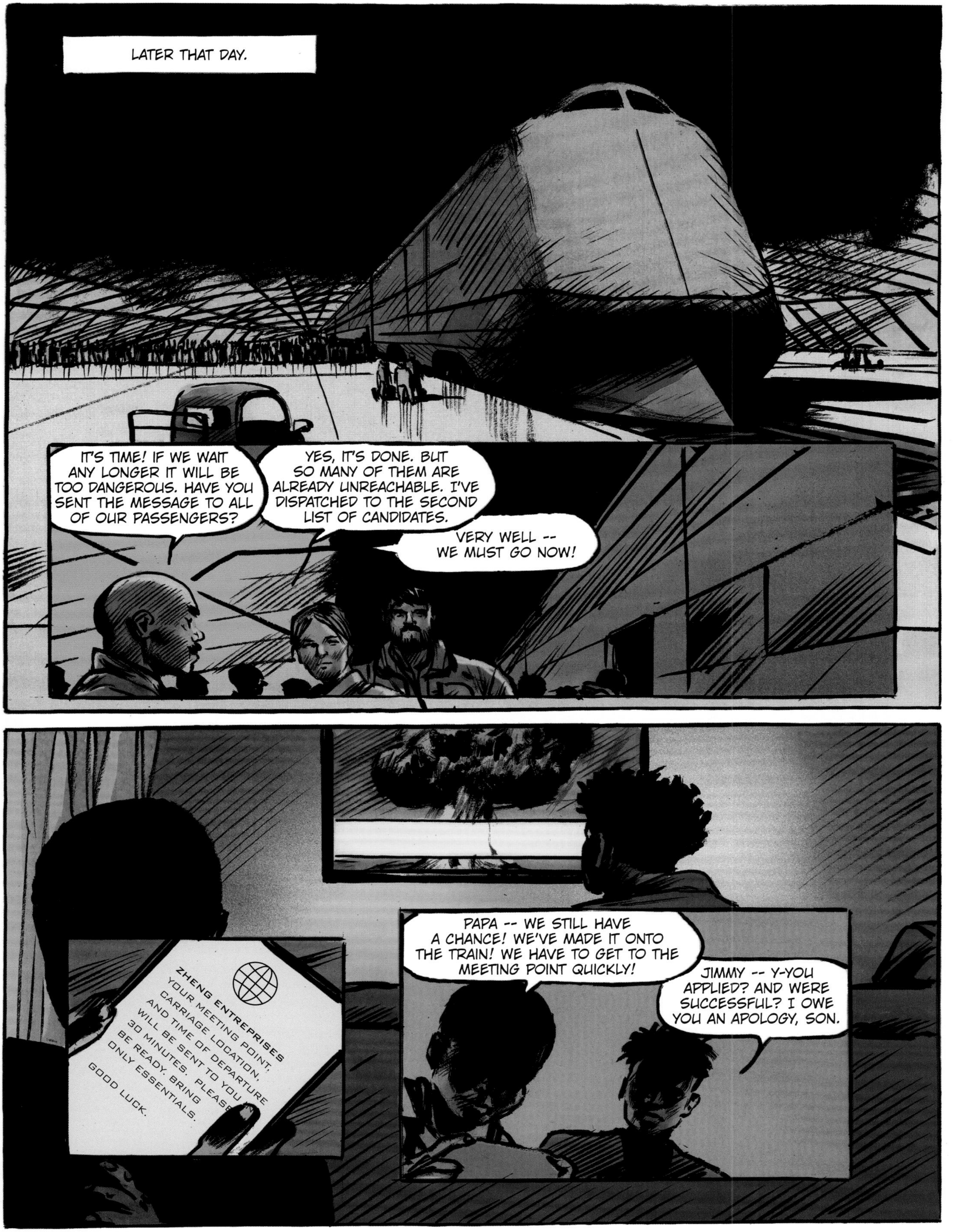
LATER THAT DAY.
IT'S TIME! IF WE WAIT ANY LONGER IT WILL BE TOO DANGEROUS. HAVE YOU SENT THE MESSAGE TO ALL OF OUR PASSENGERS?
YES, IT'S DONE. BUT SO MANY OF THEM ARE ALREADY UNREACHABLE. I'VE DISPATCHED TO THE SECOND LIST OF CANDIDATES.
VERY WELL -- WE MUST GO NOW!
ZHENG ENTREPRISES
YOUR MEETING POINT, CARRIAGE LOCATION, AND TIME OF DEPARTURE WILL BE SENT TO YOU 30 MINUTES. PLEASE BE READY. BRING ONLY ESSENTIALS.
GOOD LUCK.
PAPA -- WE STILL HAVE A CHANCE! WE'VE MADE IT ONTO THE TRAIN! WE HAVE TO GET TO THE MEETING POINT QUICKLY!
JIMMY -- Y-YOU APPLIED? AND WERE SUCCESSFUL? I OWE YOU AN APOLOGY, SON.

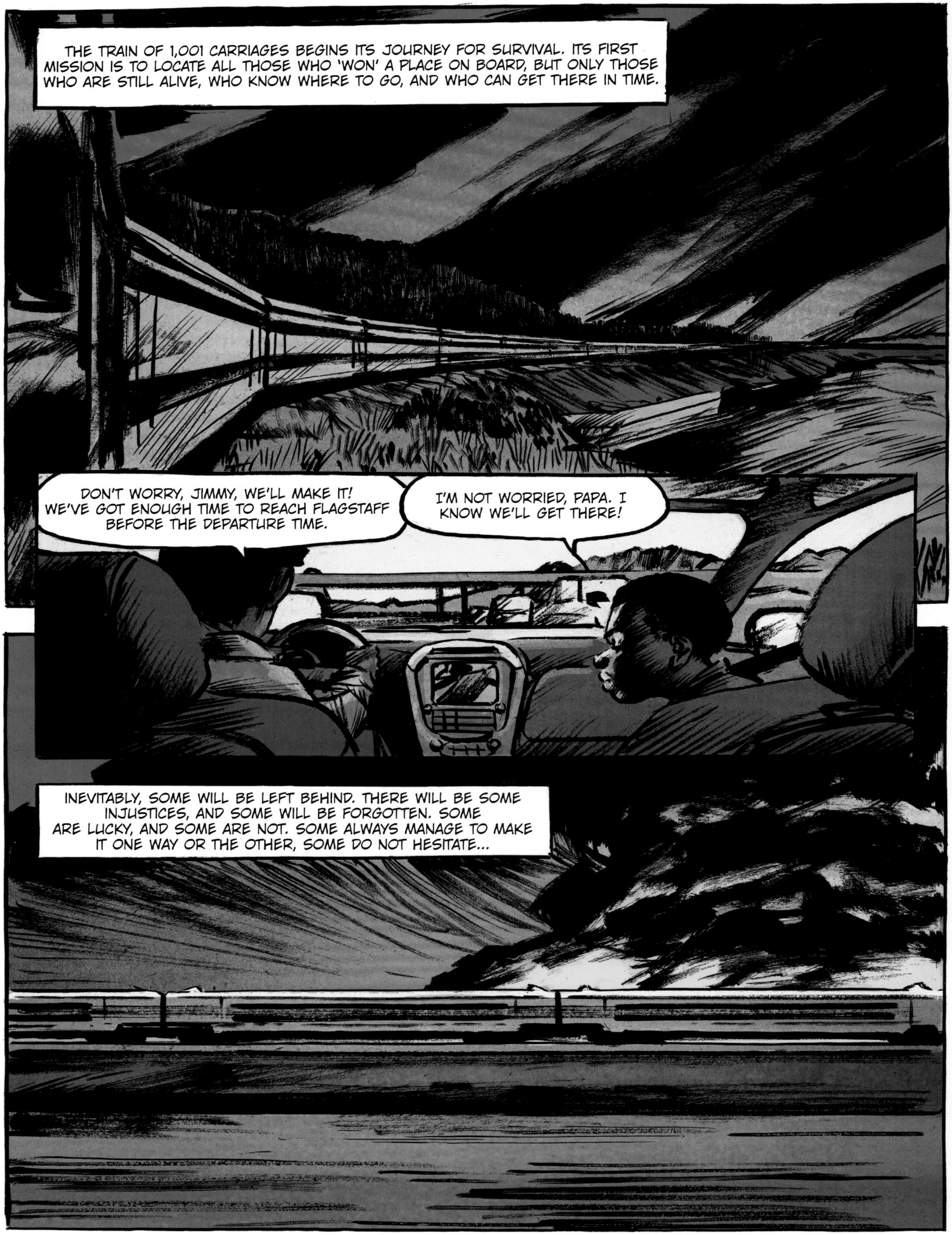
THE TRAIN OF 1,001 CARRIAGES BEGINS ITS JOURNEY FOR SURVIVAL. ITS FIRST MISSION IS TO LOCATE ALL THOSE WHO 'WON' A PLACE ON BOARD, BUT ONLY THOSE WHO ARE STILL ALIVE, WHO KNOW WHERE TO GO, AND WHO CAN GET THERE IN TIME.
DON'T WORRY, JIMMY, WE'LL MAKE IT! WE'VE GOT ENOUGH TIME TO REACH FLAGSTAFF BEFORE THE DEPARTURE TIME.
I'M NOT WORRIED, PAPA. I KNOW WE'LL GET THERE!
INEVITABLY, SOME WILL BE LEFT BEHIND. THERE WILL BE SOME INJUSTICES, AND SOME WILL BE FORGOTTEN. SOME ARE LUCKY, AND SOME ARE NOT. SOME ALWAYS MANAGE TO MAKE IT ONE WAY OR THE OTHER, SOME DO NOT HESITATE...

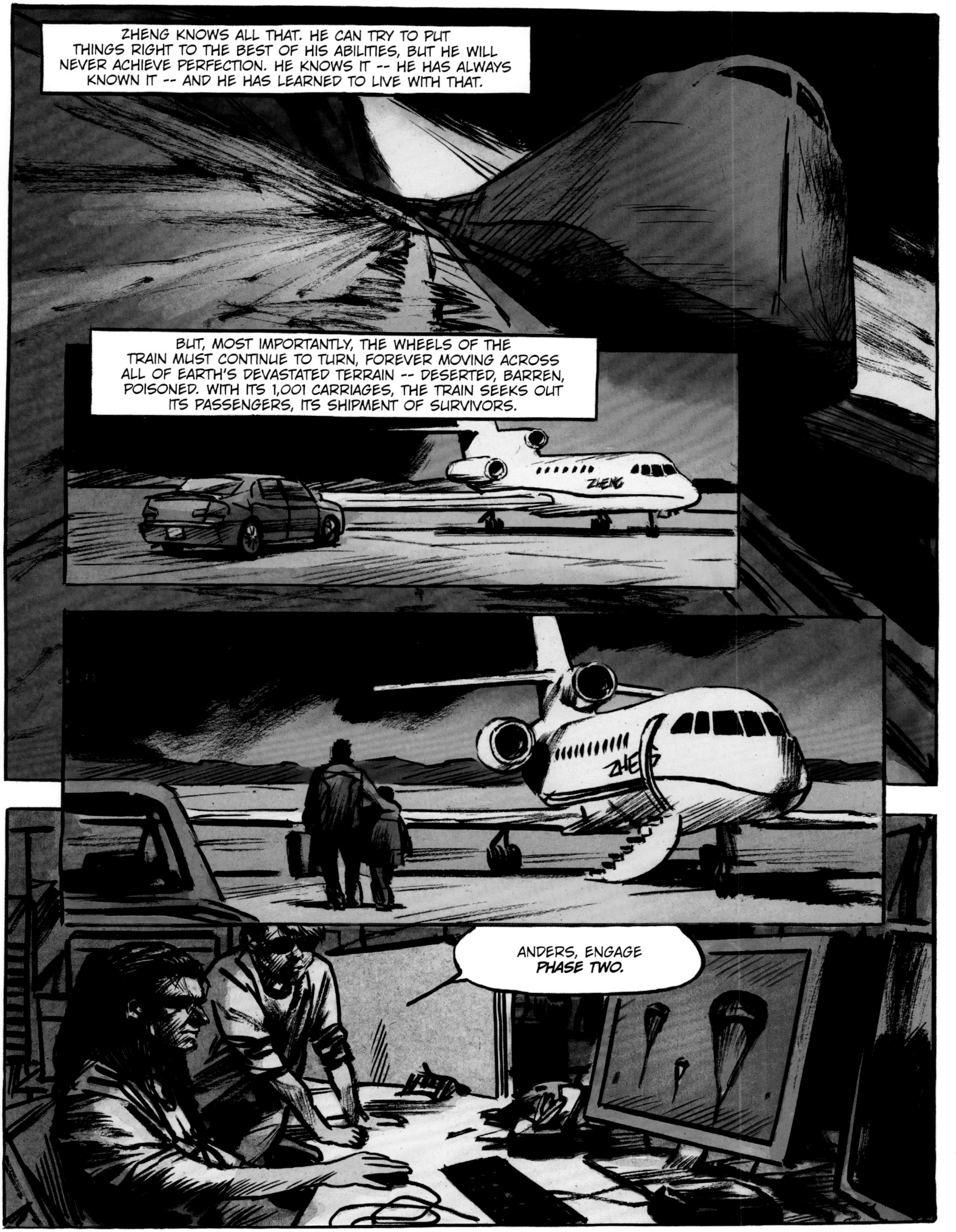
ZHENG KNOWS ALL THAT. HE CAN TRY TO PUT THINGS RIGHT TO THE BEST OF HIS ABILITIES, BUT HE WILL NEVER ACHIEVE PERFECTION. HE KNOWS IT -- HE HAS ALWAYS KNOWN IT -- AND HE HAS LEARNED TO LIVE WITH THAT.
BUT, MOST IMPORTANTLY, THE WHEELS OF THE TRAIN MUST CONTINUE TO TURN, FOREVER MOVING ACROSS ALL OF EARTH'S DEVASTATED TERRAIN -- DESERTED, BARREN, POISONED. WITH ITS 1,001 CARRIAGES, THE TRAIN SEEKS OUT ITS PASSENGERS, ITS SHIPMENT OF SURVIVORS.
ZHENG
ANDERS, ENGAGE *PHASE TWO.*

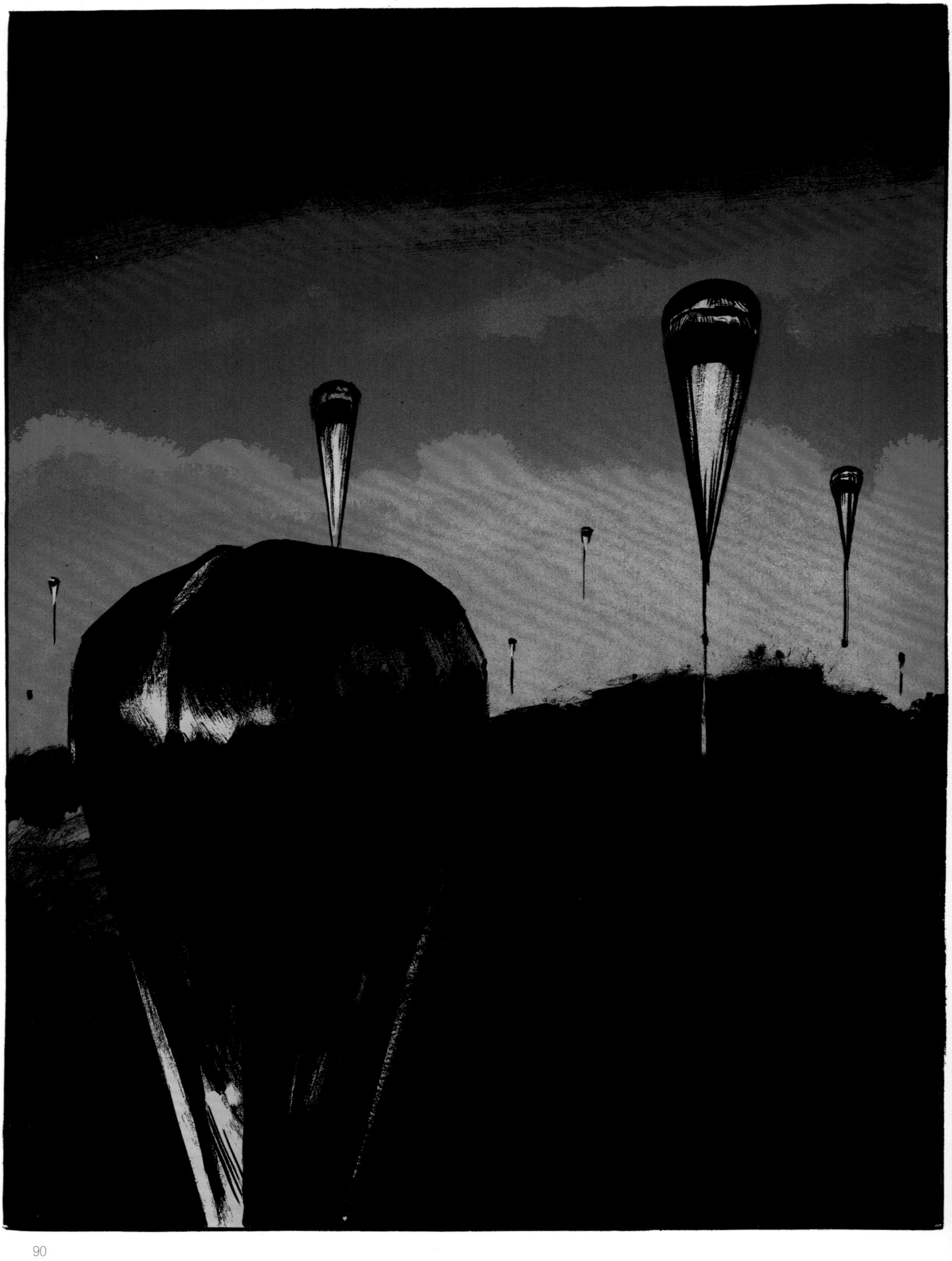

TO BE CONTINUED IN

SNOWPIERCER
THE PREQUEL
PART TWO

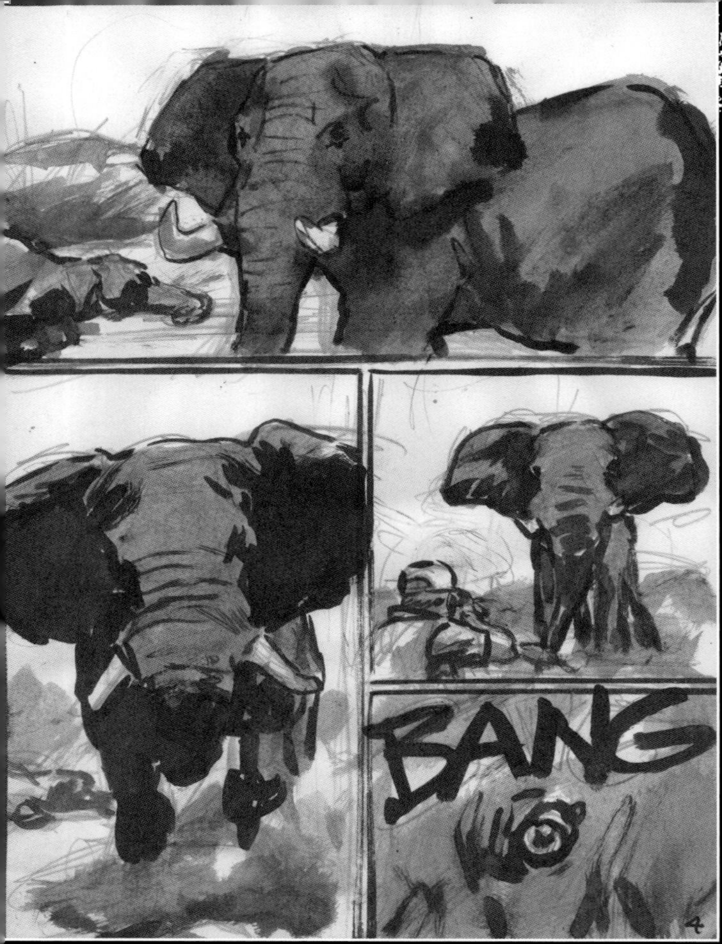
BANG

P12 ROUGH

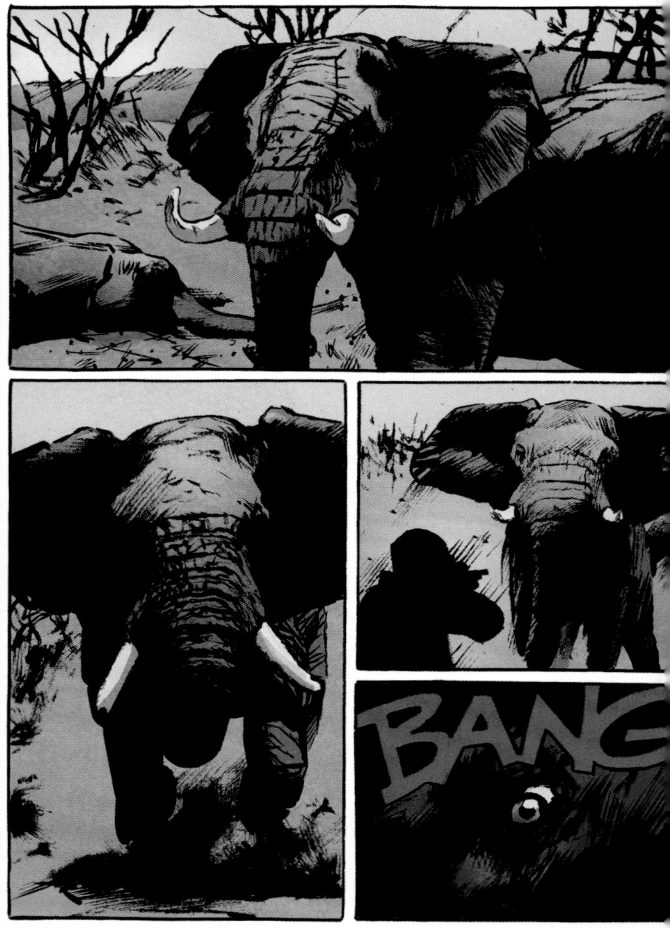
BANG

P12 FINAL ART

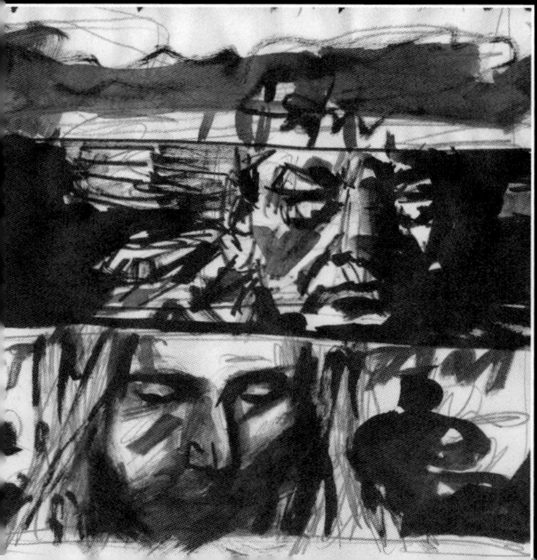

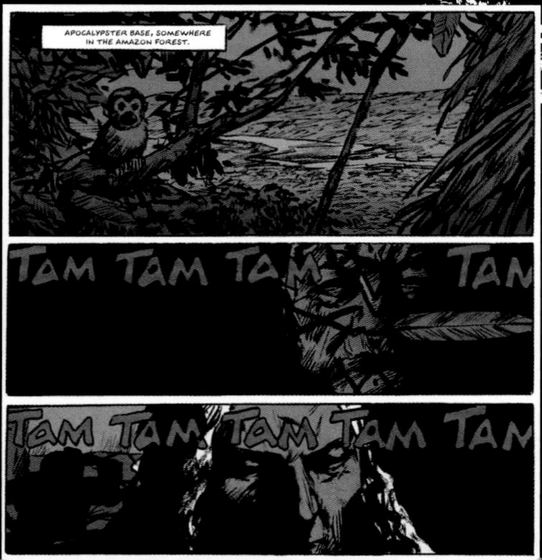
APOCALYPSTER BASE, SOMEWHERE IN THE AMAZON FOREST.
TAM TAM TAM TAM
TAM TAM TAM TAM TAM

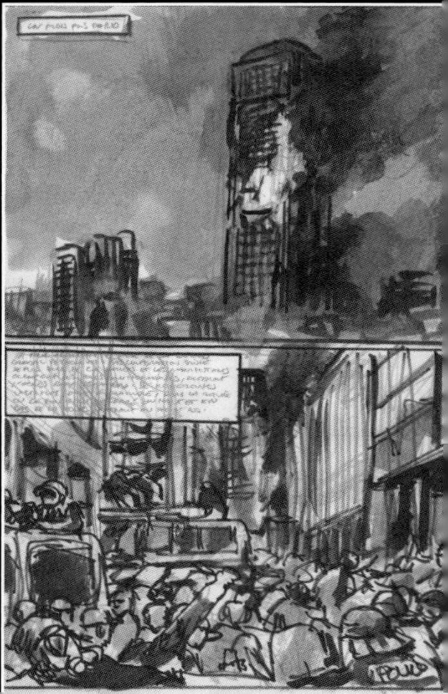

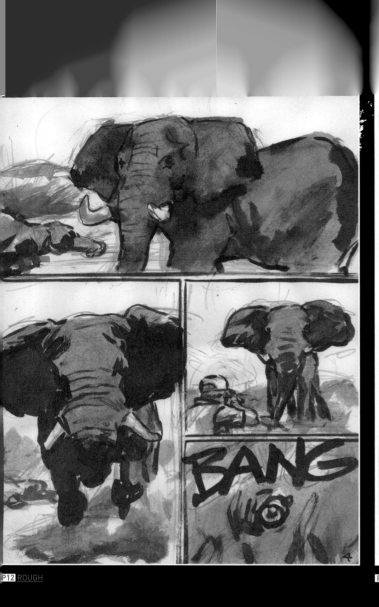

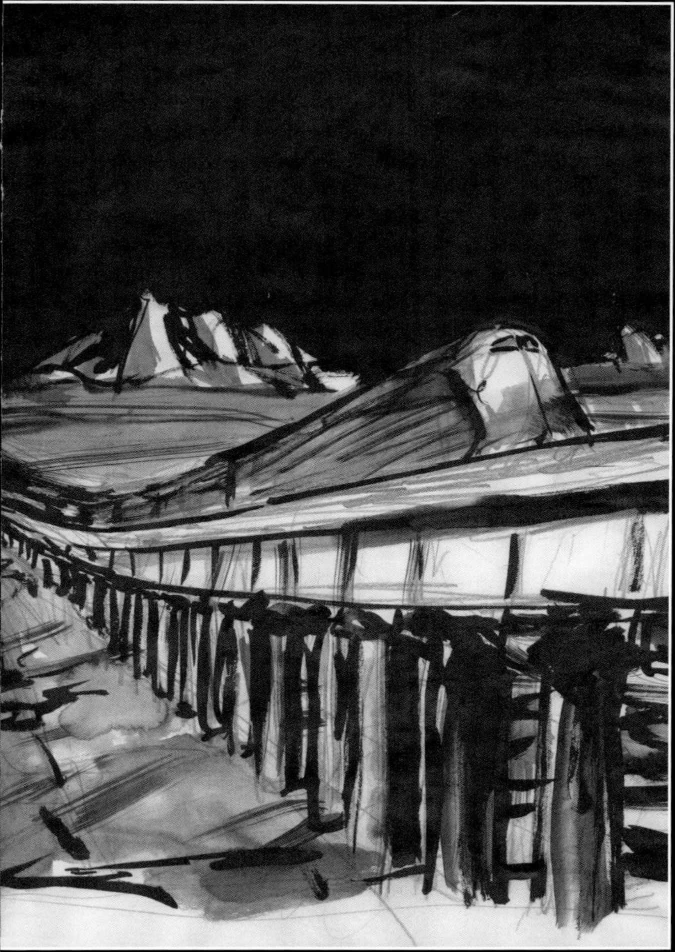

ROUGH

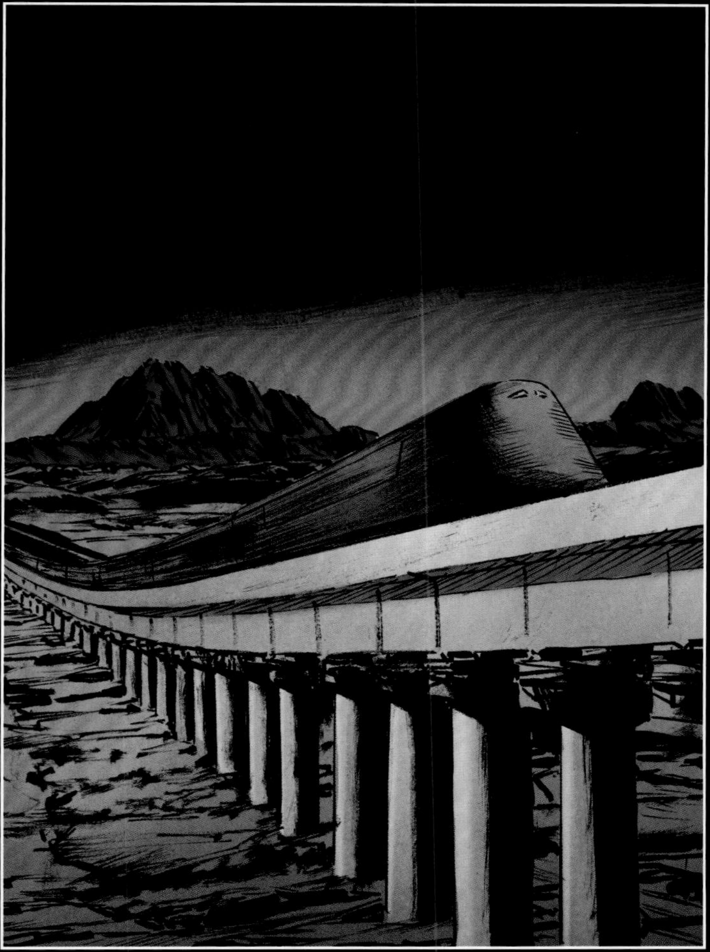

P64 FINAL ART

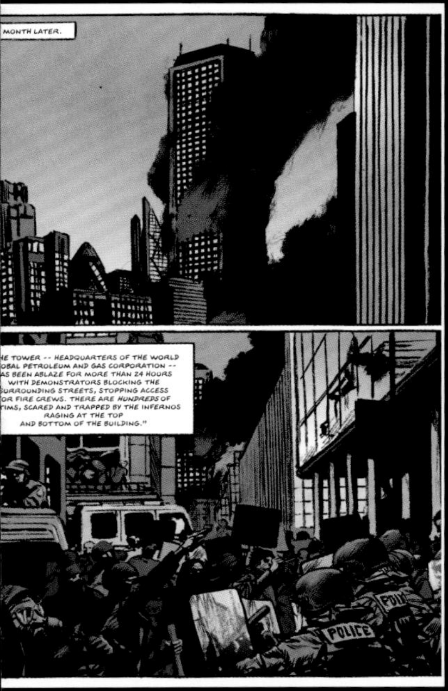
MONTH LATER.
HE TOWER -- HEADQUARTERS OF THE WORLD OBAL PETROLEUM AND GAS CORPORATION -- AS BEEN ABLAZE FOR MORE THAN 24 HOURS WITH DEMONSTRATORS BLOCKING THE SURROUNDING STREETS, STOPPING ACCESS FOR FIRE CREWS. THERE ARE HUNDREDS OF TIMS, SCARED AND TRAPPED BY THE INFERNOS RAGING AT THE TOP AND BOTTOM OF THE BUILDING."
POLICE

FINAL ART

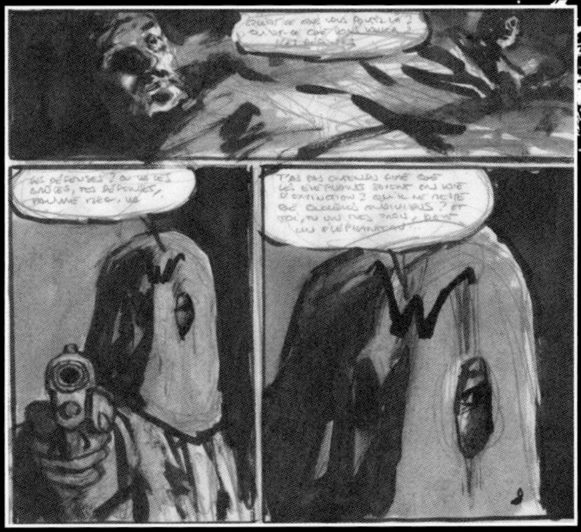

P16 ROUGH

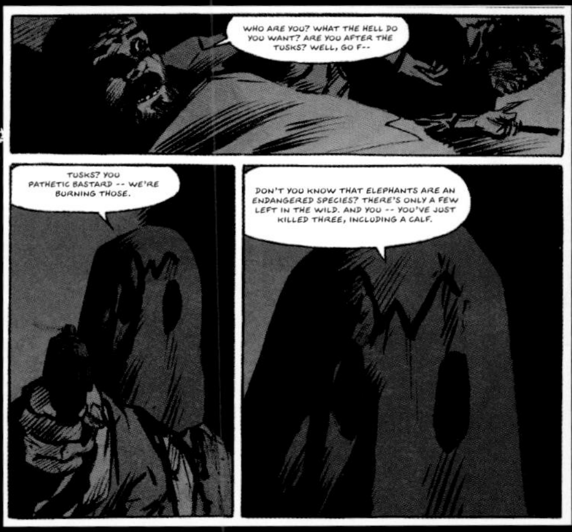
WHO ARE YOU? WHAT THE HELL DO YOU WANT? ARE YOU AFTER THE TUSKS? WELL, GO F--
TUSKS? YOU PATHETIC BASTARD -- WE'RE BURNING THOSE.
DON'T YOU KNOW THAT ELEPHANTS ARE AN ENDANGERED SPECIES? THERE'S ONLY A FEW LEFT IN THE WILD. AND YOU -- YOU'VE JUST KILLED THREE, INCLUDING A CALF.

P16 FINAL ART

AUTHOR BIOS

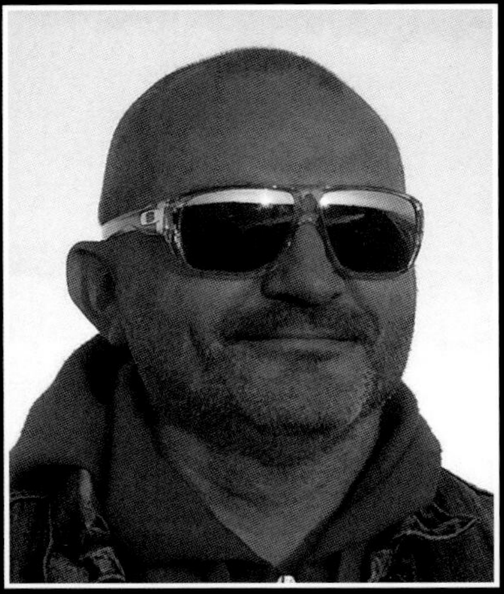

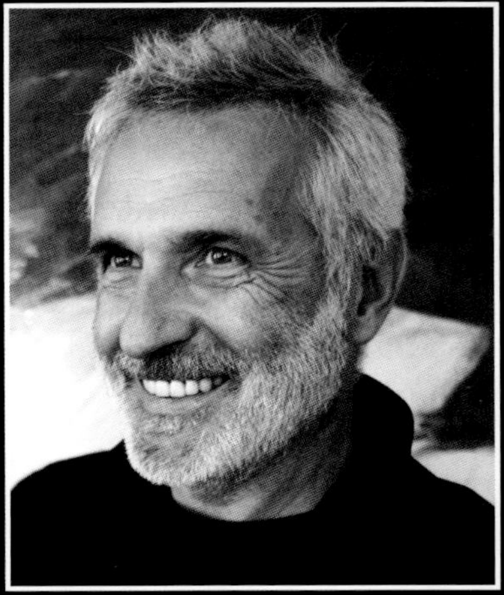

MATZ is the pen name of French writer Alexis Nolent. He is known for his comic book works *Du Plomb Dans La Tête* - adapted into the 2012 film *Bullet to the Head* - and *The Killer*, which was nominated for the Eagle Award and Eisner Award in 2007 and 2008, respectively. He has worked on a number of video game scripts, including *Splinter Cell: Chaos Theory*.

JEAN-MARC ROCHETTE is a painter, illustrator and cartoonist. He has worked across a variety of projects and genres, from science fiction comics to children's cartoons – and including adaptations of Voltaire's *Candide* and Homer's *Odyssey* – but *Snowpiercer* remains the work by which he is most popularly known.

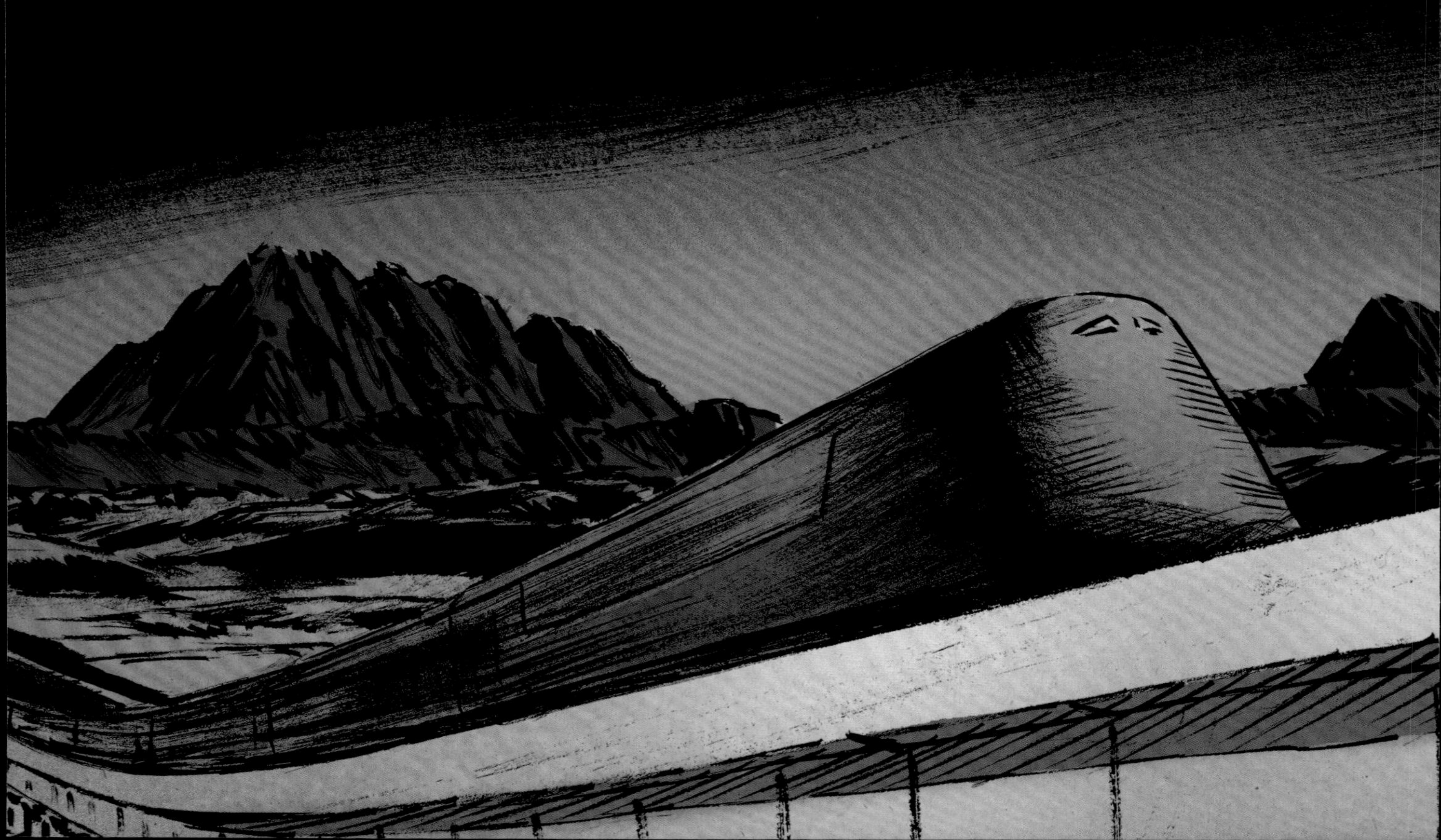

STATIX PRESS

COLLECTED EDITIONS

FROM TITAN COMICS AND STATIX PRESS

NURY
BRUNO
FROM THE AWARD WINNING WRITER OF THE BEST SELLING THE DEATH OF STALIN
ATAR GULL
ATAR GULL

Emma G. Wildford
ZIDROU & EDITH
EMMA G. WILDFORD

FROMENTAL HYMAN
The Prague Coup
THE PRAGUE COUP

THE BEAUTIFUL DEATH
MATHIEU BABLET
THE BEAUTIFUL DEATH

OLIVIER BOCQUET
JULIE ROCHELEAU
THE WRATH OF FANTÔMAS
THE WRATH OF FANTOMAS

THE GRAPHIC NOVEL THAT INSPIRED THE MOVIE
NURY × ROBIN
THE DEATH OF STALIN
A TRUE SOVIET STORY
THE DEATH OF STALIN

DEATH TO THE TSAR
DEATH TO THE TSAR

STEFANO RAFFAELE / CHRISTOPHE BEC
UNDER
SCOURGE OF THE SEWER
UNDER: SCOURGE OF THE SEWER

2021
LOST CHILDREN
2021: LOST CHILDREN

FOR MORE INFORMATION VISIT:

TITAN-COMICS.COM

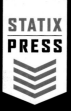

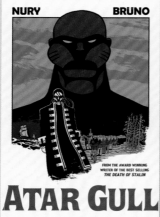

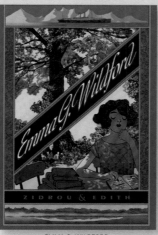

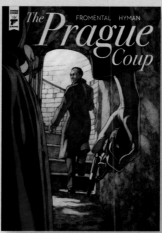

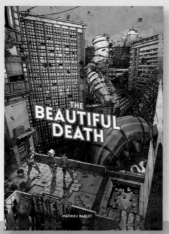

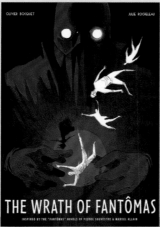

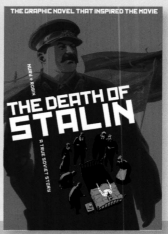

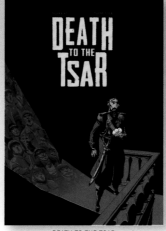

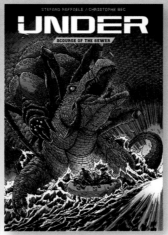

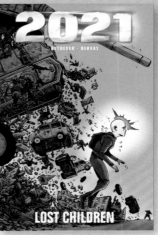

SNOWPIERCER

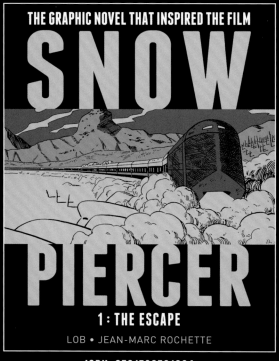

THE GRAPHIC NOVEL THAT INSPIRED THE FILM

SNOW PIERCER

1 : THE ESCAPE

LOB • JEAN-MARC ROCHETTE

ISBN: 9781782761334

THE GRAPHIC NOVEL THAT INSPIRED THE FILM

SNOW PIERCER

2: THE EXPLORERS

JEAN-MARC ROCHETTE • LEGRAND

ISBN: 9781782761365

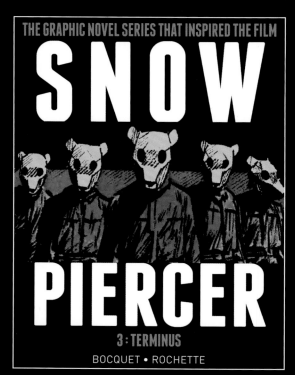

THE GRAPHIC NOVEL SERIES THAT INSPIRED THE FILM

SNOW PIERCER

3 : TERMINUS

BOCQUET • ROCHETTE

ISBN: 9781782767152

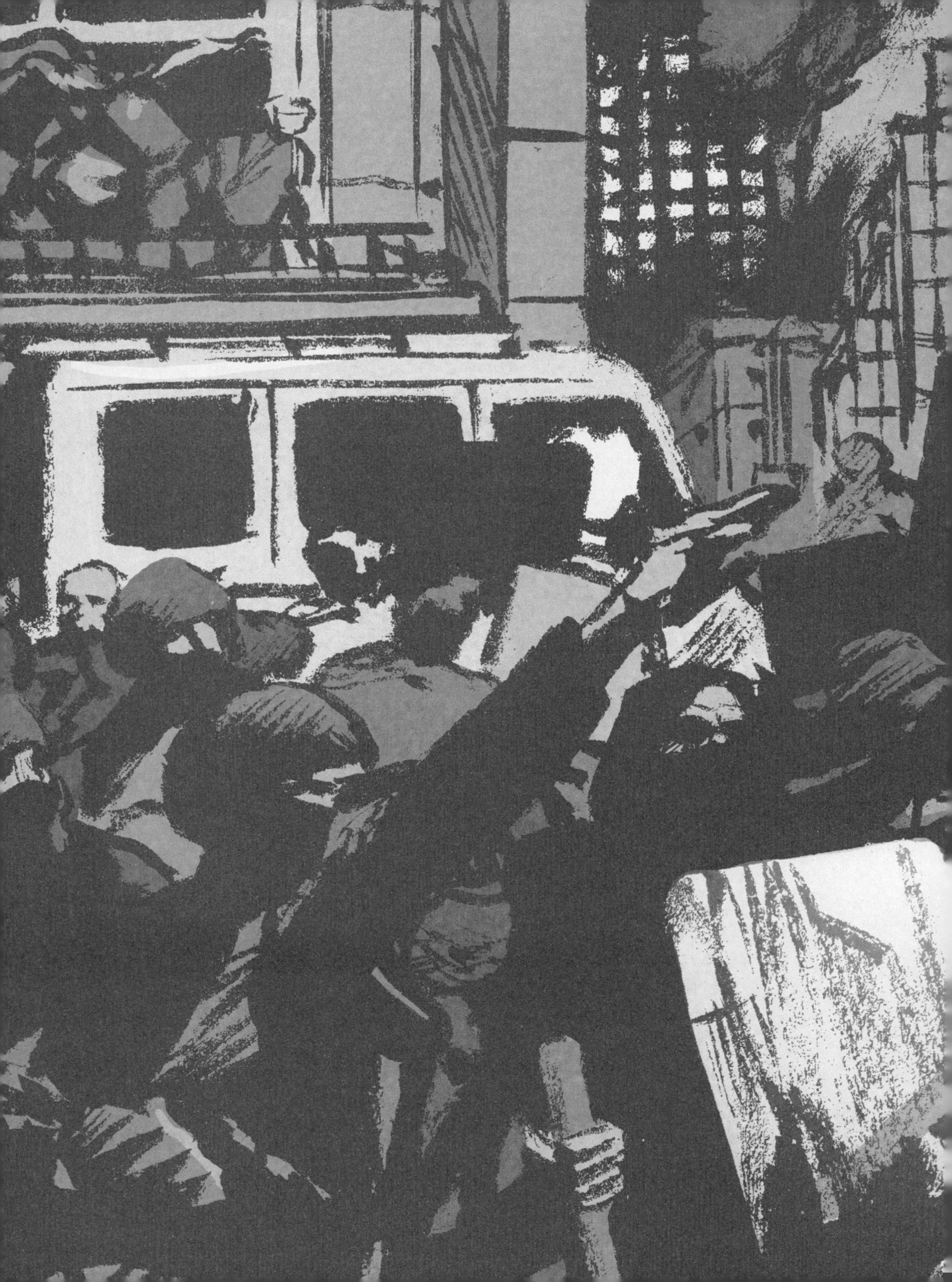